An Analysis and History
of Inflation

An Analysis and History of Inflation

Don Paarlberg

Westport, Connecticut
London

Library of Congress Cataloging-in-Publication Data

Paarlberg, Don.
    An analysis and history of inflation / Don Paarlberg.
      p.   cm.
    Includes bibliographical references and index.
    ISBN 0-275-94416-6 (alk. paper)
    1. Inflation (Finance)—History. I. Title.
  HG229.P14 1993
  332.4'1—dc20   92–17815

British Library Cataloguing in Publication Data is available.

Library of Congress Catalog Card Number: 92–17815
ISBN: 0-275-94416-6

First published in 1993

Praeger Publishers, 88 Post Road West, Westport, Connecticut 06881
An imprint of Greenwood Publishing Group, Inc.

Printed in the United States of America

The paper used in this book complies with the Permanent
Paper Standard issued by the National Information Standards
Organization (Z39.48–1984).

10 9 8 7 6 5 4 3 2 1

Copyright Acknowledgments

The author and publisher gratefully acknowledge permission to use materials from the
following:

Earl J. Hamilton, *American Treasure and the Price Revolution in Spain, 1501–1650.*
Copyright © 1934 by Harvard University Press. Reprinted by permission.

Bertrand Nogaro, "Hungary's Recent Monetary Crisis and Its Theoretical Meaning," *The
American Economic Review* 38, no. 4 (1948): 526–542.

A. W. Phillips, "The Relation between Unemployment and the Rate of Change in Money
Wage Rates in the United Kingdom, 1861–1957," *Economica* 25 (1958).

To the late
Frank A. Pearson
in partial discharge
of an ancient debt

Contents

Acknowledgments

The Department of Agricultural Economics of Purdue University, despite my retirement, provided me with office space, secretarial help, access to the library, and a research assistant.

The early research of Professor Frank A. Pearson of Cornell University, begun fifty years ago and left unfinished, undergirded the work. The study built on the 1953 doctoral dissertation of my student, Walter O. Wegner, entitled "Relationships Among Price Levels in Various Countries." This work was of critical importance to Chapter 3. David Camp, my assistant, extracted price data and prepared many of the tables.

The various libraries of Purdue University, the Congressional Library, and the Interlibrary Loan System were all essential.

Early drafts of the manuscript were read helpfully in whole or in part by Otto Doering, George Horwich, Don Paarlberg, Jr., John Sanders, Betsy Schuhmann, Karl-Eugen Wädekin, and Fred Warren. Assistance was also given by Nina Andreeva, Jules Janick, and Victor Nazarenko. My colleague James Binkley helped with some of the computations. My wife, Eva, typed repeated drafts of the work and assisted greatly in its clarification.

All these people are exonerated from errors of fact or interpretation. Heartfelt thanks to each.

Introduction

Inflation, defined as a general increase in prices, is the world's greatest robber. A covert thief, inflation steals from widows, orphans, bondholders, retirees, annuitants, beneficiaries of life insurance, and those on fixed salaries, decreasing the value of their incomes. Inflation extorts more wealth from the public than do all other thieves, looters, embezzlers, and plunderers combined.

Inflation, a Jekyll and Hyde character, is not only a great robber but also a great benefactor. Inflation is the world's greatest giver, doling out benefits to debtors, hoarders of goods, owners of property, government (for which it reduces the burden of the public debt), and, over time, owners of common stocks. The largesse thus bestowed on the debtor class and owners of property exceeds the combined total of all charities, contributions, and donations.

The reason for this inequitable behavior is that administered prices (such as returns from bonds) respond very slowly to inflation, while competitive market prices, largely determining the cost of living, surge upward. If all sectors of the economy responded to inflation in like fashion it would make little difference whether the price level was high or low, rising or falling.

A rough estimate may be made of the magnitude of inflation's arbitrary redistribution of income. In 1988 the total indebtedness—public and private, mortgaged debt and consumer credit—was approximately $6,471 billion. Inflation during the last half-century has been running at about 4 percent per year, reducing the 1988 incomes of the country's lenders by

$259 billion. This theft may be compared with $4 billion, the estimated amount of all fraud, vandalism, and robbery during 1967.

Inflation's gift of $259 billion to borrowers may also be compared with a lesser amount, $154 billion, the estimated total for all charitable contributions, religious and others, in 1984.

There is this difference between the robber inflation and the ordinary thief: inflation betrays public trust in a currency, whereas the holdup man betrays no trust, as the victim never placed confidence in him. There is also a difference between the giving of inflation and that of the ordinary philanthropist: inflation gives its benefits indiscriminately, whereas the ordinary philanthropist is moved by compassion for or a desire to advance some particular cause. Philanthropy has moral qualities; inflation has none.

Inflation charges no commission for its massive redistribution of wealth: what it takes from one it gives fully to another. Inflation is nebulous, impersonal, disembodied, and invisible. Those from whom inflation steals have difficulty in identifying the thief or even knowing that they have been robbed. Those whom inflation helps are inclined to attribute their improved circumstances to their own sagacity.

The moral and ethical aspects of inflation seldom appear in professional discussions of price-level behavior.

The inability to recognize the effect of inflation results from the money illusion, the widespread but mistaken belief that money is, over time, a stable measure of value. The error of this perception is clear; from 1933 to 1987 the U.S. dollar lost 87 percent of its value. The money illusion is in part a holdover from earlier times, when the overall level of prices tended toward a reasonable degree of stability. In part the money illusion is a fiction propagated by money-issuing authorities. The imposing architecture and the impressive interior of a financial building are intended to convey the impression of stability and trustworthiness; these structures actually house a subtle form of deceit.

Is it better that people should be in the grip of the money illusion, accepting blindly the inequities of inflation, thus reducing the accusations and invidious comparisons that would otherwise beset them? Or is it better that they should be aware of inflation's thefts and gifts, even though friction and disharmony would result from such knowledge? This writer opts for full reporting of the facts. The public purpose is seldom served by deception.

Inflation, poorly understood, is commonly attributed to erroneous causes, thereby leading to unfounded animosity between economic groups. Consumers blame food processors and distributors for price increases that result from inflation. Likewise, increases in rent are attributed to greedy landlords. Manufacturers who raise prices are accused of profiteering, even when they may be losing money. A stable price level would mean a less acrimonious society.

In most cases, inflation is a monetary phenomenon; money is the element common to every price. Myths about money add to the difficulty of understanding it. Baron Rothschild, the famous French financier, was heard to say that he knew of only two people who really understood money—an obscure clerk in the Bank of France and one of the directors of the Bank of England. "Unfortunately," he added, "they disagree." The mystery that surrounds money makes tolerable the massive redistribution of wealth that accompanies the inflationary process.

A dubious argument in favor of inflation is that it permits astute persons who understand it to manage their economic affairs so as to take advantage of those less informed people to whom inflation is a mystery. Among arguments supporting inflation, this contention must be ranked at the bottom.

Inflation has a diametric opposite—deflation, defined as a general decline in prices. Some people maintain, in a perversion of logic, that if inflation is bad, its opposite, deflation, must be good. Like inflation, deflation is no respecter of persons and is without scruples. Its effect on economic groups is the reverse of that of inflation; it steals from those who have fixed obligations and gives to those with fixed incomes. Competitive market prices plunge downward while incomes from the administered sector generally remain unchanged.

There is a further significant difference: inflation generally redistributes wealth within an increasing total, whereas deflation redistributes a shrinking amount. Trying to make long-term financial decisions with a dollar of changing value is like trying to build a structure with a rubber yardstick.

The law, which clings to the money illusion, validates the injustice of inflation and deflation. It enforces, with foreclosures and deficiency judgments, the dollar terms of contracts entered into by debtors who have already repaid the entire real value of what they borrowed. The law marks "paid in full" across the face of a contract that returns to the lender only half its real value. Inflation and deflation are forms of legal larceny. With inflation the debtor steals from the creditor; with deflation the reverse is true. (Prices, wages, income, and economic growth rate reflect the effect of changes in the price level. Real prices, real wages, real income, and real economic growth rates are these respective variables corrected in an effort to remove the effect of a changed price level.)

In earlier times, fairly stable price levels were the norm, and inflation was the aberration. During the 1930s monetary discipline was relaxed, and we entered a new Age of Inflation; inflation became the norm and stability the aberration. Institutional practices—legal, social, and economic—continue to reflect the earlier epoch, now outmoded.

Inflation results when a national government, which has a monopoly on the creation of money, issues excessive amounts of currency, based on borrowing, sleight of hand, or nothing at all. The result is inflation, often wrongly explained and poorly understood. Inflation is chosen by government in preference to taxation, which is onerous and clearly perceived. But inflation based on deficit financing is a form of taxation and has been called the cruelest tax of all. It transfers resources from the people to the government much as would taxation. The process of resource transfer is subtle but equally effective. The following quip was once popular with conservatives: "The government gives to its favorites only what it first takes in taxes from all its citizens." With deficit financing and the creation of new money this is now only partly true. In addition to taking wealth from its citizens in the overt form of taxes, the government now takes it in the deceptive form of inflation.

If the expansion of governmental services had to be accomplished by the visible means of taxation rather than by the deceitful process of printing money, the various nations of the world would have smaller governmental structures. But such is the preference for the present over the future and for illusion over reality that governments continue to expand and price levels are tilted upward.

Those who deplore inflation judge it against an ideal: a stable price level. They should judge it against its true alternatives: increased taxes or a reduction of government services.

This book deals with the Age of Inflation, the now-institutionalized process of irregularly escalating prices. It traces the history of inflation from Roman times to the present, describes the conditions of our day, and offers a tentative assessment of the future. Alternative ways of coping are described and appraised.

The logical way to deal with the problem of inflation is to stabilize the value of money, in which case both inflation and deflation would disappear, and their inequities with them. It is understood that the way of doing this is to limit the issue of money. But such a course would require more discipline than the public and public officials worldwide have been able to muster. There are those who have vested interests in inflation, and others who gain by deflation, so none of the various proposals for stabilizing the value of money has been found acceptable.

If the annual inflation rate is 5 percent and continues for five years, prices will rise about 28 percent. If the rate is 10 percent and is compounded for ten years, prices will rise from an index of 100 to an index of 259. If the rate is 20 percent and persists for twenty years, prices will rise to about thirty-eight times their beginning level. Such is the power of a geometric rate of increase. Once this virus gets into the system, powerful antibodies are required to counteract it.

The conclusion to which this writer reluctantly comes is that inflation has become endemic, in the bloodstream, reinforced by attitudes and practices that have been built into the system during the past sixty years. Public policy should be focused on restraining inflation, although these efforts come at considerable political and economic costs. Costs are lower if restraint is exercised while inflation is in the creeping stage; if restraint is withheld until inflation walks or runs or gallops, costs are enormous, as this history of inflation indicates.

Over time, and in today's setting, a zero inflation rate is probably impossible, though it has rhetorical appeal. Two-digit and three-digit rates of inflation, the Latin American types, are disastrous. Inflation kept in the lower half of the one-digit range has been demonstrated to be tolerable. Such performance is the implicit if not the explicit objective of U.S. policy. History, economics, and political reality appear to endorse present efforts to restrain inflation; total suppression seems out of the question.

The greatest obstacle to restraining inflation is that, on balance, people like a certain amount of it.

An Analysis and History
of Inflation

1

Price Histories in Brief

When you can measure what you are speaking about and express it in
numbers, you know something about it, but when you cannot measure
it, when you cannot express it in numbers, your knowledge is of a meager and unsatisfactory kind.

—Lord Kelvin, 1889

The author's hope is that we can learn something useful from a neglected
subject, price history. Most historians focus on political, social, and military
matters. For some reason economic history is given less consideration, and
price history, despite its critical importance to the citizenry, is typically an
unexplored part of that slighted sector. It may be that money and prices are
considered too crass for scholarly examination. In truth, all these aspects of
history are intertwined; the present writing may help, in small degree, to re-
dress the imbalance of attention.

Inflations are the most dramatic events of price history. By examining
them it may be possible to craft better economic policy. Patrick Henry proclaimed, "I have but one lamp by which my feet are guided and that is the
lamp of experience." George Santayana observed, "Those who cannot re-
member the past are condemned to repeat it."

Case histories follow for 15 inflations covering eighteen centuries and oc-
curring on four continents (Table 1.1). Inflation is sufficiently general that,
had space permitted, 100 cases could have been considered instead of 15.

Table 1.1
Fifteen Inflations

	Dates of Inflation[a]	Commodity Price Index at End of Upsurge (beginning date = 1)	Annual Percentage Rate of Increase
Ancient Rome[b]	150-301	200	5.6
Black Death[c]	1348-1351	2.4	5.8
Spain[d]	1501-1600	4.2	1.5
John Law[e]	1717-1720	2.0	26
American Revolution[f]	1775-1780	32	100
French Revolution[g]	1790-1796	285	157
U.S. Civil War, North[h]	1861-1864	2.1	28
U.S. Civil War, South[i]	1861-1865	91	209
Germany[j]	1910-1923	$143(10^{10})$	1174
Russia[k]	1913-1924	$171(10^{8})$	752
Hungary[l]	1945-1946	$400(10^{25})$	$3(10^{27})$
China[m]	1937-1949	$126(10^{13})$	1451
Bolivia[n]	1972-1985	$103(10^{3})$	143
Brazil[o,p]	1937-1988	$800(10^{7})$	56
United States[q,r,s]	1933-1987	7.7	3.8

[a]   Years given are from the beginning to the end of the upsurge. Most of the inflations continued, however, but in a moderate form after the end-year given.

[b]   Jones, A. H. M., 1974. The Roman Economy: Studies in Ancient Economic and Administrative History. Totowa, NJ: Rowman and Littlefield, p. 201.

[c]   Rogers, J. E. T., 1866. "A History of Agriculture and Prices in England from 1259 to 1793". Summarized by Murray, N.C., 1922. "Wheat Prices in England," in 1922 Yearbook of Agriculture. Washington, DC: U.S. Department of Agriculture, 1923.

[d]   Hamilton, E. J., 1934. American Treasure and the Price Revolution in Spain, 1501–1650. Cambridge: Harvard University Press.

[e]   Hamilton, E. J., 1936. "Prices and Wages at Paris Under John Law's System," Quarterly Journal of Economics, 51: 51–54.

[f]   Fisher, W. C., 1913. "The Tabular Standard in Massachusetts History," Quarterly Journal of Economics, 27: 452.

[g]   White, Andrew D., 1933. Fiat Money Inflation in France: How It Came, What It Bought, And How It Ended. New York: Appleton Century, pp. 44–45.

Table 1.1
(continued)

[h] Warren, G. F., and F. A. Pearson, 1935. Gold and Prices. New York: Wiley, p. 13.

[i] Lerner, Eugene M., 1955. "Money, Wages, and Prices in the Confederacy, 1861–1865," Journal of Political Economy, 63(1): 24.

[j] Warren, G. F., and F. A. Pearson, 1937. World Prices and the Building Industry. New York: Wiley, p. 42.

[k] Narodnoye, I. Gosudarstvermoye Khoziaistvo, and Statisticheski Sbornik PO GO Sudarstvennomu budgetur 1922–1923. Published by the Commisiariat of Finance. Quoted in Young, John Parke, 1925. European Currency and Finance, U.S. Senate Commission on Gold and Silver Inquiry, Foreign Currency and Exchange Investigation, ser. 9, vol. 2, p. 360.

[l] Nogaro, Bertrand, 1948. "Hungary's Recent Monetary Crisis and Its Theoretical Meaning," American Economic Review, 38(4): 526–542.

[m] Wu, Kang, 1958. Historical materials relating to the inflation in Old China and unpublished records of Central Bank of China. Quoted in Chou, Shun-Hsin, 1963. The Chinese Inflation, 1937–1949. New York: Columbia University Press, p. 261.

[n] Cole, Julio Harold, 1987. Latin American Inflation: Theoretical Interpretations and Empirical Results. New York: Praeger, p. 42.

[o] Wegner, Walter O., 1953. "Relationships Among Price Levels in Various Countries," Ph.D. thesis, Purdue University.

[p] United Nations, 1953–1988. Monthly Bulletin of Statistics.

[q] Warren, G. F., and F. A. Pearson, 1935. Gold and Prices. New York: Wiley, pp. 12–14.

[r] Wegner, Walter O., 1953. "Relationships Among Price Levels in Various Countries," Ph.D. thesis, Purdue University.

[s] United Nations, 1953–1989. Monthly Bulletin of Statistics.

The most striking aspect of the Table 1.1 is the astronomical price levels reached in Germany, Russia, Hungary, China, Bolivia, and Brazil—all twentieth-century inflations. In Germany in 1923, a postage stamp cost 100 billion marks. The author will attempt to portray how these economies functioned and how people managed to live during such periods of fantastic price behavior. Although hyperinflation is of greatest concern, one-digit and two-digit inflations are also examined.

These inflations had their similarities. Most were bound up with related and sometimes overwhelming national events: war, revolution, or natural disaster. Inflation has often been the scapegoat for other problems.

A common characterization of inflation—"too much money chasing too few goods"—applies to all these case studies. In all but one, the primary cause lay with too much money. In the single exception, the one that accompanied the Black Death, the principal source of difficulty was too few goods for the supply of money, which remained unchanged.

When national emergencies arose, governments usually inflated the currency along with and sometimes in preference to other measures: taxing, borrowing, increasing production, requisitioning, fixing prices, rationing, subsidizing, imposing austerity, and drawing down existing stocks of wealth. Inflation must be judged not by its behavior alone but also by the probable consequences of other alternatives.

All these inflations resulted in a wrenching redistribution of wealth. To the surprise of some, many of the inflations were accompanied by increased economic activity. They were officially resisted, at least rhetorically. Most of the fifteen have been completed: they rose, crested, and then leveled off, abated, or moved upward at a lesser rate. Yet throughout history the course of prices has been irregularly upward.

To the degree that foreign trade was conducted and exchange rates were allowed to fluctuate, prices in the various countries moved roughly together. Inflation in a particular country typically accompanied the depreciation of its currency or led to inflation in other countries. These outcomes tended to equate the price level of the inflating country with the price levels of its trading partners.

The inflations also had their differences, not only in magnitude and duration but also in cause and consequence. They occurred under every form of government, with every known form of currency. Yet all obeyed now-recognized principles of economic behavior; they were not departures from economic law.

Although all the inflations had shared characteristics, each had at least one unique attribute:

Ancient Rome: Inflation resulted from the debasement of precious metals

Black Death: Inflation contributed to the weakening of serfdom

Spain: Inflation resulted from the influx of American silver

John Law: Paper currency was first introduced and produced inflation

American Revolution: Continental currency contributed to winning independence

French Revolution: The inflation, though prodigious, was obscured by the world-shaking events that accompanied it

U.S. Civil War, North: The story here is not so much the inflation as the deflation that followed

U.S. Civil War, South: Defeat and disaster were accompanied by inflation

Germany: The archetype of hyperinflation

Russia: A planned inflation

Hungary: Stupendous, inept, incredible, forgotten

China: Financial mismanagement was the key element

Bolivia: A Third World country that disciplined its inflation

Brazil: Economic development accompanied and facilitated by inflation

United States: The advent of the Age of Inflation

The economic archeology underlying these historic accounts has been pursued by a group of scholars, some of whom are referred to in the footnotes to Table 1.1. These scholars were known and respected by each other but by few others. The data they compiled can be found in books now resting on library shelves, unopened for years on end, a mother lode awaiting the prospector's pick. Preoccupation with other, more popular forms of historical inquiry keeps economic history buried.

No claim can be made for the precise accuracy of statistics obtained before the middle of the nineteenth century. Prior to that date, price information can be derived only from the shards of history: ancient coins, contracts, edicts, court orders, business accounts, scraps of recorded transactions, and scattered references to prices in the literature of the times. Prior to the nineteenth century, no deliberate, sustained effort was made to record prices. But the directional change of prices was usually perceived by those who delved into this detritus, as was the general order of magnitude.

During the last century and a half virtually all modern governments have assembled price data, providing far greater accuracy and continuity. The statistics are largely wholesale commodity price indices. Because the composition of the indices used in this study has been changed from time to time, various means of splicing them together have been used to give longer time series. The general pattern of price behavior comes through clearly enough, however, despite this massaging, to permit reasonable interpretation.

Particularly noteworthy in Table 1.1 is that recent inflations have been much greater than was true earlier. This trend is attributable to two world wars, the abandonment of the gold standard, and recourse to credit and paper bank notes. Inflation of a given magnitude is a greater problem today than it was in earlier times, because economic activity was then largely of a subsistence kind, with relatively few long-term contracts. The earlier conditions made an inflation of a given magnitude more tolerable. But in today's economy, characterized by greater inflation, a largely exchange economy, and many long-term contracts, inflation is much less tolerable. We deal, therefore, with a growing problem. Strangely, the more our economic knowledge advances, the greater difficulty we have in suppressing inflation.

The story that emerges from these case studies is that inflation is generally, though not always, a monetary phenomenon. Money is half of every price quotation; if price levels go up, it is more likely that a change has occurred in the one element common to all prices—money—than simultaneously in a thousand different goods and services.

The chief casualty of this exercise is the money illusion, badly wounded but still alive. This notion that money is a unit of stable value, promoted by the monetary authorities, enforced by law, and still accepted by many people, is clearly unsustainable.

We are navigating in strange seas. Fortunately, these waters were occasionally sailed by earlier voyagers who strayed from the established sea lanes. The logs of these journeys may be helpful. We next examine them.

2

Fifteen Inflations

ANCIENT ROME: DEBASEMENT OF COINS AND INFLATION

The Great Inflation of ancient Rome is the earliest of reasonably well-documented price upheavals. Though price data are sketchy, we know enough to perceive that the escalation was enormous and widespread. Scraps of information give the basic facts. Much of the price history of ancient Rome comes from the diligent work of the eminent English scholar, A.H.M. Jones.

From A.D. 138 to A.D. 301, the price of a military uniform increased 166 times (Jones 1974). From the middle of the second century to the close of the third, the price of wheat, a good proxy for the price level, rose 200-fold (Jones 1974).

This inflation cannot be attributed to paper currency, for that form of money did not appear for another millennium. Nor was it the consequence of deficit financing; public debt as we know it had not yet been invented. Rome used a metal currency, variously gold, silver, copper, and bronze. Government business was mostly done on a cash basis.

The Great Inflation of Rome was the result of debasing the metal currency. A succession of emperors, who enjoyed a monopoly on coinage, reduced the size of the coin, hoping that their authority would serve to maintain its value—but of course it did not. Alternatively, some added a base metal such as lead into the coin, permitting the issue of, say, two coins instead of one, each having half the precious metal content of its predecessor. Thus the supply of money in the emperor's possession was increased and thereby the emperor's control of the empire's resources.

When successive governments found it difficult to raise money by taxation, they tampered with the currency. Much has changed during the intervening years, but not this. Then, as now, the ruling authorities fostered the money illusion, the myth that money is what the government says it is and that it has constant value.

Ordinary citizens of the Roman Empire joined in the debasement process. They clipped some of the precious metal from the coin's perimeter, a practice that led to the issue of coins with milled edges, which made clipping more difficult. Slaves "sweated" coins by jiggling them, hour after hour, in woolen bags, wearing off some of the gold; the bags were then burned and the gold separated from the ashes. So long as the value of the sweated gold exceeded the cost of provisioning his vassals, the slaveowner found it a profitable business. When coins such as the denarius had been so reduced in value and credibility as to lose their relevance, they were replaced by coins with a new name.

Enormous power and mystique were possessed by gold and silver in the minds of the ancients, more so than is the case today. The Roman people had high regard for the quantity of precious metal in a coin, and less regard for its claimed worth or the emperor's image stamped thereon. As the content of precious metal in the denarius declined, the coins lost value, so more of them were required to buy a given quantity of wheat or olive oil. Consequently, prices rose; or, more accurately, the value of the coins fell.

Debasement of the currency was an established practice from the early days of Rome. A coin known as the *as* originally weighed 10 or 11 ounces. By 269 B.C. it weighed 1 ounce, by 217 B.C. 0.5 ounce, and by 89 B.C. 0.25 ounce (Levi 1927). This process, prevalent under the republic, continued under the empire. During the reign of Marcus Aurelius (A.D. 161–180), the denarius was debased, its silver content falling to 75 percent of its earlier amount. In Severus Alexander's time (A.D. 222–235) it fell further, to 50 percent (Jones 1974).

From A.D. 235 to 284 anarchy prevailed, and the economy was in chaos. Usurpers would assassinate emperors and gain the throne, only to be overthrown in turn. Of the twenty-six emperors who held power during this fifty-year period, only one, Claudius, escaped violent death. Once-glorious Rome became inglorious. Inflation was at its height during this anarchic period. Devaluation of the coinage was rampant. Under Gallienus (A.D. 253–268), the "silver" coin contained less than 5 percent silver (Jones 1974).

Money was needed to run the government. How could it be raised? Taxes? With the general anarchy, collection of taxes was difficult if not impossible. Cut government costs? The chief cost was the military. With bar-

barians threatening to overwhelm the empire, military costs could hardly be cut. New conquests? It was all the empire could do to hold onto its earlier gains. Accuse the wealthy people of treason and confiscate their property? This behavior, once a common practice, had about run its course. Debasing coinage seemed the least objectionable of the alternatives.

The Great Inflation of third century Rome was not itself the problem; it was the symptom of a greater problem, the corruption of the empire. Throughout history, inflation, a believable villain, has been blamed for disasters resulting from deeper causes, too embarrassing for public officials to confess.

Volumes have been written about the decline and fall of Rome, a subject that does not directly concern this study. The Great Inflation is among the alleged causes of the fall, but it is sufficient to say that none of the leading historians who have written on this subject—Frank, Gibbon, Heitland, Kornemann, Nietzsche, Rostovtzeff, Toynbee—attributed the fall of Rome to inflation.

Whether the inflationary consequences of a debased coinage were clear to the emperors and their advisors is not known. The emergence of economics as a recognized pursuit and body of knowledge did not occur until the eighteenth century, and even now it is still evolving. The stormy seas of Rome's inflation were sailed without an economic compass. Nevertheless, it is possible to see in the Roman experience the operation of economic laws that would later be discovered. With the debasing of coins, gold was hoarded and the less valuable metals—silver, copper, and bronze—came into use; bad money drove out good money, in accordance with the principle first stated by Thomas Gresham in 1558. As the number of coins increased, the value of each was reduced, a phenomenon explained in 1852 by John Stuart Mill as *the quantity theory of money*.

The Roman economy was based more on subsistence and less on exchange than is the modern economy, so that a given rate of inflation was less of a problem than it is today. We obviously do not have detailed annual price data, but the rate of inflation appears to have been gradual in such an economy, and so it was relatively easy to accommodate. A 200-fold increase over a period of a century and a half translates into an average compounded rate of between 5 and 6 percent per year, modest by comparison with twentieth-century inflation rates in many countries. Nevertheless, in authoritarian Rome, some prices were slow to change, so over time, price relationships became utterly inequitable. From the second century A.D. until A.D. 301, the official salaries of high officials fell, in purchasing power, to one-eighth of their earlier value (Jones 1974). As a consequence, salaries were supplemented by bribes and gifts. Under the great trust fund of Nerva and Trajan, poor children in Italian cities found their annual dole reduced to 2 or 3 percent of its former purchasing power (Frank 1923). A soldier's pay had so diminished in real worth as to require the whole of his annual allowance to buy bread sufficient for only eight weeks (Jones 1974). Foraging and living off the land became the soldier's necessary means of livelihood.

The main losers from the inflation were soldiers, public officials, wage workers, recipients of public welfare, and property owners who rented their holdings at fixed rates. The gainers were borrowers, tenants with fixed rents, holders of real property, hoarders, payers of slow-to-change taxes, and the emperors, who escaped both the need to impose taxes and the necessity to curtail expenses.

The most visible event of the Great Inflation was the price-fixing edict of Emperor Diocletian. In fact, this effort at price control eclipses in modern perceptions the inflation it was intended to suppress. Diocletian, who came to power late in the third century, is identified with the inflation much as any official is identified in the public mind with a problem he addresses, even though the difficulty may have arisen in the time of the predecessor. This public perception, discernible today, helps explain why public officials are reluctant to address difficult problems.

Diocletian first tried to stabilize the currency. In this he failed, and prices resumed their upward movement (Haskell 1939). So in A.D. 301 he issued his famous edict. In the preamble to his proclamation he denounced profiteers, who "extort prices for merchandise, not four or eight-fold, but such that the human speech is incapable of describing either the price or the act" (Jones 1970).

Diocletian announced maximum prices for 700 to 800 articles and types of work and service (Haskell 1939). This remarkable document has survived, so we have the prices for millet, both ground and unground, olive oil of first and second quality, goose artificially and naturally fed, better and lesser cabbages, and so forth. Maximum wages for barbers, wagonmakers, elementary teachers, and instructors of Latin and Greek were also specified. Because the intention was to roll back inflation, most of the announced prices were below those prevailing. Stipulated prices were the same at retail as at wholesale, and no provision was made for geographic differentials. The penalty for evasion, frequently invoked, was death (Lacy 1923).

With prices in a straitjacket, markets and trade dried up. Farmers withheld their produce from the market, and food riots resulted. Wage relationships established by the edict were inequitable, so citizens refused to perform undervalued services. Further edicts followed, one of which bound farmers to the land in what amounted to serfdom. In order to retain workers in needed functions, children were bound to the same occupation as their parents. A swarm of officials worked to enforce the various regulations. A contemporary wrote, perhaps with disgusted exaggeration, that half of the men of the empire were on the government payroll (Haskell 1939).

The edict was eventually revoked by Constantine (Durant 1944). Thus reads an obituary to the edict:

For merest trifles blood was shed and out of fear nothing was offered for sale, and the scarcity grew much worse until after the death of many persons, the law was repealed from mere necessity. (Haskell 1939)

But this was not the end. Debasement of currency and inflation persisted throughout the fourth century—Diocletian's efforts had failed (Jones 1974). Gibbon tells us that sixty years after Diocletian's effort to control the cost of living, the emperor Julian made a similar attempt with no greater success (Lacy 1923).

As we shall see, the Roman inflation was but an early episode of price behavior that zigzagged upward through the centuries. What can we learn from the Roman experience? That the gold standard was no insurance against inflation. That inflation was a scapegoat for other problems. That price control was unavailing if the underlying causes of inflation were not addressed. That inflation stole from some and gave to others. That economic laws are not enacted but are inherent in the operation of the trade of goods and so are to be discovered rather than legislated or promulgated. These economic principles are timeless, and are reaffirmed in the other inflationary episodes examined below.

THE BLACK DEATH AND PRICE BEHAVIOR

During the middle of the fourteenth century, a moderate inflation overtook most of Europe. The best of limited available data suggests an approximate doubling of prices during a three-year period. This inflation, small though it was, is of interest because of the setting in which it occurred—the Black Death, which killed 20 million people, one-third of the population of Europe. The inflation was associated with a striking socioeconomic change.

The Black Death has been studied by epidemiologists concerned with the spread of infectious disease such as the AIDS virus and by those who fear the possibility of nuclear holocaust. We examine it now for a different reason. It carried the European economy far from normal intersectoral relationships and by so doing provided economists with the opportunity to examine stressed economic behavior. Some of the most useful knowledge in any discipline derives from the careful analysis of abnormal cases, whether in economics or medicine.

One of the subtle effects of the Black Death and the inflation associated with it was a weakening of the feudal system. With the numbers of serfs sharply reduced, each individual was perceived as more valuable, and workers' bargaining power increased. The serfs demanded wages along with subsistence. Employment replaced unpaid servitude; wages increased.

The Black Death was bubonic plague, caused by the bacillus *Pasteurella pestis*. The rat was the carrier. The flea, *Xenopsylla cheopis*, was the transmitter. The disease struck quickly; tumors (buboes) appeared in the armpits and groin, hence the name bubonic plague. Gangrenous inflammation developed in the throat and lungs. Dark-colored blemishes appeared on various parts of the body, giving the disease its common name. Death came soon, in some cases only a few days after symptoms first appeared.

The plague came from the Far East, where it had long been endemic and where the people had developed some degree of resistance. It came to Europe by way of Italy, the chief western terminus of the trade route from the east. Europeans had little natural resistance; in two and a half years the plague spread throughout the continent. There was then no satisfactory explanation of the cause and no effective medical treatment. The three years from 1347 to 1349 bracketed the height of the disaster; mid-year 1348 was the worst. The disease struck, waxed, crested, and waned. Then it recurred between 1357 and 1362, though with less ferocity. Lesser outbreaks occurred during the remainder of the fourteenth century. Resistance gradually developed and the dread disease receded, but there was an outbreak in London 300 years later; the Great Plague of 1665–1666 caused the death of at least 68,000 people.

It was five and a half centuries from the outbreak of this terrible disease before its cause became known. The plague bacillus was finally identified by Dr. Alexandre Yersin, a Frenchman, in 1894. In 1898 another Frenchman, Dr. Paul-Louis Simond, discovered that rats carried the bacillus and that fleas transmitted the plague from rats to man. The plague remained untreatable until the advent of sulfa drugs in the 1930s and effective antibiotics in the 1940s (Duplais 1988).

When the disease struck, prices fell, abruptly and briefly. The reason is obvious. Demand fell as the people perished, but the existing stock of goods remained while the supply of money was undiminished. Too many goods chased a static amount of money. In England, the price of wheat (a fairly good measure for general price behavior) had stood at 21 cents a bushel in 1346 before the plague. By 1348, at the height of the plague, it fell to 13 cents, a decline of 28 percent. The yearly wheat prices in England between 1346 and 1351, converted to cents per bushel, were as follows (USDA 1923):

1346	21
1347	20
1348	13
1349	16
1350	25
1351	31

Prices rose after the worst of the plague had passed. Again, the reason is manifest. Existing stocks had been drawn down. Production fell because there were fewer workers. The well-to-do classes, living in better hygienic circumstances, had survived in greater proportion than the poor who were severely victimized by deplorable sanitary conditions. The rich continued to make demands, bidding for a reduced supply. The static amount of money chased too few goods. During the three-year period from 1348 to 1351 the price of wheat rose to 2.4 times the plague-depressed level.

During autumn 1349 the cost of threshing wheat in England nearly doubled. James Edwin Thorold Rogers (1908), the great English historian, reported that during the whole period from 1350 to 1400, wages for threshing grain in England increased 60 percent in eastern counties, 73 percent in midland counties, 48 percent in southern counties, and 59 percent in northern counties. English wages retained their gain after the plague subsided. According to Rogers, prices rose throughout Britain.

The general wage pattern in England was also evident in Navarre, Spain, though increases were of somewhat lesser magnitude. Hamilton says that during the plague years, 1347 to 1349, wages averaged 19 percent above those of 1346, the year before it struck. During the twenty years beginning with 1351, wages averaged 40 percent above the levels reached during the three plague years. The index numbers of wages in Navarre, 1346–1351, (1421–1430 = 100), were as follows (Hamilton 1936):

1346	15
1347	16
1348	15
1349	24
1350	—
1351	20

In both England and Spain there were unavailing governmental efforts to restrain the wage and price increases associated with the Black Death. After several decades the effect of the plague on prices and wages diminished, and other forces, currency changes among them, became more important in price determination.

The Black Death had strikingly different effects on the various classes. Best off were the surviving rich people who inherited the wealth of their deceased relatives and lived in unbridled self-indulgence. The peasants and laboring people, who had been greatly reduced in numbers, were much sought after, which explains the increase in wages. Bowsky describes the phenomenon of "two masters running after one journeyman." Landlords were perhaps the most adversely affected. As they bid strongly for peasants to work their land, the landlord's return fell to 50 (Rogers 1908) or even 25 percent of its earlier level (Bowsky 1971). Feudalism and the manorial system never fully recovered from the effects of the Black Death. Rogers (1908) states, "The plague, in short, had almost emancipated the surviving serfs." The status of the merchant class was improved along with that of the peasants. Though the grief and anxiety associated with the Black Death were probably without parallel, in the light of history the resulting social and economic changes must be regarded as advantageous.

Fourteenth-century Europe was a Malthusian society; that is, population numbers pressed against the food supply and were thereby held in check. After the Black Death had reduced the numbers of consumers, the food discipline was temporarily lifted. In time (there were no vital statistics and so we cannot know how long), the population of Europe was restored to Malthusian status. Rogers notes that this occurred with remarkable rapidity: "In a short time the void made by the pestilence was no longer visible." The Black Death provided a brief respite from the Malthusian curse.

What can be learned from this terrible experience that will shed light on our inquiry into price behavior? Some conservative economists are fond of saying, "Only government can cause inflation." Not so during the Black Death. Government did nothing to cause it. Others suggest that inflation is always a monetary phenomenon. But the inflation associated with the Black Death came from the goods side; money was unchanged. In this respect, it differs from the inflation of ancient Rome.

Often, inflation is considered a form of economic pathology, needful of therapeutic treatment. During the Black Death, however, the rising prices, which were moderate as inflations go, had remedial, not deleterious effect. They served to stimulate needed production and deter consumption. Fortunately, price and wage controls failed, but the market worked.

Inflation had profound effects on the structure of the economy. The Black Death reduced the power of the landed gentry, weakened the feudal system, helped develop the merchant class, and elevated the status of the common man. Institutional changes were brought about not by the force of arms or edict but through the agency of changing prices.

It is sometimes said that great aberrations invalidate the accepted principles of economics, but nothing we learn about the Black Death supports this contention. Supply, demand, and price appear to have functioned in a manner consistent with the economic principles formulated four centuries later. Nothing so establishes the validity of a principle as seeing it verified during a time of stress. Such are the scraps of economic lore salvaged from one of the greatest catastrophes of history.

SPAIN, SILVER, AND THE PRICE REVOLUTION

During the sixteenth century prices in Spain more than quadrupled, rising at an average rate of 1.5 percent per year (Table 2.1).

The Roman inflation was set off by the debasement of scarce gold and silver. The inflation of the Black Death was caused by a dearth of goods. Inflation in Spain was different from both of these; it sprang from a superabundance of precious metals.

From 1501 to 1600, 17 million kilograms of pure silver and 181,000 kilograms of pure gold flowed into Spain, the outpouring of the fabulously rich treasures and mines in Mexico and Peru (Warren and Pearson 1935). The tonnage of incoming silver exceeded that of gold by nearly 100 times. In addition to official quantities, smuggling was estimated at perhaps 10 percent over the official receipts (Hamilton 1934). Relative to the previously existing stocks, the increment of gold and silver from the new world must have been large. In any case, the influx of precious metals set off a price revolution, a four-fold increase of prices in Spain with lagged advances in other European countries. The rise was gradual enough that the different sectors of the Spanish economy were able to accommodate the change reasonably well; the maladjustments that accompany abrupt price changes were not encountered.

E. J. Hamilton, then of Duke University and later of the University of Chicago, made a study of this inflation with the help of his wife, Gladys. To assemble data on imports of gold and silver together with records of prices and wages, the Hamiltons examined contemporary Spanish documents, hospital records, royal edicts, laws, the volume of gold and silver imports, and demographic data. They studied institutional changes and their social consequences. The Hamiltons' research efforts make the sixteenth-century Spanish experience what is perhaps the best documented price history of an early epoch.

When the Spanish price revolution struck, Europe was firmly committed to the mercantilist idea that precious metals were the true form of wealth,

Table 2.1
Index Numbers of Commodity Prices in Spain, 1501–1600 (1573–1581 = 100)

Year	Index	Year	Index	Year	Index
		1540	58	1580	103
1501	33	1541	56	1581	104
1502	36	1542	60	1582	107
1503	37	1543	61	1583	109
1504	38	1544	60	1584	110
1505	41	1545	59	1585	111
1506	47	1546	65	1586	107
1507	46	1547	63	1587	111
1508	45	1548	66	1588	108
1509	39	1549	71	1589	113
1510	39	1550	69	1590	114
1511	40	1551	69	1591	113
1512	38	1552	71	1592	117
1513	39	1553	70	1593	113
1514	40	1554	72	1594	114
1515	41	1555	71	1595	114
1516	41	1556	72	1596	117
1517	40	1557	80	1597	124
1518	43	1558	81	1598	133
1519	43	1559	78	1599	135
1520	42	1560	79	1600	137
1521	46	1561	87		
1522	51	1562	91		
1523	49	1563	90		
1524	49	1564	89		
1525	50	1565	92		
1526	50	1566	90		
1527	53	1567	91		
1528	51	1568	92		
1529	53	1569	90		
1530	57	1570	94		
1531	57	1571	98		
1532	55	1572	97		
1533	51	1573	99		
1534	54	1574	98		
1535	49	1575	104		
1536	54	1576	96		
1537	53	1577	94		
1538	57	1578	98		
1539	56	1579	108		

Source: Hamilton, 1934.

and that possession thereof should be the first objective of national policy. The export of commodities was seen as one means of acquiring, in exchange, a growing supply of precious metals. Mining was a worthy pursuit. Piracy and conquest were alternative means of acquiring precious metals and were actively pursued, seemingly with no pangs of conscience. A stock of gold and silver was viewed as a source of national prestige, a way of outfitting armies and navies, a method of adding to the splendor of court and church, and a means of importing desired articles from distant lands.

The early mercantilists had no well-developed idea of how an increased supply of precious metals would affect commodity prices, or, if they did, they communicated little about it. When Spanish prices rose, wage earners were displeased with the rising cost of living, and exporters found it difficult to sell in foreign markets. Any explanation of these difficulties that lay blame on the abundance of gold and silver, which were supposed to be the source of nothing but good, found no enthusiasm on the part of the mercantilists. Instead, other explanations were offered: ostentation, luxury, idleness of women, foreign influence, depopulation, excessive numbers of unproductive priests and nuns, profiteers, tariffs, the enclosure of grazing land, poor crops, high pasture rent, and excessive beef slaughter. In their research, the Hamiltons found fewer than 1,000 words devoted, over a period of 100 years, to the influence of imports of precious metals upon prices.

The first scholar to demonstrate by careful analysis that the American mines were the principal cause of the price revolution was the Frenchman Jean Bodin, who in 1568 published his *Response au Paradoxe de Malestroit Touchant l'Encherissement de Toules Choses* (Hamilton 1934). Apparently the first Spanish economist to attribute the price revolution to the influx of American treasure was Martin Gonzales de Cellorigo, who published in 1600 his *Memoriale de la Politica Necessaria y Util Restauración á la Republica de España.* Not until much later, with John Stuart Mill, Irving Fisher, John Maynard Keynes, and others, were the theoretical aspects of money and price levels thoroughly probed. The Spanish price revolution, like the Roman inflation and the inflation associated with the Black Death, were experienced without understanding what was happening to prices and why.

In simplest terms, the reason for rising prices was that precious metals, in increased supply, experienced a loss in unit value in accordance with the now familiar economic principle of diminishing utility. More units of the precious metals were required to equal the value of a quantity of wheat or a month's work, so prices and wages rose. That the change lay more with the money than with the wheat or the labor was a subtlety not readily apparent, then as now. This obscurity was cultivated by the officials, who shared their belief with the people that precious metals had constant value over time.

Strangely, silver did not circulate widely in Spain. Spain was not a country noted for the production of material wealth, so the silver was exchanged for goods imported from the other European countries. Some of it was traded for the exotic goods of the Far East, that vast sinkhole for precious metals. Much of it went to supply Spanish military adventuring in Europe, the New World, and North Africa. Some of it was fashioned into ornamentation of religious shrines. The Spanish, ever suspicious of competitive markets, established official prices for silver at such levels that, although it was the official money, it was perceived to have greater value when hoarded than when exchanged. There was such a scarcity of circulating silver that a bronze currency called *vellon* was issued for domestic use—again, the classic case of bad money driving out good money.

The importation of precious metals, with the upcreep in the price level, stimulated the economy. In these circumstances there was no need for currency devaluation (Hamilton 1934). An old adage states that if prices will not rise on their own, some form of public policy will be used to make them rise. In sixteenth-century Spain there was no such need; prices rose on their own. The sixteenth was the only century in history that did not witness serious departures from parity in one or more forms of Castilian money.

The initial incidence of the inflation was in Andalusia, where most of the American treasure arrived. The next most rapid advance in Old Castile—Leon and Valencia, which were more distant, was somewhat less rapid.

Efforts were made to restrict the flow of silver out of the country, but these were only partially successful. The gold and silver entered neighboring nations by trade and by piracy. Price changes in France followed very closely those in Spain. Prices rose in England somewhat more slowly than they did in France and Spain. The price of wheat, internationally traded, rose concurrently in Spain, France, and England. The extent of the advance in prices in England was recognized by that keen observer, Benjamin Franklin, who at age twenty-three wrote: "As these metals have grown much more plentiful in Europe since the discovery of America, so they have sunk in value exceedingly; for instance in England, formerly one penny of silver was worth a day's labor, but now it is hardly worth a sixth part of a day's labor." (Warren and Pearson 1935). Prices were very high in Mexico and the Andes, where precious metals were abundant and other goods scarce.

In Spain there were official efforts, feeble for the most part, to restrict the price increase. But as in Rome and fourteenth-century Europe, these generally were unavailing. When the flow of silver from American mines began to diminish around 1600, prices in Spain continued to rise, supported by a debasement of the circulating money.

Hamilton (1934) reports that Spain flourished under the stimulus of rising prices and lagging wages until near the end of the sixteenth century. Only a limited effort was made, however, to invest any substantial amount of silver in productive enterprises. According to the mercantilist notion, precious metal was wealth itself—what need to build factories and to improve agriculture? The greatest good was already in hand.

In the sixteenth century, the time of the inflow of treasure and the consequent price revolution, Spain was noted for attempted conquest (the "invincible" Armada), religious fervor (the Inquisition), the Golden Age (in literature, Cervantes; in painting, El Greco), and royal ostentation (the excesses of Phillip II). Sixteenth-century Spain, buoyed by the inflow of silver, was the greatest, richest, farthest-flung empire on earth. The Spanish monarchy ruled Spain, the Netherlands, Milan, Naples, Sicily, Sardinia, the Philippines, the West Indies, most of South America, part of North America, and all of Central America. In central Europe, Spain was allied with the Holy Roman Empire. The Spanish court of this age was the most splendid, and the Spanish aristocracy was the proudest in the world. Nonetheless, this grandeur was but an excrescence, built on illusions of permanence and the economic fever associated with inflation and the influx of precious metal.

Assisted by the abundance of gold and silver, wealthy families became yet more wealthy. The manorial system, in retreat elsewhere, became entrenched. The Industrial Revolution, which transformed northern Europe, was turned aside. The Protestant Reformation failed to cross the Pyrenees. The treasure from America precluded the need for change. The institutions that had been in place before the inflow of precious metals were strengthened and exported to the New World. By the time the inflow of treasure tapered off, the political and social structure that it supported had become well established and remained so, clinging to what was left of past glories (Kennedy 1987). Spain went into a slow eclipse, from which, several centuries later, it is beginning to emerge.

The Spanish inflation offers the following insights:

- Money was shown not to be synonymous with wealth.
- Inflation, which was gradual, accommodated growth.
- Incoming silver relieved the pressure for institutional change.
- Basing the money system on precious metals did not assure price stability.
- Spain could not retain to herself the precious metals that flowed in from abroad.
- Inflation, which began in Spain, spread to other trading nations.
- Efforts to restrain price increases were unavailing.
- Failure to understand economic principles did not prevent them from operating.

- The money illusion, which cherished myth, was weakened for all who were sufficiently open eyed to observe what was happening.

JOHN LAW AND PAPER CURRENCY

From 1717 to 1720 commodity prices in Paris doubled in what became known as "John Law's inflation." The index numbers of commodity prices in Paris, 1717–1720 (1716–1717 = 100), were as follows (Hamilton 1936):

July 1717	96
July 1718	97
July 1719	116
July 1720	191

The story of John Law and his paper money reads like the script of a low-budget movie, but it is a documentary, not a fantasy. Law has been called "the father of paper money," which is hardly true; like the litter of a vagrant dog, paper money has many fathers. The significance of this period comes not from the inflation itself, which was modest, but from the advent of paper money and the accompanying chaos in the financial markets.

The three inflations we have considered all occurred with what might be called "full-bodied" money: gold, silver, copper, or bronze, each of which had intrinsic value. Had these metals not been declared money, they still would have had substantial value in the arts, the crafts, and other uses. There was some cost involved in the production of these monies. They all had to be dug from the earth, smelted, and coined, so there were natural restraints on the quantity produced. True, the coins could be clipped, sweated, and blended with baser metals, thus requiring more units than before to exchange for a day's labor or a quantity of wheat, bringing about inflation, as discussed above, but there were limits.

Paper money has no such limitation. It costs next to nothing to produce and can be turned out in enormous quantities. With the advent of paper money, the limit on the amount of the circulating medium shifts from the parsimony of the mines to the conscience of the public officials, a much softer discipline. Paper money, which may be called "token money," "fiat money," or "credit money," is therefore much more prone to inflation than is full-bodied money. This is vividly shown by the inflationary history of the world during the nearly three centuries since paper money came into general use.

Full-bodied money, like gold or cattle or tobacco, develops naturally through the functioning of the market, without the intervention of central government. A fiat money like paper, on the other hand, requires monopoly of the money-making power and can be validated only by the decree of strong central authority. The ascendancy of paper money during the twentieth century is both cause and consequence of growing governmental power. A part of the conservative effort to return to the gold standard derives from a dislike for strong central government.

The first users of paper money were the Chinese, who produced what was called "flying money" in 177 B.C. Paper money was introduced into Europe by the Arabs in the sixth century. But use of paper money in the Western world was limited until efficient ways of making paper were brought from the Near East during the Crusades. Even so, the ease of counterfeiting precluded general use until the invention of the printing press, which standardized the paper notes and facilitated the identification of bogus bills. The American colonists, denied gold and silver by England, resorted to paper money. It remained for John Law, the imaginative Scotsman, to demonstrate the potentialities and the limitations of this form of currency.

John Law was born in Scotland in 1671, the sixth of thirteen children. His father, William Law, was a goldsmith. As was customary for such artisans, William issued receipts to those who supplied him with gold. A receipt constituted a claim on the gold it represented, and was payable in gold on demand. People came to prefer the receipts to the gold; they were easier to carry about and were readily denominated in different amounts. The receipts were transferable and so facilitated trade. Goldsmiths thus were the first bankers.

It had been learned through experience that more receipts could be given out than the amount of precious metal held by the goldsmith, since all the demands would probably not be made at the same time. Banking, with its deceptive fractional reserve system, was thus born. The capability of creating money out of nothing had been discovered. John Law, the goldsmith's son, having gained early exposure to the perils and promises of banking, was impressed that the value of currency lay not in its intrinsic worth but in public confidence.

When Law was thirty-four he anticipated his career by publishing *Money and Trade Considered with a Proposal for Supplying the Nation with Money*. His idea was to issue paper notes based on land as security, bearing 3 percent interest, and passing as legal tender. He would thus convert a fixed asset, land, into liquid form, thereby stimulating economic activity and expediting commerce. Law tried to get acceptance of his idea within his own country, but the canny Scots would have no such nostrum, nor would the stolid Dutch, then known for their reputable banking system. Not until 1714, when he went to France, did he find a country receptive to his idea. "I shall," he said, "make gold out of paper."

But that is to get ahead of the story. First, Law himself. He was brilliant, handsome, and of commanding presence. He was variously and sometimes simultaneously a gambler, a speculator, a wastrel, a visionary, an innovator, a reformer, a humanitarian, an idealist, and a pragmatist. Politically he was a state socialist. His economic beliefs defy classification except that he was antimercantilist. His religious beliefs were negotiable; at the height of his career he renounced his Protestantism and embraced the Catholic faith, thereby qualifying himself for a cabinet position in the French government.

At age twenty-three, Law had a dispute with a man named Edward Wilson, whom he killed in a duel. He was tried and sentenced to death. With the help of friends he escaped from jail, jumping thirty feet from his window, sustaining only a sprained ankle. A fugitive from Britain, he made his way to Holland, where he was fascinated with the venerable Bank of Amsterdam and the renowned East India Company. He began reading treatises on money, banking, and trade—an undertaking full of portent.

In Paris he took up with Lady Catherine Knollys Seigneur, who was married to but neither living with nor divorced from a French husband who disappeared into the mists of history. Law was devoted to her for the rest of his life. She bore him a son, named John, and a daughter, named Mary Catherine after her mother.

John Law had come to France in 1714, a rich man with a personal fortune of 1.6 million livres, acquired by astute financial dealings. The France to which he came was on the brink of economic collapse. Louis XIV, the Sun King, had engaged in unbridled extravagances and exhausting wars, leaving the country with staggering debts and ruined credit. Commerce was stagnant, workers were unemployed, and agriculture was in distress. Commodity prices had declined, reflecting and adding to the difficulty.

In 1715, Louis XIV, having reigned for seventy-two years, finally died. Louis XV, his successor, was then five years old. The Duke of Orleans, allegedly a gambling associate of Law's, was named regent. Impressed with the Scotsman's financial genius, the regent agreed with Law's proposal to establish a private institution, the Banque Générale, with capital stock of 6 million livres, the equivalent of about 250,000 British pounds, a small beginning. The date was 2 May 1716. The stock bore 4 percent interest. The bank was authorized to make loans, to receive money on deposit, to discount commercial paper, and to issue notes that were redeemable in gold on demand. With a stroke of genius, Law specified that redemption would be in the weight and fineness of the gold at the time of issue; French memories were vivid with recent reductions in the gold content of their currency, which had been cut by 30 percent during the two years that preceded establishment of Law's bank. Bank shares sold readily. The public, confident that the notes could be converted to gold and preferring the notes because of their convenience, at first made no effort to claim the gold.

Eleven years after he had written his treatise on money and trade, Law was able to put a version of his plan into operation, not in his own land but in another. The essential elements of his original idea were clear in the operations of his bank. Though an impulsive man, he held to his original concept with great tenacity.

The bank's principal borrower was the State, to which Law's bank issued notes. With these notes, the State paid its expenses and reduced its debt. In October 1716, tax collectors were ordered to make their remittances payable with notes of the bank, thereby making them legal tender.

This first small injection of paper currency was not sufficient to lift French prices, which had been in irregular decline. During the two years following the establishment of Law's bank, commodity prices in Paris fell 8 percent. For price and wage data we are indebted to that remarkable scholar, Earl J. Hamilton.

Although the Banque Générale did little to alleviate the lethargy of the French economy, it did help the French government meet its debts and thus demonstrated the utility of a paper currency. John Law's reputation was mightily enhanced. If he had stopped at that point he would have been celebrated rather than reviled by history. But this success was not enough for Law, who had grandiose plans. Law's ambitions were aided and abetted by his sponsor, the regent, a man of minimal scruples and less-than-towering intelligence.

In August 1717, the Banque Générale organized under its auspices a mining and colonization company entitled the Compagnie des Indes Occidentales, also known as the East Indian Company, the Western Company, the Mississippi Scheme, the Mississippi Bubble, the Louisiana Bubble, and The System. The capital of this concern was 100 million livres, 200,000 shares of 500 livres each. The company had obtained from the Crown a grant of the Province of Louisiana, which, it was claimed, was rich with gold, silver, and precious stones. Hopeful allusions to the Spanish experience in the New World are here discernable. Parties of colonists were formed to explore this allegedly favored land (in part Louisiana swamps) and transport its treasures to France.

On 4 December 1718, the Banque Générale became the Banque Royale, offering enormous windfall profits to its shareholders. Law was the director of the renamed bank, and the king guaranteed the notes. Dividends were promised at 12 percent, later raised to an incredible 40 percent (Hamilton 1936). The bank presses poured out notes. Law, now virtually without restraint from the Parlement and with the support of the regent, took on additional enterprises. He absorbed the French tobacco monopoly and acquired the privilege of coining money. He took over tax farming, a state enterprise by which entrepreneurs paid the state for the right to extract taxes from the citizens. Finally, he undertook to convert the national debt, some 1.5 billion livres, to shares of stock in his company.

The economic base for this superstructure of credit, particularly the Louisiana venture, was exceedingly weak. Vast sums of money and a long period of time were needed if Louisiana were to be developed. The subsoil of the Mississippi delta was soggy mud, not sparkling ore of gold or silver. Colonists were reluctant to volunteer for settlement; judges sentenced thieves, prostitutes, and beggars to deportation to Louisiana. Only the 4 percent interest on the loans went toward developing the watery wilderness.

Law faced the question of how to pay dividends on the stock of his unproductive company. He solved this problem with the revenue obtained by selling more stock. He originally sold 200,000 shares of his company; this he more than trebled to 624,000. The money that poured in from these new sales accommodated the paying of dividends and contributed to the perception that his company was flourishing. It was the pyramid scheme, to be exploited by Charles Ponzi in the United States in 1920.

To foster the perception that his company was flourishing, Law circulated propaganda about successes in Louisiana. He bought, for his own account, futures in his own company, paying 33 percent above the current rate and conveying the impression that he alone knew about forthcoming successes. He restricted the purchase of new stock to holders of original issues, thus making stock purchases a seeming privilege. He expanded the issue of notes by 30 percent during the first four months of 1719. By September that year the amount of paper bank notes in circulation was ten times the amount of gold and silver in the Banque Royale's vault; Law's fractional reserves were being stretched to the breaking point (Minton 1975).

The expansion of credit had a positive effect on economic activity. Economic growth occurred, and commodity prices increased. Commodity prices in Paris, which had been falling, doubled during the three years between the establishment of the Banque Royale in August 1717 and the peak of the boom. This advance confirmed John Stuart Mill's belief, to be enunciated later, that, other things equal, changes in prices vary in proportion to changes in the quantity of money in circulation. In accordance with Professor A. W. Phillips' principle, affirmed by economic historians, rising French prices were accompanied by a business expansion (Galbraith 1975, Hamilton 1936, Hyde 1969, and Minton 1975).

The inflation in commodity prices, paralleled by an increase in wages, was modest and of brief duration. It was completely overshadowed by a spectacular increase in the price of bank stock. Inflation in prices of financial instruments during a period of little inflation in commodity prices was amply demonstrated in the United States in 1929.

France had no established market for trading in securities, and trading in stock took place in the Rue Quincampoix, a little street not much longer than a football field. It became the scene of an increasingly hysterical pit of auctioneers and speculators. Law encouraged the bull market with rumors, promises, and manipulations. In January 1720, he put into circulation 1 billion livres of paper money, nine times the amount afloat the year before (Minton 1975). Bank shares had been issued at 5,000 livres each (Hamilton 1936). Subsequent shares were issued for differing amounts. They rose irregularly to forty times their nominal price (Angell 1930). This enormous increase took place within a span of a little more than three years. The market reflected a form of pathology that establishes price not on returns but on anticipation of further price increases. Shares were bought on margin; a buyer could put up as little as 10 percent of the cost and had twenty months to pay off the balance. Shares could be sold within a month, before any payments came due. They fluctuated wildly in price. A rumor that the Spanish had ravaged Louisiana sent shares tumbling. Law would release optimistic information to overcome adverse market movement. Thousands of people converged on Paris from the provinces to make money on Law's bank shares. A waiter made 30 million, a chimney sweep 40 million, a clerk made an 86 percent profit during his lunch hour (Minton 1975).

Law himself profited from the speculation, though seemingly he did nothing illegal. Prospering, he acquired the duchy of Mercoeur, the estate of Tancarville, and seven houses in the Place Vendôme. Law was the most celebrated man in Europe. Prominent people dressed like him and tried to deport themselves in his manner. A Scottish poet, Allan Ramsay, wrote a panegyric about him that reads:

> The grateful Gauls your Mem'ry will revere,
> And glorious in their Annals you'll appear:
> Who formed them Banks, their sinking credit rais'd,
> Whilst Your warm Fancy in Mississippi Blaz'd . . .
> O More than Man!"

Riding the crest of power and popularity, Law moved to bring about wholesale social change, revealing his reform-minded self. He asked that the peasants be given the uncultivated lands of the clergy, that tolls be abolished, tariffs reduced, and the grain trade be freed of restraints. He began to finance public works and industry with his loans and notes. He was ennobled by a grateful sovereign; he was made the first (and only) Duc d'Arkansas, and on 5 January 1720 was made comptroller-general of France. Nevertheless, the end was very near.

The collapse came for no other reason than that the boom could not continue. Any speculation, whether in land or in stock—or in tulips as in Holland in 1634—that is based not on the earning power of the asset but on the expectations of further price increase is bound eventually to fail. The event that precipitates the decline may be great or trivial; the critical element is that expectation of further increase somehow vanishes. So it did with Law's bank stock.

An early rumbling of difficulty came in the first part of 1720 when the Prince of Conti sent a huge bundle of notes to be redeemed in hard currency. The notes were redeemed but seriously drew down the bank's reserve. The regent, much concerned, ordered the prince to turn back a considerable share of the precious metal he had received. But the seeds of doubt had been planted. Others began converting Law's paper into gold and silver, moving it to England and Holland. The price of bank stock weakened. On 22 February 1720, in an effort to bolster the sagging market, Law announced the amalgamation of the Banque Royale and the East Indian Company—but to no avail. In a further effort to stem the decline, the bank offered, on 5 March 1720, to buy its own stock at 9,000 livres a share, considerably above the market value, and shareholders rushed forward to sell. Law printed a billion and a half more livres to pay for the shares, vastly increasing the amount of currency in circulation and aggravating the inflation of commodity prices, which increased 68 percent in twelve months' time.

Law saw that something major had to be done. With his support and that of the regent and of the former minister of finance, an edict was issued on 21 May 1720. The value of paper money was to be diminished by 50 percent over six months. The price of bank shares would be forced down from 9,000 to 5,000 livres during the same period. To the holders of paper money and bank shares, this was a seismic shock. The public scrambled to get rid of as much paper as possible. The rush on the bank was so great that the institution was compelled to close its doors for ten days. On one night in July, 15,000 frantic individuals were tightly wedged in the Rue Vivienne. When dawn broke, 16 had died of suffocation.

There is anecdotal material to the effect that commodity prices rose tremendously during the later months of the Mississippi Bubble and fell catastrophically thereafter. There are tales that the value of bank stock fell to zero and that the paper money became worthless. "Not so," maintained Hamilton, surely the most careful scholar to examine the price record. He reports a mere doubling of commodity prices during the three years of the bank's glory days. Regardless of anecdotal wit or charm, historical accuracy is better served by painstaking scrutiny of the empirical record.

By autumn 1720, both paper currency and stock certificates had fallen sharply in value. Excess notes were publicly burned, leading the sardonic Voltaire to observe, "Paper currency has now been restored to its intrinsic value!" Speculators who specialized in holding paper over long periods, however, bought up notes and stock. In later years these people made a tidy profit. Hamilton says the holders of bank notes and East Indian Company stock apparently received on the average about two-thirds of the nominal value of their claims.

It was the people of means who were broken by a late entry into the market at or near its crest. They lost as much as 95 percent of their presumed wealth. A ditty of the day portrays the plight of one such:

My shares which on Monday I bought
Were worth millions on Tuesday I thought.
So on Wednesday I chose my abode:
In my carriage on Thursday I rode;
To the ball room on Friday I went;
To the workhouse next day I was sent.

The tales of catastrophe that characterize the Mississippi Bubble come largely from the small percentage of the total population who lost by speculation and who wrote and spoke out of proportion to their numbers. The common people, who worked for wages and tended their shops, were much less affected. During the inflation, commodity prices in Paris doubled, as has been told, and wages rose 61 percent, changes that were relatively modest. With the deflation, from August 1720 to August 1721, commodity prices fell 30 percent and wages declined 17 percent. From 1721 to 1725, commodity prices rose 8 percent. These are substantial changes but hardly beyond the coping ability of the French people, who have experienced far greater changes before and since.

On 10 October 1720, the French government formally marked the end of "The System." It declared that in their present discredited state the notes constituted a hindrance to trade and that consequently, as from the beginning of November, the use of gold and silver would be resumed in all commercial transactions (Hyde 1969). Notes stopped circulating, coins gradually took their place, and by December the country had apparently returned to a specie basis. When the bad money was banished the good money emerged.

Following the collapse of his bank and company, John Law was dismissed from his office and stripped of his property. In fear for his life, he fled to Belgium and then to Venice, where he lived nine more years. He died on 21 March 1729, a poor man, at age fifty-eight. He said, "I am like the fabulous hen which laid the golden egg, but which, when it was killed, was found to be like any ordinary fowl."

John Law's venture with paper money was a pioneering experience. As well as anyone else, before or since, he demonstrated its utility and its dangers. Despite the bursting of his Mississippi Bubble, his undertaking had sufficient attractiveness that after him paper money came into increasing use. If the experience of John Law's paper money had been as disastrous as sometimes represented, the world would hardly have made paper and credit the centerpiece of modern finance.

H. Montgomery Hyde, who on the whole is favorably inclined toward Law, appraises Law's experience thus:

Neither by tradition nor by education nor by legislation were the French people properly prepared for the gigantic credit experiment which Law launched upon the country. He moved too quickly for public understanding and with characteristic impatience neglected to explain all the steps in the program as he should have done. That he subsequently realized this fault there is no doubt. "If I had the work to do over again," he wrote from exile in 1723, "I would proceed more slowly but more surely and I would not expose the country to the dangers which must necessarily accompany the sudden disturbance of generally accepted financial practice."

Interestingly, while France was picking up the pieces of the Mississippi Scheme, England was experiencing the collapse of a somewhat similar venture, the South Sea Bubble, a financial scandal that burst in 1720. Apparently, financial speculation was contagious. The Spanish success with New World treasure was so impressive that France and England sought to repeat it.

Law's parting words to the regent, after being relieved of his post as comptroller-general, were these: "Sire, I acknowledge that I have made great mistakes. I made them because I am only human, and all men are liable to err. But I declare that none of these acts proceeded from malice or dishonesty, and that nothing of that character will be discovered in the whole course of my conduct."

The John Law story is not just about inflation. It is also a story about ambition, innovation, greed, folly, and economic theory—all companions of inflation. It would be a good introduction to a course in money and banking if professors had the courage to teach it.

Some conservatives observe from the John Law story that paper money is a snare and a delusion. Bolder people see in this experience evidence that paper currency, if it were intelligently managed, could promote economic growth while holding inflation to a tolerable level.

THE AMERICAN REVOLUTION AND CONTINENTAL CURRENCY

During the American Revolution, prices, quoted in Continental Currency, rose to high levels, variously reported to be 30, 40, 100, or more times the prewar level. There is much anecdotal material but little statistical information. The best documented of these uncertain statistics is a report of a tabular standard for measuring depreciation of the Continental Currency. This is an early example of indexation, used as a basis for paying soldiers in the colony of Massachusetts. The table shows the depreciation of the currency, a reasonable proxy for the rise in prices. The computation shows that by January 1780, over four years after the Continental Currency was first issued, it took 32.5 units to equal the Spanish dollar, into which it was nominally convertible (Table 2.2).

The chaotic price and monetary history of the American colonies begins much earlier. The American colonies were short of money. England, in the grip of mercantilism, prohibited the export of gold and silver and required the colonies to pay with coin for articles they bought from the mother country. Parliament also prohibited the colonies from coining money. There were attempted restrictions, from time to time, on the use of paper money and the issue of bills of credit. This dictatorial and inconsiderate treatment of the colonies, little mentioned by the historian, was one of the causes leading to the Revolutionary War.

The colonists acquired some gold coin by trading with the Spanish colonies, but this was insufficient for their needs. Consequently, they early relied on commodity money: wampum, beaver pelts, deer and raccoon skins, gunpowder, bullets, tobacco, indigo, sugar, rice, corn, and cattle. Two of these commodity monies, wampum and tobacco, are worth comment.

Wampum was Indian money, also used for ornaments, made from cockleshells. Small pieces were broken from these shells, which were then ground and polished. Holes were drilled with sharp stones so that shells could be strung together. A skilled Indian could make thirty-five to forty individual pieces in a day. Wampum became legal tender from Massachusetts to Virginia (Lester 1939). To the colonials it had no value other than as money. With their iron tools, the colonists made prodigious amounts of this money, so its value fell sharply, with the result that commodity prices rose enormously. In 1662, Rhode Island refused to accept wampum as payment for taxes (Hepburn 1924).

Table 2.2

Depreciation of the Continental Currency, 1777–1780, Based on Prices of Beef, Indian Corn, Wool, and Sole Leather

	Rate of Depreciation, Date of First Issue = 1				
	Beef	Corn	Wool	Sole Leather	Mean
1777					
Jan.	1.142	1	1.50	1	1.16
Feb.	1.142	1	1	1	1.03
Mar.	1.142	1	1	1	1.03
Apr.	1.142	1	2	1	1.28
May	2.284	1	2	1	1.57
June	2.284	1.50	2	1	1.69
July	2.284	2	2	1	1.82
Aug.	2.284	2.50	2.50	2.25	2.38
Sept.	2.284	3	2.50	2.25	2.50
Oct.	2.284	3	6	4	3.82
Nov.	2.284	3	6	4	3.82
Dec.	2.857	4	6	4.50	4.34
1778					
Jan.	3	4.50	6	4.50	4.50
Feb.	3.580	4.50	6	4.50	4.64
Mar.	3.714	5	6	4.50	4.80
Apr.	4.285	6	6	4.50	5.19
May	4.714	8	6	4.50	5.80
June	5.142	8	6	4.50	5.91
July	4.857	10	6	4.50	6.34
Aug.	4.714	10	6	4.50	6.30
Sept.	4.857	10	6	6.75	6.90
Oct.	4.857	10	6	6.75	6.90
Nov.	5.142	10	6	6.75	6.97
Dec.	5.142	12	6	6.75	7.47
1779					
Jan.	6.285	13	7.50	6.75	8.38
Feb.	6.857	14	7.50	9	9.34
Mar.	12	15	7.50	9	10.87
Apr.	15.428	16	9	9	12.35
May	20.571	18	9	9	14.14
June	20.571	20	10	13.50	16.02
July	22.285	40	15	13	22.57
Aug.	22.285	30	11.25	18	20.38
Sept.	20.571	22.50	11.25	13.50	16.95
Oct.	20.571	22.50	12	13.50	17.14
Nov.	22.285	25	21	27	23.87
Dec.	24	40	30	27	30.25
1780					
Jan.	30 for 1	40	30	30	32.50

Source: Fisher, 1913.

Another commodity money was tobacco. Though never an official currency, it was used to pay church dues, official fees, fines, and court charges. It was an unsatisfactory money, as it was bulky, perishable, seasonal in supply, variable in quality, and subject to increased or decreased quantity, depending on the size of the crop. When the tobacco crop was large, the value per pound fell so that it took more pounds of tobacco to buy a given article, and commodity prices rose. During 1620–1621 settlers paid 100 pounds of tobacco each for "young and uncorrupt girls" brought from England. A little later the supply of young girls must have decreased or the demand for them increased or the supply of tobacco increased or the demand for it decreased; in any case the price rose to 150 pounds (Lester 1939)—an early case of inflation.

Debtors wanted tobacco to be abundant and cheap, which was inflationary, so they could easily meet their obligations. The clergy and local officials who were on fixed salaries wanted tobacco to be scarce and of high value so that prices of the articles they bought would be low and they could live well. Efforts were made to control the planting of tobacco to stabilize its value, but the British Crown forbade this early effort at monetary stabilization. The growing use of paper money led to the abandonment in 1733 of tobacco as currency.

Massachusetts issued paper money in 1690, printing the equivalent of 7,000 English pounds sterling (Bogart 1927). This was the first paper money in America and the first in the British Empire, and it provided the model that gave John Law the inspiration that led to the French paper money inflation of 1720. These colonial bills were used to pay soldiers for the expedition against the French in Canada. When the money began to depreciate, prices rose by 50 percent (Felt 1839). The colony called in a portion of the issue and promised redemption of the remainder.

With Queen Anne's War and the second campaign against Canada, 1702–1714, paper money again depreciated. By 1714, the price of wheat had advanced 60 percent. Paper money continued to depreciate, and by 1749, wheat was three times the price it had commanded five years earlier.

The price increase had a differential effect on various sectors of the economy. It was well received by farmers but opposed by local creditors and by the crown. Wages lagged behind the rise in commodity prices. Those on fixed incomes were disadvantaged. Massachusetts Governor Belcher pointed out that "the loss has more heavily fallen upon widows and orphans, upon ministers of religion, and upon such as spend their time to serve the public" (Felt 1839).

In 1749 Massachusetts redeemed its paper currency at a ratio of 7.5 units of paper money to one in specie. This "generous" redemption was made possible by a grant from the English Parliament to recompense the colony for its expenditures during King George's War (Bullock 1900). With the withdrawal of paper money (it was burned), deflation occurred. Wheat fell in price from 50.3 shillings per bushel to 4.8 shillings. The historian Felt (1839) reported: "To those who earnestly sought the extermination of such currency, it was a fire of joy—but for many who cast long and lingering looks for its continuance, it was a fire of sorrow."

Despite the disapproval of the mother country, the colonies all issued paper money. Amounts were excessive and depreciated relative to sterling. Paper money was made legal tender, and exchange rates against sterling were fixed by law. Nevertheless, there was a dual price system, one in paper money and one in pounds sterling. At their maximum depreciation, paper monies of the following colonies reached these ratios to sterling:

South Carolina	7 to 1
Connecticut	8 to 1
North Carolina	10 to 1
Massachusetts	11 to 1
New Hampshire	24 to 1
Rhode Island	26 to 1

Largely because of Benjamin Franklin's leadership, colonial Pennsylvania had better experience with paper money than did the other colonies. As a member of the legislature, Franklin voted for the issue of paper money and, as a printer, produced it. Pennsylvania first issued paper money in 1723 (Macfarline 1896). According to Franklin, the quantity "increased from the first issue of 15,000 pounds to 600,000 pounds or near it" (Sparks 1836). Apparently the amount issued was related to the increase in trade, for it resulted in only a moderate price increase. During approximately a half-century preceding the Revolutionary War, the index of prices in Pennsylvania rose about 60 percent (Warren and Pearson 1931). Franklin wrote regarding paper money, "It was well received by the common people in general; but the rich men disliked it" (Franklin, undated). Franklin maintained that Pennsylvania's paper currency was stable in value: "Nor has any alteration been occasioned by the paper money, in the price of the necessaries of life, when compared with silver" (Franklin 1764). Adam Smith, that keen observer, wrote in his *Wealth of Nations*, "Pennsylvania was always more moderate in its emissions of paper money than any of the other colonies. Its paper currency, accordingly, is said never to have sunk below the value of gold and silver." Bezanson (1935) noted that from 1730 to 1775 the exchange rate of the Pennsylvania currency against the pound sterling moved within a narrow range of 19 percent.

Price behavior varied geographically because each of the colonies had its unique situation and issued its own paper money. By the time of the Revolution, the colonies had considerable experience with paper money and the price behavior associated with it.

In the Declaration of Independence Thomas Jefferson eloquently characterized the many grievances the colonies had against the mother country. The oppressive monetary policies of the Crown are not named, however. For some reason—perhaps aversion to vulgar monetary matters—Jefferson omitted their mention. Yet these policies must have been deeply resented, especially by the laity, to whom financial consideration mattered so much.

War requires the transfer of resources from civilian to military purposes. This transfer may be accomplished in nine ways, depending on the circumstances:

1. Increasing production, with government acquiring the increment

2. Requisitioning men and goods without compensation, a method both ancient and modern

3. Borrowing from the citizenry, thereby transferring purchasing power from the private to the public sector

4. Acquiring goods from abroad

5. Postponing investment in plants and infrastructure

6. Taxing, whereby purchasing power is transferred from the individual to the state, making possible the purchase of goods needed in wartime

7. Rationing goods and fixing prices, a method much in favor

8. Spending of savings accumulated by the sovereign, permitted by earlier excess of revenues over expenditures, a method used by medieval kings

9. Debasing the coinage if on a metallic standard or inflating the circulating medium if fiat money is in use. This permits the state to bid goods away from the citizenry

Increasing production, requisitioning, borrowing from the public, obtaining goods from abroad, postponing investment, taxing, rationing, and fixing prices reduce what would otherwise be wartime's upward pressure on price levels. Injecting additional money into the income stream by creating new money is frankly inflationary. Governments, past and present, finding themselves at war, typically employ as many of these alternatives as are useful to achieve the greatest possible contribution to the war effort while holding the economic hardship of the citizenry to a tolerable level.

When war broke out, the colonies hesitated hardly at all in choosing among these various policies. Their treasuries were empty, their credit was poor, and the revolution was itself a statement against heavy taxation and arbitrary governmental action. They had experience in the use of paper currency, and they issued it in large volume.

On 22 June 1775, less than a week after the Battle of Bunker Hill, Congress provided for the first issue of paper money, known as the Continental Currency. Nominally convertible into Spanish dollars, the notes were given credibility by the supposed backing of the government-owned public lands of the West. The amount was not to exceed 2 million Spanish dollars (Phillips 1972). During the next 4.5 years, there were forty issues of Continental Currency aggregating $242 million (Dewey 1931). The Continental issues were almost equaled by issues of the various colonies that in total amounted to $210 million. Both the Continental Currency and the monies of the colonies were systematically counterfeited by the British and others.

With these paper currencies, the embattled colonies acquired arms, provisioned the army, paid the soldiers, and met the ordinary expenses of government. Supplied with these new monies, the Continental Congress bid goods away from the civilians, thus forcing up prices and diverting material from peacetime to wartime use.

At first the Continental Currency was received willingly, but by the end of 1776 it had begun to depreciate. By 1780 the ratio to specie was 32.5 to 1, and by May 1781 it had ceased to pass as currency. Barber shops were papered with notes. "Not worth a Continental" is a phrase traceable to that time.

Quotations on price behavior during the revolution are difficult to find, partly because newspapers, dependent on imported newsprint, ceased publication or curtailed the size and frequency of issue.

Perhaps the best indication of the degree of inflation is given by the "tabular standard" introduced by the state of Massachusetts for paying soldiers. The rate of currency depreciation was determined by the average prices of beef, corn, wool, and sole leather. In January 1777, the soldier received $1.16 in currency for every dollar due. By January 1780, he was receiving $32.50 for every dollar.

Exactly how much prices rose is difficult to assess. Hard-money prices apparently increased somewhat in response to international forces. The currencies of the various colonies depreciated more than did the Continental Currency. Whether quoted prices were in terms of Continental Currency or the currency of one of the colonies was often unspecified. With the exigencies of war and poor transportation, prices varied from one area to another.

Then as now, blame for advancing prices was laid at the doorstep of profiteers. In March 1778, this assessment was made in Boston:

One Great Reason of the present Excessive Prices of Provisions in this Town arises from the Avarice, Injustice, and Inhumanity of certain Persons within 20 miles of it, who purchase great Part of the same of Farmers living at a greater Distance and put an exorbitant Advance on it. (Davis 1905)

Price controls and sumptuary laws were voted but, as previously noted, they were generally ineffective (Webster 1791).

The variety of impacts of rapid inflation were not much different from those of earlier and later times. Ramsay (1789) describes it thus:

The aged who had retired from the scenes of active business . . . found their substance melting away . . . The widow experienced a frustration of all . . . (her deceased husband's) well-meant tenderness. The blooming virgin who had . . . a liberal patrimony, was legally stripped of everything but her personal charms and virtues . . . such were the evils which resulted from paper money . . . It was at all times the poor man's friend . . . all kinds of labor very readily found their reward . . . expending their money as fast as they received it, they always got the full value . . . The poor became rich, and the rich became poor. Money lenders . . . were injured. They who were in debt and possessed property of any kind could make the latter extinguish the former . . . A small part of the production of a farm would discharge long outstanding accounts . . . The dreams of the golden age were realized to the poor man and the debtor, but unfortunately what these gained was just so much taken from others.

An indication of the degree of inflation is provided by a resolution passed by Congress in January 1780 recommending that the various colonies regulate prices "not to exceed 20-fold of the prices current through . . . 1774" (Phillips 1972). Only two months later, on 18 March 1780, when the paper dollar had fallen in value to only one or two cents, Congress adopted a plan for reducing the Continental Currency to one-fortieth of its nominal value, or 2.5 cents per dollar (Bullock 1900), a value that indicates a fortyfold price increase. Ramsay (1789) described the demise of the Continental Currency thus: "Like an aged man expiring by the decays of nature, without a sigh or a groan, it fell asleep in the hands of its last possessor." Peletiah Webster (1791) wrote:

Thus fell, ended, and died the Continental Currency, aged 6 years . . . The most powerful state engine, and the greatest prodigy of revenue, the most mysterious uncontrollable, and the most magical operation, ever known . . . expired without one groan or struggle.

By 1781 the war was over, won with the help of the Continental Currency. Benjamin Franklin, then in France as U.S. ambassador, assessed this value to the currency:

The effect of paper currency is not understood on this side of the water. And indeed the whole is a mystery even to politicians; how we have been able to continue a war for four years without money and how we could pay with paper that had no previously fixed fund appropriated specifically to redeem it. This currency, as we manage it, is a wonderful machine. It performs its office when we issue it; it pays and clothes troops and provides victuals and ammunition; and when we are obliged to issue a quantity excessive, it pays itself off by depreciation. (Van Doren 1945)

Following the repudiation of paper money there was a brief period of postwar prosperity; then depression set in. Commodity prices fell to the prewar level in Boston and to slightly above the prewar level in New York, Philadelphia, and Charleston. "Houses were scarce; rents were exorbitant, and landlords made no repairs. Labor was scarce when peace was made but unemployment accompanied the depression" (Spaulding 1932). Many ex-soldiers were imprisoned for debt. The New York Assembly defeated, passed, and then repealed insolvency acts. Lawyers became the most hated group. Sheriffs auctioned off foreclosed farms. Manufacturing industries closed their doors.

In New England, farmers who had borrowed money at wartime prices found it impossible to pay their debts. Discontent was manifested in Shays's Rebellion, which was put down by force of arms. Massachusetts finally recognized the injustice of requiring repayment with scarce currency and legalized a moratorium for debtors (Sumner 1874).

So the United States won its independence, financing its war with irredeemable paper. As prices rose and fell, benefits and penalties were scattered indiscriminately among its citizens. In retrospect, it might have been possible to reduce the inequities had the paper currency been retained and so managed as to hold prices at approximately their wartime level. Price relationships had come into rough adjustment at that level. There was no need to force them down by wiping out the entire supply of paper currency, thus bringing on depression. The prewar price level had no special merit—no price is high or low except by comparison.

After World War II, U.S. monetary affairs were so conducted as to maintain something like the price level reached during the war. Thanks to the wisdom of our monetary officials, the nation thus averted the price collapse and the postwar depression that had followed each of our earlier major wars.

Decisions regarding monetary policy are sometimes made by salaried people who, reasoning from their own circumstances, consider that things would be better if prices were forced down. The desire to restore earlier price levels is powerful, reinforced by a vague idea that economic justice lies in reestablishing an earlier relationship. People seek to apply to economics a concept more appropriate to physics—what goes up must come down—though even there, with objects hurtling into space, the notion is flawed.

We can learn from experience with the Continental Currency that paper money and its attendant inflation, despite the admitted inequities, can be a powerful engine for marshalling material goods in the hands of government during a national emergency. The Continental Currency, often judged harshly, comes off reasonably well if compared to its alternatives, which were uniformly bleak.

THE FRENCH REVOLUTION AND THE ASSIGNATS

During the French Revolution, prices in France rose to 285 times their earlier level, an increase that exceeded by about 150-fold the inflation associated with John Law's paper money inflation seventy years earlier. The world-shaking events of the French Revolution so far eclipsed the price increase associated with it that awareness of that price rise has almost vanished.

"Madmen in authority, who hear voices in the air, are distilling their frenzy from some academic scribbler of a few years back," wrote John Maynard Keynes. The madmen of revolutionary France included Robespierre, Danton, and Carnot, leaders of the Reign of Terror. The voices they heard were those of Rousseau and Voltaire. Rousseau (1712–1778) wrote *Social Contract*, the veritable textbook of the revolution, which begins, "Man is born free but is everywhere in chains." These chains Rousseau attributed to inept government. Voltaire (1694–1778) was a vigorous critic of the church. The crown and the church were the underlying institutions that gave stability to France. With these two institutions under withering attack, the country was ripe for revolution.

The causes of the revolution, according to various writers, were the new thought that flowed from Rousseau and Voltaire; the growth of a new entrepreneurial class that found no ready place in a society controlled by the church, the nobility, and the landholders; a weak sovereign, Louis XVI, discredited for his lavish life-style and beset by a bankrupt treasury; grinding poverty among the lower classes; and severe drought in 1788, which increased prices and brought the poor people to the threshold of famine.

On 14 July 1789, the people of Paris revolted and successfully stormed the Bastille, a fortress-prison. The country was left without an effective government. There were efforts to establish control, all imbued with the drive for a new order. The National Assembly, the Legislative Assembly, the Convention, and a Committee on Public Safety succeeded one another in a desperate quest for governance. Prussia and Austria, old regimes that feared the spread of revolutionary ideas, sought to help put down the French uprising. War against the revolutionists broke out in April 1792.

King Louis XVI was guillotined on 21 January 1793. The Reign of Terror is dated from then until the death of Robespierre on 28 July 1794. According to Bax (1907), of the 2,750 victims of Robespierre's Terror, only 650 were of the upper or middle classes. Many of the victims were workingmen and tradesmen, accused of violating the Law of the Maximum, a price-fixing edict. During the last three weeks of Robespierre's rule, 1,125 persons were executed in Paris alone. The extreme disruption of the revolution is illustrated by an incident in 1793: a dancer, Mlle. Candeille, was garlanded as the "Goddess of Reason" and borne to the Cathedral of Notre Dame, where, amid music, tricolor, and virgins dressed in white, the worship of reason was inaugurated, supplanting the worship of God.

In the end, the terror devoured its parents as well as its children. Robespierre was guillotined, Marat was stabbed to death, and Danton was executed.

After the terror, a counterrevolution set in, sometimes called "The White Terror," which had excesses of its own. It was climaxed by the coming to power of Napoleon, the military dictator, on 10 November 1799.

The price behavior during this period swung from a prerevolutionary deflation, 1770–1787 (Labrousse 1876); to inflation, 1789–1796 (White 1876); and back to a postwar deflation, 1797–1807 (White 1876).

Early in 1789, the French nation found itself in deep financial trouble characterized by a heavy debt and a deep deficit, partly the result of having helped to support the American revolution. Growing disquiet in the country precluded a tax increase. What to do? Marat, in his newspaper, *Friend of the People*, advocated printing paper money, the medium of exchange associated with John Law early in the century. Arguments for paper money were persuasive:

- *It would have solid backing.* The first issue, proposed at 400 million livres, constituted only about 20 percent of the value of the confiscated church property on which it would be based. This, it was said, was better than undeveloped Louisiana, the backing for Law's currency.

- *The failure of Law's money was no precedent.* The contention was that paper money in the constitutionally governed country would escape the hazards of paper money under a monarchy.

- *There was no alternative.* On 17 June 1789, the National Assembly declared all taxes illegal. Borrowing was impossible. Precious metal had gone into hiding, and no other course was open.

Benjamin Franklin, architect of Pennsylvania's successful paper currency and supporter of fiat money during the American Revolution, was America's minister to France from 1776 to 1785. Very likely the successful American experience with paper money, related by Franklin, predisposed the French to its use.

Necker, the able minister of finance, opposed paper money. But after the storming of the Bastille, there was no stopping it. In April 1790, a decision was made to issue 400 million livres of paper money. The revolutionists had confiscated the vast property of the church, with an estimated value of at least 2,000 million livres. (A livre was the equivalent of $1.25 in 1965 American dollars.) The church property, the accumulation of 1,500 years, consisted of princely estates in the country, bishops' palaces, and urban buildings which composed between one-fourth and one-third of the real property of France. The expropriated church property was used as backing for the notes, called *assignats*, these having assigned value based on the newly acquired land. The first issue bore 3 percent interest.

Andrew Dickson White argued that the chief resistance to the issuing of paper money is the initial opposition, and that once this has been overcome, successive issues come more readily and in progressively larger amounts, thus resulting in a geometrically escalating price increase and bringing about either hyperinflation or draconian restraint (White 1876). In France, 1790–1796, it was the former. In the United States, 1979–1982, it was the latter. By early 1796 the assignats in circulation totaled, in nominal value, something like twenty times the original estimated worth of the supporting expropriated church property.

The revolutionists were anxious to place the seized church property into the hands of the common people both to broaden the basis of land ownership and to absorb the excessive number of assignats. The former church property moved slowly, however. The common people lacked the money to buy, and the wealthy were reluctant to purchase for fear that, once purchased, their newly acquired property would be expropriated.

Some of the wealthy fled the country, taking with them what valuables they could. Their estates were then confiscated by the revolutionary government. An estimate in 1793 placed the value of these confiscated large estates at 3 billion francs, an amount comparable to the value of the expropriated church property.

As with John Law's experience seventy years earlier, the first effects of the paper currency were helpful. The government was able to meet its obligations. A part of the national debt was retired. The new currency lubricated the wheels of trade. Production rose, and employment increased. Had the issue of new paper currency ceased after this first success, printing of the assignats might have been considered a statesmanlike venture. Intoxicated with success, however, the architects of the revolution printed addi-

Table 2.3
Depreciation of a 100 Livre Paper Assignat in Terms of the Number of Gold Livres for Which It Would Exchange, 1790–1796

Original issue, April 1790	100
Dec. 17, 1791	80
Late 1791	68
Early Feb. 1792	60
Late Feb. 1792	53
Aug. 1795	11
Sept. 1795	8
Nov. 1795	4
Dec. 1795	3
Feb. 1796	1
Last quotation	0.7

Sources: White, 1876.

tional assignats. If some were good, more must be better. Assignats seemed a painless way of financing the government, far better than taxes, which had been outlawed, or borrowing, which was impossible.

The initial contention was that the assignats, because they bore interest, would be preferred to specie, but the assignats soon fell to a discount. Gold and silver were hoarded, the bad money driving out good money in accordance with Gresham's principle.

The depreciation of the assignats can be measured two ways: one, as in Table 2.3, is by the ratio of assignats to specie; the other is directly by price behavior. We examine both; they are in a sense mirror images of one another. Prices for different commodities rose by different amounts. While the inflation was in progress, the price of wood rose to 125 times its earlier level while the price of shoes increased forty-fold.

Whereas Law's inflation was one of financial instruments, the revolutionary inflation had to do with commodities. The two sectors can display different behavior, as we see in the various inflations examined in this study.

The first assignats had been issued with the image of King Louis XVI prominently displayed. After his execution the new assignats bore different images. For a time the notes bearing the king's picture commanded a premium over the later issues; to many people, particularly the nobility, the revolution seemed so unlikely to succeed that they felt the royal house would be reinstated and, out of honor, would redeem the currency that bore the king's image. The hopes of the aristocrats were illusory; the revolutionists repudiated the assignats issued under the king.

When the assignats failed, the revolutionists sought new means of financing the government. A forced loan died at birth. A national bank was proposed, but this idea quickly expired. The government turned to a new form of paper currency, mandats, backed by the now publicly owned real estate that had been confiscated from wealthy people who had fled the country. Mandats were represented as "fully secured" and "as good as gold," but even before the mandats could be issued they fell to 35 percent of their nominal value. The people had simply lost faith in paper currency. The mandats then fell to 15 and soon after to 5 percent of face value, and finally to 3 percent in August 1796, six months after their first issue. The 2,500 millions of mandats went into a common heap together with the 45,000 millions of assignats.

Inflation acquired its special advocates, particularly those who had borrowed money or purchased the confiscated lands; they wanted plenty of cheap money to meet their obligations. Among the chief beneficiaries were speculators and the war profiteers.

The estates of many among the aristocracy were devastated. On 18 May 1796, a young man complained to the National Convention that he, the heir of his deceased father, had been paid his inheritance in assignats, and had received scarcely 1/300th of the real value of his share.

Wages lagged as prices rose, repeating a familiar pattern. Those on salaries and fixed incomes found their purchasing power cut to the bone. Shrewd people put as much of their resources as possible into objects of permanent value. The working class had no such foresight or skill or means. Most of the assignats, when they expired, were in the hands of the common folk.

A special attribute of the inflation was that it obscured the natural workings of the economic system, thereby weakening the observed link between performance and reward. A consequence was a loosening of morals, a rise in gambling, a surge of speculation, and an increase in conspicuous consumption on the part of those who reaped windfall profits.

Tradesmen were accused of causing the price increase, an explanation that was readily accepted by the revolutionary leaders, who were happy to see attention shifted away from the excessive issue of assignats. Citizens raided the shops. The revolutionary leader, Roux, declared, amid applause, that "shopkeepers were only giving back to the people what they had hitherto robbed them of." Prudhomme's newspaper Les Revolutions de Paris declared in 1791 that prices "will keep rising until the people shall have hanged a broker."

Other explanations of rising prices were that the Bourbon family had drawn the currency out of the country, that the British were putting counterfeit assignats into circulation, and that imports were too great and exports too little.

So came price control, the Law of the Maximum. On 29 September 1793, price control, which had earlier been applied to grains, was extended to all foods. There were four rules:

1. The price of each article of necessity was to be fixed at 1⅓ of its 1790 price.
2. All transportation was to be added at a fixed rate per league.
3. Five percent was to be added for the profit of the wholesaler.
4. Ten percent was to be added for the profit of the retailer.

Penalties for violation ranged from fines and imprisonment to death. The Law of the Maximum sent more people to the guillotine than did the uprising against the aristocracy.

At official prices, many farmers could not afford to produce, and some tradesmen could not operate. Commerce dried up, barter developed, and the Law of the Maximum was widely violated. People sought to withdraw from enterprises that had been made unprofitable, but the government passed a law binding them to their work. The Law of the Maximum intended not just a halt to the price rise; it sought a substantial rollback as well. It was an effort to undo with one hand what was being done by the other. In December 1794, after only fifteen months of existence, the Law of the Maximum was repealed. This represented a victory of the conservative element over the revolutionary Jacobins.

The Law of the Maximum had held the price increases in partial check and made possible the purchase of necessities by the people in the towns and cities during the winter of 1793–1794, but this was at the expense of farmers and tradesmen. On balance, inflation, difficult though it was, was preferred to price control with its associated shortages.

Initially, the entrepreneurial class and the hired workers had joined in revolutionary opposition to the royalty, but with the royalty vanquished, the confrontation shifted to one between the entrepreneurs (bourgeoisie) and the workers (proletariat), the classical polarity described by Marx. The Law of the Maximum set up this new confrontation, and the entrepreneurs won it.

With decontrol, pent-up economic forces were released, accompanied by resurging inflation. Prices soared, and there were food riots in spring 1795. A final increase of prices brought events to a climax. A counterrevolution set in. The paper currency was burned, prices fell, and specie came out of hiding. There came a surprising return to conditions in which capital and labor could expect reasonable remuneration. Napoleon set the tone when he said, "While I live I will never resort to irredeemable paper." The transition to order was difficult, but less so than many had expected.

In Hegelian terms, the revolution was thesis, the counterrevolution antithesis, and the subsequent fusion of French political, economic, and social complexities the synthesis.

The French Revolution, with its chaos and its inflation, proved less disruptive to the country than many had thought. During the revolution and the inflation, France effectively pursued a war against Prussia and Austria. Soon after the revolution, Napoleon conducted a series of military campaigns that subdued much of Continental Europe. These things hardly could have happened if, as some contend, the French economy had been wrecked by the inflation. Perhaps the major lesson we can learn from this event is the amazing resilience of human beings and the force of continuity of their national existence.

The French Revolution scarcely could have occurred without paper money inflation. To those who on balance think well of the revolution, Galbraith for example, this is an endorsement of paper money. To hard-money people such as Andrew Dickson White, paper money can have no justification.

THE AMERICAN CIVIL WAR, NORTH: INFLATION AND DEFLATION

During the American Civil War, prices in the North rose to more than twice their prewar level (Table 2.4). Although interesting, this result is not the major subject of this section. The Civil War provided an opportunity to document three special types of price behavior. One, the most familiar, was the problem of inflation; another was deflation, the price pattern that came after inflation had crested and the price level was forced down. The third was relatedness, and it provided the lesson that nations are not autonomous as regards their price behavior, but that there is a world price framework to which a trading nation is in some fashion bound and from which it can depart only temporarily and in degree.

This section contains very little on the war itself; the facts of that cataclysmic event are well known. President Lincoln, in his second inaugural speech, stated its cause: "One eighth of the whole population were colored slaves, not distributed generally over the Union, but localized in the Southern part of it. These slaves constituted a peculiar and powerful interest. All knew that this interest was, somehow, the cause of the war."

Financial conditions were in disarray before the war. Expiration of the Second Bank of the United States in 1836 left the field of banking entirely to the states. Private banks sprang up in the depths of the forest, issuing notes with variously claimed authority and little backing. With its migratory gold reserves so manipulated as to be in place when the bank

Table 2.4
Index Numbers of Wholesale Prices of All Commodities in the North,
1860–1896

1910-14 = 100			
1860	93	1880	100
1861	89	1881	103
1862	104	1882	108
1863	133	1883	101
1864	193	1884	93
1865	185	1885	85
1866	174	1886	82
1867	162	1887	85
1868	158	1888	86
1869	151	1889	81
1870	135	1890	82
1871	130	1891	82
1872	136	1892	76
1873	133	1893	78
1874	126	1894	70
1875	118	1895	71
1876	110	1896	68
1877	106		
1878	91		
1879	90		

Source: Warren and Pearson, 1935.

examiner arrived, wildcat banking was the essence of soft money. At the time of the Civil War, an estimated 7,000 different bank notes were in circulation. An estimated 5,000 counterfeit issues were in use (Galbraith 1975). The paper money inflations of the American Revolution and the French Revolution were still within public awareness. The financial disasters associated with John Law and his paper money were among the apprehensions of conservative bankers. Hard money was the rallying call of conservative financial people. Zeal on the part of the dominant financial interests for a strong gold-based currency may never have been greater than during and after the Civil War.

This zeal was augmented by the precarious state of financial affairs. On 4 March 1861, when the Lincoln administration took office, the treasury was practically empty, the administrative departments were disorganized, customs receipts were almost at a standstill, the public debt was increasing, and government credit was ebbing (Dewey 1968).

The federal need for new money to meet the demands of war was acute.

During the first full year of the war, federal expenditures were seven times greater than annual prewar outlays, and in the last year of the war almost twenty times greater (Studenski and Krooss 1952). Federal expenditures were 26 percent of the gross national product in 1865 as compared with 2 percent in 1861.

The practical sources of new money were taxation, borrowing, or printing paper currency. All were difficult. A sharp increase in taxes would have alienated a public whose support was vital to the war effort. With the uncertain future, bonds were hard to sell. Paper money was anathema to the hard-money interests.

In the end, the federal government yielded to the various interests; the war was financed mainly by paper money and loans. In the North, only 22 percent of total financial resources came from tax revenue (Studenski and Krooss 1952). The net debt of the federal government at its peak was $2.8 billion, thirty-three times greater than the prewar debt and equal to more than half the national income.

In February 1862, after a hard fight, Congress passed a bill authorizing the issue of $150 million in legal tender U.S. notes, quickly named "greenbacks" because of the green ink with which they were printed. In July 1862, another $150 million issue was voted, and in 1863 still another $150 million was authorized. With the passage of time this method of financing the war gained in acceptance in accordance with the principle laid down by Andrew D. White cited in Section 6. Authorization of the last issue of greenbacks passed the House the day it was presented and passed the Senate the following day by a vote of thirty-eight to two.

The uncertain future, military and monetary, led to apprehension regarding the currency. In the closing days of 1861, paper money could no longer be redeemed in gold, and specie payment was suspended. The new greenbacks were quickly discounted against gold. Regular dealings in gold began on the New York Stock Exchange on 13 January 1862. Gold was purchased to compensate foreign suppliers who insisted on being paid in gold. There were of course speculators in gold. It was considered patriotic for loyal citizens to sell their accumulated gold and so hold down the premium of gold over greenbacks.

The discount against greenbacks was greatest in 1864, when a $100 greenback note was worth only $49 in gold (Table 2.5). This was reflected in the U.S. price level. The exchange rate against England and France remained stable in terms of gold, but more U.S. greenbacks were required to buy an English pound or a French franc—at the peak, about 2.6 times as many. American prices, quoted in domestic currency, necessarily rose. Full convertibility of paper currency into gold was not achieved until eighteen years after the discount began.

Table 2.5
Gold Value of $100 in Paper Currency in the United States, 1861–1879

	Dollars
1861	100
1862	88
1863	69
1864	49
1865	64
1866	71
1867	72
1868	72
1869	75
1870	87
1871	90
1872	89
1873	88
1874	90
1875	87
1876	90
1877	95
1878	99
1879	100

Source: Warren and Pearson, 1935.

With the onset of the war, prices began to rise. In August 1864, the price index rose to more than twice the level prevailing before the war. This must be considered a modest rise, taking into account the magnitude and duration of the war. The resolute efforts of the hard-money interests to protect the currency and hold the line against inflation were responsible for this performance.

Prices in Europe changed relatively little during the war. Wesley C. Mitchell (1960) shows that from 1860 to 1865, domestic prices rose in the United States 104 percent, in England 6 percent, and in Germany 1 percent. The increase in the United States was related to the increase in the gold price of the greenbacks.

Mitchell, in his classic study *A History of the Greenbacks*, originally published in 1903, reported the impact of the inflation on various sectors of the northern economy. From 1860 to 1864, textiles quadrupled in price as a result of the dearth of cotton. In general, wholesale prices rose more than did retail prices. The inflation imposed a heavy tax on working men, estimated by Mitchell at one-fifth or one-sixth of real income. Salaries of male school teachers in Boston rose only 25 percent, whereas the overall price level more than doubled, so their real salaries were reduced by 40 percent. Farm laborers suffered as well; their real wages fell by about 25 percent. Government employees found their slender wage increases outstripped by the price increase, and many quit their jobs. Nominal house rents rose by about 65 percent, but in real terms they fell sharply.

The soldiers' sacrifices comprised not only fighting and dying; in real terms their pay was almost wiped out. Soldiers' pay was $13 a month at the outset of the war (Dewey 1968) and later was raised to an inconsequential $16. The soldiers' purchasing power, low to begin with, fell 43 percent.

The rate of interest, contracted for some future period and strongly subject to custom, failed to keep up with inflation. Lenders arranging for loans in April 1862, to be repaid a year later, contracted for 6 percent interest. To obtain the customary rate of return on his loan, the lender would have needed 50 percent interest (Mitchell 1960). The money illusion plus the expectation of a short war kept the interest rate from rising; almost no inflation premium was added. As a result of the erosion of the value of loaned money, credit operations diminished and cash business increased.

Entrepreneurs thrived. The number of business failures, which had totaled 2,733 in 1860, fell to 510 in 1864 (Mitchell 1960).

The author Delmer, in 1864, reported price increases for the various sectors of the economy (cited in Bresciani-Turroni 1937). Though crude and somewhat arbitrary, the listing is indicative (prewar price level equals 100):

Stipend for intellectual work	110
Wages of unskilled operatives	120
Wages of skilled operatives	130
Land	140
Handmade articles	150
Machinemade articles	160
Articles for direct consumption	160
Raw materials	170
Securities redeemable in gold	190
Precious metals	200

The inflation accomplished what was necessary during the emergency: it obtained the required resources for the war effort by diminishing the standard of living of the people, thereby diverting materials and services to the demands of the war. The profits of entrepreneurs, so derided by the populace, encouraged the needed production of war goods.

Because almost everyone found that his nominal income advanced to some degree, even though real incomes shrank, inflation gave a feeling of "prosperity." Holders of property saw the value of their real estate increase. Borrowers found it easier to repay their loans. It is difficult for a people, imbued with the money illusion, to emancipate themselves from a pleasurable sensation when the money value of their incomes and their property increases. Perception is stronger than arithmetic. That real incomes may be declining and real net worth diminishing is difficult to comprehend during a time of inflation. Inflation may be the most subtle and effective way of obtaining the sinews of war.

The Postwar Deflation

From the peak in prices in 1864 to the low in 1896, a period of more than thirty years, the price level fell 65 percent in a gradual and irregular decline. The decline resulted primarily from two causes. The dominant cause was the appreciation of the greenbacks, which, during a period of eighteen years, rose from a 61 percent discount to par with gold (Warren and Pearson 1935). This appreciation, the result of hard-money policies pursued by the prevailing financial interests, put U.S. prices, which had been high in terms of greenback currency, back in line with world prices.

The other cause of the decline was the decline in the world price level generally, which carried prices in the United States, a trading nation, down with those of other nations. From 1872 to 1878 prices in terms of gold declined as follows (Pearson 1948): United States, 29 percent; England, 20 percent; Germany, 19 percent; France, 17 percent. The world price declined because the supply of gold, which served as a monetary base for the above countries, increased at a lesser rate than did the volume of transactions it supported. Trading countries experience similar but not identical price behavior, an expression of the economic law known as "the law of markets" or "the law of one price." An official who likes to think of his country as autonomous with respect to matters of money and price is inclined to downplay this relationship; however, empirical evidence supports the similarity of price level behavior in different countries (Hamilton 1934; Warren and Pearson 1935, 1937; Mitchell 1960; Wegner 1953).

The decline in the price level was the setting for a classic battle over monetary matters. The battle pitted farmer versus financier, debtor versus creditor, West versus East, radical versus conservative, soft money versus hard money. On the one side were the common folk, who borrowed money and produced goods, but with deflation they saw the return for their goods declining, the value of their physical assets diminishing, and their debts harder to repay. On the other side were the financial people and the salaried class, who, with declining prices, saw an increase in the value of their salaries, their savings, and their income from loan repayments. This narrow gratification was reinforced by the conviction that they, as members of the largely eastern establishment, stood resolutely for sound money against the soft-money preference of the inflationists of the West.

The battle focused largely on the greenbacks. The hard-money interests wanted to retire them; the soft-money advocates, responding to the declining price level, wanted to continue and increase the greenback money supply. The immediate question was whether to resume the payment of gold at the face value of the greenbacks. Some said that payments could not be resumed—there was insufficient gold. Some wanted to cremate the greenbacks, as had been done with the assignats during the French Revolution. Some recommended retiring the greenbacks gradually, so as to reduce the shock. Others said, "Do nothing and grow up to them." Horace Greeley, ignoring these problems, said, "The way to resume is to resume." The battle was something of a standoff; the country retired some $50 million of the $450 million that had been issued, a small proportion. In effect, the country did grow up to the supply of greenbacks; in fact, it outgrew them, as a child may grow into and out of a pair of pants. Despite the deflationary pain felt by the farmers, the country grew at a fairly steady pace during the second half of the nineteenth century, thereby convincing the hard-money people of the validity of their economic policies.

A series of Western protest movements, all of which focused on the dearth of money, developed during the three decades after the Civil War: the Greenback Party, the Granger Movement, the Farmers' Alliance, and the Populist Party. The Democratic Party co-opted a number of these causes. Most prominent among the protest movements was the effort, led by William Jennings Bryan, to monetize silver at established official prices of sixteen ounces of silver equaling one ounce of gold. This campaign was defeated. Had it won, the price decline would have been alleviated. The price of silver was in a longtime decline relative to gold (Warren and Pearson 1935). Although in 1867 the ratio of silver to gold had been sixteen to one, by 1896 it was thirty-one to one, and in 1989 it was seventy-one to one. Had the country monetized silver at sixteen to one, cheap silver (the bad money) would have driven out high priced gold (the good money) in accordance with Gresham's principle and, in effect, the nation would have been on a silver standard. Commodity prices, quoted in terms of a monetary unit of diminishing value, would not have fallen as they did (Friedman 1992). Prices would have risen, as they did in China and Mexico, countries that were on a silver standard (Paarlberg 1942).

There were financial crises: the panics of 1866, 1873, 1884, and 1893. Our forefathers, more frank than we, called these panics what they were. In succeeding years, with an effort to downplay the apprehension associated with these events, they became "depressions," or "recessions," or "growth corrections."

Price level behavior had an important effect on the outcome of presidential elections. There were eight presidential elections between the end of the Civil War and 1896, a period of irregularly declining prices. Five of these elections were preceded or accompanied by low or declining prices; in four of the five the incumbent party was turned out of office. There were three elections preceding or during which the general price decline was temporarily interrupted by rising prices; in all these cases, the party in power was returned to power (Pearson and Myers 1948).

The conflicting perceptions regarding price level behavior have present relevance. Bankers, editors, congressmen, television commentators, and salaried professionals, mostly with fixed incomes, are hurt by inflation. They write and speak out of proportion to their numbers and create the perception on the part of the public, more vocal than heartfelt, that any degree of inflation is bad. But the common folk, more numerous than the elite and better treated by inflation, deem a certain amount of it to be good. At a time of inflation, if it is of modest magnitude, they reflect on their financial circumstances, which are better, or are perceived to be better, and return the incumbent party to office. Politicians generally sense this, despite their condemnation of rising prices. It is difficult to explain on any other basis why inflation is tolerated in so many countries that have the popular vote.

The fairest peacetime price behavior, as most people will affirm but that no financial system has thus far been able to provide over an extended period, is a generally stable overall level of prices, with the prices of individual goods and services free to fluctuate in response to changes in their respective supplies and demands.

In monetary terms, the Civil War attested the utility of a moderate rate of inflation and the disutility of deflation thereafter. It gave adequately documented evidence of the relationship of one country's price behavior to price behavior in the rest of the world. It showed that when a trading country's currency depreciates, it increases its price level relative to the price levels of other countries that maintain their currencies unchanged. These lessons, empirically demonstrated, appear to have been only partially learned by the practitioners of monetary policy.

The question as to whether to resume gold payment for the greenbacks was the wrong question. With the world basing its monetary system on gold and with the country tied to the world price level, the right question would have been whether to resume gold payment at the prewar equivalent for the dollar—the seemingly sacred 23.22 grains of fine gold—or at a smaller amount, say half as much. If the gold content of the dollar had been cut in half (and Congress had the constitutional authority to do so), the following significant effects would have ensued: the exchange rate of the dollar against the rest of the world would have been altered, gold payment could have been resumed quickly, the Civil War level of domestic prices to which citizens had generally become adjusted would approximately have been continued, most of the postwar deflationary pain would have been averted, and the United States would have continued to relate its prices to those in other trading nations. The volume of U.S. international trade at that time was of limited dimensions, so that the dollar could have been devalued without severe disruption to the trade of other nations.

Nevertheless, the hard-money advocates, who were then dominant, felt not only their own self-interest at stake but also perceived ethical justification in forcing deflation and resumption of the prewar exchange value of the dollar. Hence, policies were chosen that resulted in deflation, thus repeating the error that was made after the Revolution, that would be made after World War I, and that, thanks largely to the ideas of John Maynard Keynes, would be avoided after World War II.

Whether to resume or not to resume gold payment was the wrong question. It proved impossible to give the right answer to the wrong question. The right question, which would have been whether to change the gold equivalent of the dollar, seems not to have been asked.

THE AMERICAN CIVIL WAR, SOUTH: INFLATION AND DISASTER

The Civil War ended four years after it had begun, with the surrender of General Lee to General Grant at the Appomattox Court House in Virginia. In four years, prices in the South had risen to more than ninety times the prewar level. The general price index of the eastern section of the Confederacy was as follows (first four months of 1861 = 100) (Lerner 1955, 24):

1861	121
1862	388
1863	1,452
1864	3,992
April 1865	9,211

The miracle of the Confederacy, like the miracle of Rome, was not that it fell but that it survived so long.

As in the North, the increased financial needs of the Confederacy were met largely by printing paper currency. An estimated $30 million of confederate notes were in circulation at the close of 1861. A year later, this had risen to $200 million. The issues continued but the amounts are conjectural, and the total outstanding was beclouded by refunding laws. The stock of money increased eleven-fold from the first quarter of 1861 to January 1864 (Lerner 1955). Galbraith (1975) estimated that the Confederate note issue was about $1 billion, with borrowing equal to about $330 million. Officials printed the currency as needed and used it to bid goods and services away from the people. As in the North, the Confederacy used paper money inflation to transfer goods and services from peacetime to military use.

The velocity with which money turned over increased as people hastened to be rid of it before its value depreciated further. Prices increased more rapidly than the supply of currency. Statistics on prices, the volume of currency in circulation, and the rapidity of turnover are obscured by the multiplicity of currencies in use (Pearson 1948). Notes were issued by individual states, cities, railroads, turnpikes, and banks. Further complications came from the increase of barter, the dearth of paper with which to report markets, and as the war dragged on, the shrinking area within which confederate notes were accepted.

Confederate notes quickly depreciated in terms of gold. By December 1861, gold commanded a 20 percent premium. By January 1863, three confederate notes were required to buy one gold dollar. By December 1863, twenty were required, and by March 1865, sixty-one; the confederate dollar was worth a little less than two cents (Pearson 1948). The collapse of the Confederacy in April 1865 rendered the notes worthless, along with confederate bonds and loans.

Prices in the Confederacy increased throughout the war at an almost constant rate of 10 percent per month (Lerner 1955).

The blockade caused cotton and tobacco, low in price, to pile up on Southern wharves, while imported items such as coffee, kept out by the Northern navy, were scarce, and prices rose rapidly. The ratio of prices of imported to exported goods, one to one before the war, fluctuated around a level of three to one or four to one (Lerner 1955).

The chaotic conditions that accompanied the depreciation of the currency are well summarized by an old confederate soldier: "Prices were so high that nobody could see them . . . Before the war I went to market with money in my pocket and brought back my purchase in a basket; now I take my money in a basket and bring home the things in my pocket" (Eggleston 1875).

Prices rose about twice as fast as wages (Lerner 1955). Southern businessmen made large profits. Rising prices and huge profits were blamed on speculators, extortioners, and impressment agents: "a band of harpies preying on the vitals of the Confederacy" (Lerner 1955). The government enacted price controls, but these became more and more unrealistic (Lerner 1955). The following were ceiling prices in the Confederacy as a percentage of going market prices:

June 1863	66
July 1864	53
October 1864	37

Confederate soldiers fared no better than the soldiers of the Revolution, and worse than the Federals. The confederate soldier's pay was fixed at $16 per month and was raised in 1864 to $18 (Pearson 1948). Pay was in depreciated currency; towards the end of the war, soldiering in the confederate army amounted to unpaid service.

When the war was over, the price level in the confederate states gradually and painfully realigned with prices in the North. Achieving this confluence amid the havoc left by the war was the task of Reconstruction. There were immense economic, social, and political problems. A lost war, a lost generation of young men, the loss of property in the form of slaves, a devastated countryside, and a deflation that brought prices down to a fraction of their earlier level—such was the burden borne by the South. Deflation in the North, though difficult, scarcely compared to that in the South.

GERMANY AND THE CLASSIC INFLATION

The classic inflation was that of Germany in 1923—"classic" because it was the first documented hyperinflation, the one that most often comes to mind with the word *inflation*. (The common definition of hyperinflation is that given by Phillip Cagan: price increases exceeding 50 percent per month.) The German experience remains in the front rank among such price phenomena despite a rash of inflations that followed it, two of which rose higher—Hungary in 1946 and China in 1949.

Lionel Robbins, the great English economist, says of the German inflation, "It destroyed the wealth of the more solid elements of German society; and it left behind a moral and economic disequilibrium, apt breeding ground for the disasters that followed. Hitler is the foster child of the inflation" (Bresciani-Turroni 1937).

Dimensions of the Price Increase

In December 1923, the index of prices of forty basic commodities in Germany, with prewar value equal to 100, reached a level of 143 trillion (Table 2.6). Professors Warren and Pearson undertook to portray the price experience of Germany with a conventional page-sized chart with an arithmetic scale. Of necessity the 1923 experience was truncated; in a footnote the

Table 2.6
Index Numbers of Wholesale Prices of Forty Basic Commodities in Germany in Currency, 1910–1923 (1910–1914 = 100)

1910	97
1911	96
1912	102
1913	101
1914	104
1915	146
1916	180
1917	182
1918	218
1919	465
1920	1,561
1921	2,174
1922	45,205
1923, Jan.	391,214
1923, Feb.	727,024
1923, Mar.	640,635
1923, Apr.	698,553
1923, May	1,148,659
1923, June	2,540,133
1923, July	9,506,115
1923, Aug.	158,685,207
1923, Sept.	2,894,282,836
1923, Oct.	764,082,765,567
1923, Nov.	79,259,400,758,685
1923, Dec.	142,905,055,447,917

Source: Warren and Pearson, 1937.

authors explained that the peak in 1923 would have been 2 million miles above the top of the chart.

The inflations that accompanied or followed World War I came after a century of relative price stability, so that there was little understanding regarding inflation and little coping ability. The German experience was the most notable.

The Setting

Germany had been defeated in the war. Harsh terms were imposed by the victorious Allies. Germany lost one-seventh of its prewar territory and one-tenth of its population. All colonies were lost, and its fleet and army were reduced to token size (Ringer 1969). Lost too were one-third of Germany's coal production, three-quarters of its iron-ore capacity, 40 percent of the blast furnaces, and 10 percent of the iron and steel foundries (Laursen and Pedersen 1964). In addition, reparations were demanded from Germany, fixed in 1921 at 132 billion gold marks. John Maynard Keynes wrote that the burdens laid on Germany by the peace settlement were beyond her capacity to bear. The report of the Dawes committee in 1924 confirmed this view.

Germany had borne the cost of the war chiefly by borrowing. By 1918 the country was well established on an inflationary track. By the time of the armistice, November of that year, prices had already risen to 2.5 times their prewar level. There was an escalating increase thereafter; prices trebled within the next year and more than doubled during the next twelve months. A surge began in November 1921, when prices rose to forty times their prewar levels. There came something of a pause for a few months and then a sharp uptilt. In November 1922, the spiral picked up speed, and by mid-1923 hyperinflation had begun, accelerating until the end of the year when stabilization was imposed. The inflation first crept, then walked, then galloped, then halted.

Paper Money

Whatever may have been the underlying reasons for the inflation, the operative cause was the printing of enormous quantities of paper money (Table 2.7).

Whatever share of inflation the Reichsbank did not cause, it accommodated. The president of the bank during the inflation was Rudolph Havenstein, who held that office from 1908 until his death 20 November 1923. He apparently did not originate the policies that produced the inflation; he seems merely to have acquiesced to them. The dubious distinction of fueling the engine of inflation during and after World War I appears to be lodged with Karl Helfferich, a bank director who served as secretary of the treasury during 1915 and 1916. He was an aggressive leader of the right-wing Nationalist Party during the Weimar period (Ringer 1969), and later, in an about-face, became one of the chief sponsors of the 1923 currency reform.

The chief engine of inflation was governmental lending to business and industrial borrowers at fantastically low rates, accommodated by pumping out enormous sums of paper money that speedily depreciated, permitting the borrowers to repay their loans in cheapened marks.

The official annual discount (interest) rate was as follows (Bresciani-Turroni 1937):

1915–1922   5 percent

July 1922	6 percent
August 1922	7 percent
September 1922	8 percent
November 1922	10 percent
January 1923	12 percent
April 1923	18 percent
September 1923	90 percent

The rise in prices was such that private lenders to small borrowers were getting 30 percent per day, whereas business and industrial borrowers were paying the official bank rate, 12, 18, or 90 percent per year. The private rate was 120 times the official rate. The incentive to borrow from the government under such circumstances was compelling almost beyond belief. When inflation is expected, an inflation premium normally is added to the

Table 2.7
Circulation of the Reichsbank, Billions of Paper Marks in the Form of Treasury and Loan Bank Notes, 1922–1923

1922, Jan.	5,807
1922, Feb.	4,634
1922, Mar.	6,273
1922, Apr.	3,899
1922, May	4,902
1922, June	14,605
1922, July	13,083
1922, Aug.	23,240
1922, Sept.	21,829
1922, Oct.	41,056
1922, Nov.	77,787
1922, Dec.	238,481
1923, Jan.	380,902
1923, Feb.	708,305
1923, Mar.	1,147,004
1923, Apr.	1,484,270
1923, May	1,802,215
1923, June	2,866,837
1923, July	3,987,474
1923, Aug.	14,176,000,000
1923, Sept.	941,064,000,000
1923, Oct.	114,874,000,000,000
1923, Nov.	1,996,265,000,000,000
1923, Dec.	202,232,341,000,000,000

Source: Young, 1925.

interest rate. In Germany during this period, the private trade was much more inclined to do this than was the government.

A passage from Bresciani-Turroni, who was on the staff of the Reichsbank during this tempestuous period, vividly portrays the issue of paper marks to meet the demand for loans:

Towards the end of October 1923 the special paper used for the notes was made in thirty paper mills. The printing works of the Reich, in spite of its great equipment, was no longer sufficient for the needs of the Reichsbank; about a hundred private presses, in Berlin and the provinces, were continually printing notes for the Reichsbank. There, in the dispatch departments, a thousand women and girls were occupied exclusively in checking the number of notes contained in the packets sent out by the printing press. One of the more extraordinary documents in the history of the German inflation is the memorandum of the Reichsbank, published in the daily papers of October 25th, 1923. In this the issuing institution announced that during the day notes to the total value of 120,000 billions of paper marks had been stamped (a billion = $1,000,000^2$) [sic]. But the demand during the day had been for a trillion (a trillion = $1,000,000^3$) [sic]. The Reichsbank announced that it would do its utmost to satisfy the demand and expressed the hope that towards the end of the week the daily production would be raised to half a trillion. [The terms "billion" and "trillion" used by Bresciani-Turroni differ from U.S. usage.]

Anecdotal material regarding the hyperinflation is abundant. People rushed to dispose of their money before it depreciated. One man ordered two bottles of beer at the same time, fearful that if he ordered them one at a time, the second would cost him more. Another man took his money to the grocery store in a wheelbarrow, intending to buy food for his family, but a thief came by, tipped out the money, and ran off with the wheelbarrow.

Notes were issued in denominations of 1,000, 2,000, 5,000, 10,000, and 100,000 billion marks. These latter, stamped on one side only, were the highest issued. Toward the end of November 1923, a kilogram of bread cost 428 billion paper marks, a kilogram of butter 5,600 billion marks, a newspaper 200 billion, a tram ticket 150 billion, and postage for an inland letter 100 billion.

A strange new malady appeared: "digit fatigue." How many digits in the price of a loaf of bread, a postage stamp, a glass of beer, a sack of coal? How many digits today as compared with last month or last week? How many likely next week? The inflation required reckoning for which there had been no mental conditioning.

The inflation took on a life of its own. Whatever the individual causes, their combined force served to spiral inflation upward. The dominant factor determining the price of any durable item was not so much its present ability to meet a need as what it might cost to meet the need of a week or a month hence.

A vicious circle was established, the elements of which augmented one another in a pattern of causation and interdependence: the exchange depreciated, internal prices rose, note issues were increased, the added quantity of paper money reduced once more the value of the mark in terms of gold, prices rose again, and so on. Speculation and anticipation entered this circle at all its links. The German circumstances became pathological, like a rapidly growing cancer in the human body. Inflation was out of control and headed for the stratosphere.

Effects of the Inflation

If one views the German inflation in simple macroeconomic terms, it is possible, except in its ultimate chaos, to judge it with some leniency. Despite defeat on the battlefield, Germany's economy performed remarkably well during most of the inflation, and employment was high. An estimate of employment as a percentage of the labor force in Germany for selected dates, 1913–1923, is as follows (Laursen and Pedersen 1964):

1913	97
1919	96
1920	96
1921	97
1922	99
1923	90

The dominant political and industrial elite were able to retain power. The German industrial plant was rebuilt after the destruction of the war. When one examines particular sectors and the experience of individual families, however, the injustice and inequity of the inflation are so flagrant as to wipe out any alleviating effects.

The "new rich" rode the inflation to great wealth, borrowing heavily at low interest rates, investing in property or goods, and repaying their loans in cheapened marks. Chief among these was Hugo Stinnes, who was involved in multiple businesses: coal, lignite, petrol, iron mining, blast furnaces, steelworks, engineering works, electrical works, shipyards, forests, cellulose, banks, insurance, transport, ocean and inland shipping, merchant firms, newspapers, and inns. The "new rich" lived in a flagrantly extravagant manner, in vivid contrast to the lives of the poor. In this fertile soil, Hitler sowed the seeds of his revolution.

The "old rich," holders of securities, lenders of money, owners of rental properties, possessors of savings, and those who lived on dividends and interest, were at risk of total financial collapse. Regulation of rents made some houses valueless because rents did not cover upkeep, and owners were forced to sell. Prices of old stock shares, those issued before the inflation, lost 75 percent of their value.

The government virtually wrote off its entire internal debt and revalued old corporate bonds, mortgages, bank accounts, and life insurance policies up to only a 25 percent maximum (Hirsch and Goldthorpe 1978).

On the whole, farmers did reasonably well. They had their own food while the prices of what they sold rose with the inflation and mortgage burdens declined.

Prices rose faster than wages, so real wages fell. In the middle of 1921, real wages were about 90 percent of the prewar level, but by late 1922 they were at 50 or 60 percent. Meerwarth's studies (cited in Bresciani-Turroni 1937, p. 302) indicate that by the end of 1922, real wages were less than the calculated subsistence minimum.

In summer 1923, the labor unions, encouraged by desperate workers, succeeded in indexing wages to the cost of living; however, by the time the money was spent, a week or a month later, its value had eroded. Following indexation, inflation accelerated. The utility of indexation may be judged accordingly.

Government employees suffered a sharp decline in real income. In September 1923, upper-class employees had only 44 percent of their prewar salaries, the middle class 58 percent, and the lower class 80 percent.

The professional and academic classes—students, tutors, writers, and artists—were reduced to penury and misery. Scholars sold their books to buy bread.

The numbers of poor people increased. To relieve their distress, local governments sometimes provided small subsidies. Excluding the unemployed, there were 5,632,000 such recipients toward the end of 1923.

Feeble efforts were made to control prices, but the attempts were overwhelmed.

The inflation was accompanied by a greater mortality rate due to tuberculosis, an increase in emigration, and a rise in crime, the number of which rose by 45 percent from 1913 to 1923. The inflation generated profound moral disturbance.

Allegations and Denials

Although the immediate cause of the inflation was the printing of paper money, the underlying causes, real and alleged, were the subject of intense argument. German leaders rested blame not on paper money or their own actions, but elsewhere. The various controversies we next examine.

A Shortage of Goods

A ready explanation of the inflation and certainly a contributory factor was the war and the subsequent shortage of goods. Germany lost territory and production capacity after the war. A generation of workers had been greatly reduced in numbers. Although men and territory and production capacity had been lost, however, there was a diminution in the goods needed to supply a now smaller country; the two tended to offset each other. Somewhat surprisingly, total production in Germany held up well until the very end of the inflation. Production of iron and steel was below the prewar level but increased from 1920 until the chaos of 1923. Agricultural production during the period 1921 to 1923 showed considerable stability.

The layman's explanation of inflation is that it results from too much money chasing too few goods. In Germany the supply of goods, though badly distributed, was on the whole sufficient. The cause of inflation lay mostly with the superabundance of money.

Reparations

The burden of reparations was enormous—132 billion gold marks. The Allies contended that the Germans inflated their currency deliberately to reduce the real burden of reparations. Yet reparations were specified in gold marks, and paper-based inflation could not of itself significantly reduce the burden. True, the rise of the dollar in the international exchange market was greater than the increase in domestic German prices, thereby encouraging exports to earn the foreign exchange with which to pay the reparations (Warren and Pearson 1937). The widespread belief was that inflation speeded up because the French occupied the Ruhr industrial valley in 1923, crippling the German economy (Galbraith 1975). This has partial truth, but inflation was well underway before the occupation of the Ruhr. The occupation added fuel to what was already a firestorm.

In one respect, inflation and the associated depreciation of the mark did reduce the burden of reparations. Sennholz (1979) contends that during these difficult years, Germany actually procured gratuitously from abroad large quantities of raw materials and foodstuffs. Depreciation of the mark was instrumental in this maneuver. Foreign individuals and banks bought at least 60 billion paper marks that the Reichsbank had floated abroad at an average price of one-fourth gold mark for a paper mark. The ultimate depreciation of the paper mark to one trillionth of its earlier value in effect repudiated these foreign claims. Thus, says Sennholz, foreigners suffered losses of some 15 billion gold marks, or some U.S. $3.5 billion, eight times more than Germany had paid in foreign exchange on reparations. In July 1922, reparations payments in foreign exchange were suspended and the depreciation of the mark continued. In fact, inflation picked up speed.

Balance of Payments

Bresciani-Turroni, perhaps the most respected of the writers who dealt with the German inflation and a high German official during those troubled years, reported that the prevailing opinion among German economists was that the inflation was caused by a disturbance of the balance of payments resulting from the payment of reparations (1937). The reasoning was as follows: the need to export goods to pay reparations required the mark to fall against other currencies, thus resulting in a price increase within Germany, which required the printing of more paper money to sustain transactions within the country. This explanation had enough theoretical and empirical support to make it believable; at any rate, it was the rationale used by the Reichsbank to justify printing paper notes.

Speculation Against the Mark

The burden of reparations, along with the printing of so much paper money and the speculation against it, caused the mark to fall in the international exchanges (Table 2.8). Incidentally, an avid speculator against the mark was John Maynard Keynes, who foresaw the decline of the mark, went short, and made a fortune (Galbraith 1975). To what degree the fall of the mark was the result of forces emanating from abroad and to what degree it came from causes within the country can hardly be determined. One readily can see the attractiveness to the Germans of lodging responsibility with other countries.

The German controversy over economic policy involved reparations, the balance of payments, the terms of trade, and the depreciation of the mark, all tied up with the inflation. To the Germans, these linked causes had their origin in the burden of reparations. According to the foreign nations, these related events had their source in the printing of new money.

Efforts to Avoid Revolution

The revolution had come to nearby Russia. The Weimar Republic, itself the result of a revolution, clung tenaciously to power, fearful of another revolution. One view held by the ruling elite was that a new revolution might come from unemployment and a shortage of goods. They believed that rising prices stimulated production and increased employment. Therefore, to

Table 2.8
Marks per Dollar, Selected Dates, 1914 and 1919–23, Monthly Averages

1914, July	4
1919, Jan.	9
1919, July	14
1920, Jan.	65
1920, July	40
1921, Jan.	65
1921, July	77
1922, Jan.	192
1922, July	493
1923, Jan.	17,972
1923, July	353,412
1923, Aug.	4,620,455
1923, Sept.	98,860,000
1923, Oct.	25,260,208,000
1923, Nov. 15	4,200,100,000,000

Source: Ringer, 1969.

prevent revolution, many thought that inflation should be encouraged to keep the economy booming. Powerful industrialists propounded this view, finding comfortable accommodation of self-interest with national imperative. Politicians, fearful of revolution and subservient to the industrialists, found the argument convincing and reassuring. This attitude contributed to inflationary policies or at least reduced opposition to them.

Blame Focused on Special Groups

The inflation increased the real wealth of those who anticipated and took advantage of it, chiefly those astute people who borrowed, leveraged themselves, and engaged in financial manipulations. This kind of activity was widely attributed to the Jews, who allegedly promoted inflation and profited by it. Hitler capitalized on animosity toward the Jews and used it in his rise to political power.

With the mark falling to abysmal levels, German possessions of various kinds, including art objects, were attractive to foreign buyers, who bid up their prices in terms of marks and acquired German displeasure for contributing to inflation and robbing the country of its treasures. Holders of financial assets moved them out of the country in anticipation of their deterioration, thereby arousing the indignation of the citizenry and giving rise to the charge that the supply of money was thus reduced, necessitating the printing of yet more bank notes. Speculators and hoarders were charged with reducing the supply of goods on the market and thereby adding to inflation.

All these explanations for economic woes were popular within Germany as they lodged the responsibility either with foreigners or with domestic groups that were held in low repute.

An Unbalanced Budget

An unbalanced budget is characteristically associated with inflation. The German budget was badly in deficit during the war, and the government was neither willing nor able to increase taxes adequately during the war or later. After the war, government expenditures increased as a result of deficits incurred by nationalized industry and the expansion of social services (Sennholz 1979). Increased government services were largely met by printing money. The deficit grew irregularly with time.

The percentage of expenditures covered by revenue in Germany, 1914–1923, was as follows:

1914	84
1915	87
1916	79
1917	66
1918	69
1919	30
1920	34
1921	44
1922	38
Jan.–Oct. 1923	10

The Crisis

A number of events came together to produce a crisis and bring the inflation to an end.

Political and Military Events

In January 1923 the French entered the Ruhr Basin, first provoking armed German response and then "passive resistance" at enormous German financial cost. By the end of August 1923 taxes were imposed to cover this cost, thus angering the citizenry. On 8 November 1923, Hitler, enraged with the loss of the war, the occupation of the Ruhr, and the widespread distress, tried and failed to seize the Bavarian government in what became known as the "Beer Hall Putsch." By late 1923 Germany was at a boiling point.

The Mark Had Lost Credibility

With the declining credibility of the mark, various monies and non-monies came to serve as the media of exchange. Currencies of other countries came into use. By autumn 1923, 2,000 kinds of emergency money were in circulation. Barter occurred, both domestically and internationally, thus bypassing use of the depreciating currency.

The Economy Was in Shambles

Although moderate inflation provided stimulation to the economy, hyperinflation was devastating. In November 1923, unemployment stood at 23 percent of the labor force, and real wages fell to 56 percent of the pre-war level. In 1923, coal mining was 44 percent of prewar output (Laursen and Pedersen 1964). Hans Luther, minister of finance, wrote: "the effective starving in the towns and the impossibility of continuing economic activities on the basis of the paper mark was so obvious in the days preceding November 16 that a dissolution of the social order must have been expected almost from hour to hour."

Leadership Changed

Hans Luther replaced Rudolph Hilferding as minister of finance in October 1923. Rudolph Havenstein, president of the Reichsbank, died on 20 November 1923 and was replaced by Hjalmar Schacht. Karl Helfferich, chief architect of inflation policies, had a change of heart and helped design a currency reform. These changes put the German government on a new track.

The Budget Was Balanced

Confirming the new resolution to end the inflation, the Reich budget was balanced to the amazement of all. This was done by a strict cutting of expenditures and the introduction of new taxes.

The Monetary Disease Had Run Its Course

The inflationary balloon had been punctured in Austria. Monetary excesses had reached their limits. The inflation ceased.

The Miracle of the Rentenmark

The German government finally banked the inflationary fires with an ingenious ploy: an interim currency was introduced to bridge the transition to a new permanent unit. On 15 October 1923, the rentenmark was substituted for the old mark at a rate of a trillion to one.

The new rentenmark was declared to be backed by a first mortgage on all the land and the physical assets of the Reich. This idea had its ancestry in the history of the French assignats but was in fact more fraudulent. In France in 1789 there was visible backing for the assignats in the form of land freshly taken from the church; conceivably assignats might be exchanged for such property. In Germany there was no way that rentenmarks could be exchanged for German property, which was legally in other hands (Galbraith 1975). The difference was that the Germans, weary of inflation, wanted to believe in their new money, whereas the French, preoccupied with other matters, wished to disbelieve in theirs.

The new rentenmark bore the words "constant value," a phrase the people desperately wanted to believe. The new money was accepted, even though it was an inconvertible paper currency. It was spent at a reasonable rate rather than at a headlong pace. Emission of the rentenmark was limited by decree. An attempt was made by the government to exceed the specified quantity limit that had been imposed, but this was beaten back by the management of the new Rentenbank, now stalwart in support of monetary stability. This greatly strengthened confidence in the new money.

According to Helfferich, the experiment with the rentenmark was made without having created the conditions for monetary recovery, that is, the solution of the reparations question and improvement of the economic and political situation. The attempt was "a leap over a ravine, the other edge of which was obscured by clouds." Even the minister of finance, Hans Luther, author of the stabilization decree, described his work as that of "one who builds a house, beginning with the roof." Nevertheless, it worked. The will to believe made the myth of stability self-fulfilling. This was "the miracle of the rentenmark." The German government was on the way toward a sound currency.

The shift from the panic of inflation to the stability of prices, money, and the economy was amazingly rapid. Unemployment, which had stood at 10 percent in 1923, declined to 6.4 percent in 1924 and to 3 percent in 1925 (Laursen and Pedersen 1964, Galbraith 1975). Total production and union wage rates rose:

	1926	1927	1928	1929
Total production (1928 = 100)	71.5	97.2	100.0	101.3
Wages, pfennig per hour, unskilled labor	66.6	71.5	78.5	82.9

On 30 August 1924 the reichsmark replaced the rentenmark and was in use by 11 October 1924. Paper marks could be converted into the new currency at a rate of one trillion to one.

The fine gold equivalent of the reichsmark was the same as that fixed for the old mark in 1875. Its ratio of value to the rentenmark was also fixed: one rentenmark equal to one reichsmark. Actually, the German monetary system was on a dollar exchange standard. On April 1930, the directors of the General Council of the Reichsbank obliged the bank to convert notes, at its discretion, into German gold money, gold ingots, or foreign exchange. Germany was again on a sound money basis. When the bad money could no longer circulate, the good money replaced it.

The shift from raging inflation to price stability was thus made with towering success. Any debts that were incurred with the paper mark could be repaid with the rentenmark at a ratio of one trillion to one. There was no need to reduce the innumerable fixed prices because stabilization at the inflated level was in effect a continuance of the old price level. This was entirely different from deflation (Warren and Pearson 1935). From 1924 to 1929, the price level of basic commodities averaged only 33 percent above the prewar level and fluctuated within a narrow range of eight points above and four points below its average.

The postinflation experience of Germany (nondeflation from a stratospheric level) was much easier than the U.S. post–Civil War experience (actual deflation from a moderate price increase). Credit for this performance is generally given to Hjalmar Schacht, allegedly a financial genius, who was commissioner of the currency and who, after the death of Rudolph Havenstein, became president of the Reichsbank. A controversial person, Schacht became minister of the economy under Hitler and helped Germany avoid the worst effects of the Great Depression. He was removed from the Reichsbank presidency in 1939, made ambassador to Turkey, and incarcerated in a concentration camp during the last year of the war. He was accused but acquitted of being a war criminal (Galbraith 1975). When, during his trial, it appeared that he might be found guilty, the quip among the Allies was that Schacht should be compelled, before he was executed, to write a report on how he had stabilized the currency.

Nothing in the German experience with inflation denies the validity of the quantity theory of money. It does refute the contention of certain early monetary theorists, particularly Ricardo (1817) and Mill (1848) that money is neutral, without force of its own, not really entering into the determination of price, and that the supply of money is identical with the demand for goods. This error has been corrected by various writers, but the residue of it remains, nourished by some in the financial community because it appears to alleviate their responsibility for the cycles of inflation and deflation. According to this monetary myth, changes in prices are caused solely by changes in the supply of goods and the demand for goods.

The Price Theory of Warren and Pearson

More than half a century ago, professors G. F. Warren and Frank A. Pearson of Cornell University offered an explanation of price behavior that has continuing validity despite the absence of wide acceptance. They contended that the price of a good or service is a ratio between the value of a given amount of that good or service and the value of a given amount of money (Warren and Pearson 1935). The value of a good or service is itself a ratio, and may be written thus:

$$\text{value of a good or service} = \frac{\text{demand for the good or service}}{\text{supply of the good or service}}$$

The value of money, also a ratio, may be written:

$$\text{value of money} = \frac{\text{demand for money}}{\text{supply of money}}$$

The price of a good or service may be written:

$$\text{price of wheat} = \frac{\left(\dfrac{\text{demand for wheat}}{\text{supply of wheat}}\right)}{\left(\dfrac{\text{demand for money}}{\text{supply of money}}\right)}$$

All these factors vary and their separate causality is difficult to assign. The price level is simply the aggregation of various individual prices.

In Germany in 1923, the supply of money increased prodigiously. The demand for money was greatly diminished; people rushed to dispose of it before its value fell yet further. With an enormous increase in the supply of money and a diminution in the demand for it, the value of money fell to an abysmal level, and many monetary units were required to buy a good or a service.

The assumption that money has a constant value is an error, claimed Warren and Pearson—again, the "money illusion." This money illusion may be expressed thus:

$$\text{price of a good or service} = \frac{\left(\dfrac{\text{demand for the good or service}}{\text{supply of the good or service}} \right)}{1}$$

Though critically in error, the illusion gave little trouble so long as the value of money remained reasonably stable, but when severe inflation occurred, its error became obvious.

The Warren-Pearson explanation of price behavior accommodates the various forms of money, whether precious metal as in Rome, tobacco as in the colonies, or paper as in Germany. It relieves an analyst of the necessity of claiming that the supply of bread or the demand for bread could have, at the height of the German inflation, boosted the price of bread to 1.4 trillion times its prewar level. The Warren-Pearson theory addresses the price level directly, whereas the other economic theories, developed mostly before the Age of Inflation, address the price level only tangentially.

The Warren-Pearson idea is really very old. It reaches back before Mill and Ricardo, the nineteenth-century theorists who stripped money of its essence and declared it to be passive.

Retrospect

The German inflation was related to a number of factors: a lost war, a blizzard of paper currency, the vindictiveness of the Allies, flawed economic theory, the threat of revolution, timorousness on the part of the German politicians, anachronistic behavior of Reichsbank officers, greed on the part of the industrial opportunists, speculation against the mark, and a psychology that became self-fulfilling.

Perhaps the lesson to be learned from this major inflation is that its effects were primarily on individuals rather than on aggregates, that it had social, political, and military as well as economic consequences, that its impact was more delayed than immediate, and that it must be understood in terms of psychology as well as objective fact. One legacy of the German experience is the abhorrence of inflation, discernible in German monetary policy from that date to this.

THE RUSSIAN REVOLUTION AND PLANNED INFLATION

Reporting the Russian inflation before, during, and after the Revolution of 1917 presents conceptual and statistical problems. How does one discern price behavior in a country that was trying to outlaw money, prices, and trade? What happens in an impoverished economy when rationing and allocations are substituted for the market? What forms do inflationary forces take when they are suppressed? The government, though mistrustful of the market, was driven by necessity to use what it had to of the price system. Only some official prices (which probably understate the degree of price increase) and some fragmentary records of the black market are available.

The forces that would have caused inflation in a market economy, in this centrally directed system, produced shortage, chaos, an upward progression of official prices, and a wildly fluctuating set of illegal prices. The best available information indicates that the price index in February 1924, with a prewar value equal to 1, stood at a level 17.1 billion times higher than eleven years earlier (Table 2.9).

The revolution had multiple causes: a lost war, exploitation of the poor, an autocratic czar, and Marxist zeal. For our purposes—an examination of price behavior—the revolution can be broken into five phases: the events resulting from the war with Germany, 1914–1917; the Revolution of 1917; the civil war or War Communism, 1918–1920; the New Economic Policy, which began in 1921; and the collectivization of agriculture undertaken in 1930.

Events Resulting from the War with Germany

World War I broke out in 1914. Prewar Europe had been divided into two tense camps. On one side was the Triple Entente, consisting of Russia, France, and Great Britain, who had agreed to defend each other against attack. On the other side was the Triple Alliance, consisting of Austria-Hungary, Germany, and Italy, also bound to support one another. On 1 August 1914, Germany declared war on Russia, a rival for influence in the Balkans.

The war was a disaster for Russia. Two and a half million Russian soldiers were killed (Ambramovitch 1962), and huge chunks of territory were lost in the central and north sectors (Heenan 1987). Russian soldiers at first fought bravely, but as word of the looming revolution, with its proposed redistribution of land, reached the front, soldiers deserted in great numbers. From 1 March 1917 to 1 August that same year, there were 170,000 desertions. In the nine postrevolutionary months, 1,183,988 evacuees failed to return to the front (Heenan 1987). Many of these deserters were peasants; they went back to the rural areas, intent on acquiring land for themselves in the wake of the revolutionary upheaval.

The country was ill prepared to fight the Great War. Because peasants were drafted into the army, food production declined (Haensel 1930). Transportation was difficult and fuel scarce.

Table 2.9
Index Numbers of Retail Prices in Russia, 1916–February 1924 (1913 = 1)

1916, Jan.	1.43				
1917, Jan.	2.94				
1918, Jan.	20.8	1920, Jan.	2,420	1922, Jan.	288,000
1918, Feb.	27.0	1920, Feb.	3,090	1922, Feb.	545,000
1918, Mar.	33.0	1920, Mar.	3,810	1922, Mar.	1,153,000
1918, Apr.	43.2	1920, Apr.	4,770	1922, Apr.	2,524,000
1918, May	57.5	1920, May	5,780	1922, May	4,162,000
1918, June	70.6	1920, June	6,570	1922, June	5,087,000
1918, July	88.6	1920, July	8,140	1922, July	5,795,000
1918, Aug.	101.0	1920, Aug.	9,070	1922, Aug.	5,589,000
1918, Sept.	93.5	1920, Sept.	9,230	1922, Sept.	5,995,000
1918, Oct.	93.5	1920, Oct.	9,620	1922, Oct.	7,342,000
1918, Nov.	107.5	1920, Nov.	10,500	1922, Nov.	11,561,000
1918, Dec.	135.0	1920, Dec.	12,000	1922, Dec.	16,972,720
1919, Jan.	164	1921, Jan.	16,800	1923, Jan.	21,240,000
1919, Feb.	203	1921, Feb.	21,600	1923, Feb.	27,700,000
1919, Mar.	258	1921, Mar.	27,600	1923, Mar.	31,100,000
1919, Apr.	336	1921, Apr.	35,700	1923, Apr.	39,260,000
1919, May	414	1921, May	42,700	1923, May	54,740,000
1919, June	516	1921, June	62,000	1923, June	79,930,000
1919, July	656	1921, July	80,700	1923, July	117,569,000
1919, Aug.	750	1921, Aug.	80,300	1923, Aug.	194,830,000
1919, Sept.	814	1921, Sept.	76,400	1923, Sept.	335,360,000
1919, Oct.	923	1921, Oct.	81,900	1923, Oct.	659,840,000
1919, Nov.	1,360	1921, Nov.	95,500	1923, Nov.	1,101,070,000
1919, Dec.	1,790	1921, Dec.	138,000	1923, Dec.	2,314,081,000
				1924, Jan.	5,400,000,000
				1924, Feb.	17,100,000,000

Source: Young, 1925.

The czarist government and Kerensky's brief provisional government met the war's financial problems in typical fashion—by inflating the currency. At the beginning of the war there had been 1.6 billion ruble notes in circulation. By 1 January 1917, this number had increased more than five times to 9.1 billion. On 1 March that year, the time of the fall of the czarist regime, circulation had risen to 10 billion. Under eight months of the Kerensky government and up to the time of the October Revolution, it almost doubled again, to 19 billion (Haensel 1930).

Prices of consumer necessities rose three-fold between 1913 and January 1917, and 2.5 times more by October of that year. The country was on the inflation track before the November revolution.

The Revolution of 1917

The initial stage of the revolution lasted eight months from its outbreak in November 1917 to the beginning of War Communism in June 1918. During that period, according to official USSR statistics, retail prices increased seven-fold.

The revolution developed in rapid stages. In February 1917 there were uprisings in Petrograd, and on 14 March, Czar Nicholas, beset by problems beyond his coping ability, signed his resignation (Reed 1919). A provisional government was headed by Prince Lvov. In June, Alexander Kerensky, minister of war, ordered an offensive against Germany, an unpopular move that failed miserably. Power was gained by the soviets; councils of workmen formed in accordance with Marxist theory. Then came the "July Days," when the Bolsheviks, under Lenin, sought to take over the government but were turned back; Lenin fled to Finland. Later that month Kerensky, a Socialist, became premier. Lenin returned from Finland in October and convinced the Bolsheviks that they should seize the government. "All power to the soviets!" was the cry. On 7 November 1917, the Bolsheviks took the Winter Palace in Petrograd, headquarters of the provisional government. By 15 November, the revolutionaries controlled Moscow as well.

When the Bolsheviks took over the government they had fewer than 100,000 members, not quite one Communist per thousand of the population. Only by a combination of popular support and strict discipline could so small a group dominate so large a country.

The Lenin government hoped that the Russian Revolution would precipitate similar revolutions in other countries and bring about a worldwide communistic system. To this end, they supported political cells in many nations and trained, in Russia, potential revolutionaries from other countries, notably China.

The French Revolution was clearly influential in communist thought. On 17 January 1918, the Soviet government published a "Declaration on Rights of Working and Exploited People," modeled on the French revolutionists' "Declaration of the Rights of Man" more than a century earlier (Nove 1969). The rallying call of the Russian Revolution was "Land, Bread, Peace," reminiscent of the French slogan "Liberty, Equality, Fraternity." Interestingly, the French declaration had been primarily political, whereas the Russian slogan was essentially economic. As the Russian Revolution drew on the French experience, so subsequent revolutions in Latin America, Africa, and Asia drew on the Russian model.

The initiative was in the hands of Lenin and the Bolsheviks. They took over a country defeated in war, ravaged by hunger, and torn by revolution. To some this would have been a thoroughly disheartening prospect, but for

Lenin it was the kind of chaos vital to the creation of a new communist world.

The Bolsheviks had the power. They outlawed all other political parties—seventeen in Petrograd alone (Reed 1919). They expropriated all the land, confiscated food from the peasants, nationalized industry, killed the czar, liquidated the nobility, suppressed the church, abrogated the debts of the old Russian government, and substituted central decision making for the market process. They negotiated a separate peace with Germany and sealed it with the Treaty of Brest-Litovsk, which they later annulled.

To achieve mastery, the Bolsheviks required command over resources, thus necessitating a huge budget. This was achieved mostly by printing paper money; taxation and borrowing had little part in government finance. In 1918 the government printed 36 billion rubles, doubled from the 19 billion of the Kerensky government (Haensel 1930). This currency was inconvertible, thus differing from most of the paper currencies considered here, which had at least some backing, however tenuous. Despite the necessity of using it, Lenin held his paper currency in contempt, calling his notes "colored pieces of worthless paper" (Nove 1969).

According to some versions of Soviet economic policy, the original idea was to continue printing currency until Soviet notes possessed absolutely no value, thus allowing money to commit suicide. This was deemed an appropriate fate, since the ideal communist world would be operated without money, with the people producing in accordance with their ability and consuming with regard to their needs (Hubbard 1936). John Maynard Keynes wrote: "Lenin is said to have declared that the best way to destroy the capitalistic system was to debauch the currency. Lenin was certainly right. The process engages all the hidden forces of economic law on the side of destruction, and does so in a manner that not one man in a million is able to diagnose" (Hazlitt 1965). The Russian revolutionary economist Preobrazhensky described the printing press as "the machine gun of the Commissariat of Finance which poured fire into the rear of the Bourgeoisie system" (Lindberg and Maier 1985). Professor Leonid N. Yurovsky, chief of the Currency and Foreign Exchange Bureau in the Commissariat of Finance of the Soviet Government, wrote in his article "The Currency Problem in Soviet Russia" that "money was not to play any part in the economic system" (Young 1925). The issue of paper currency escalated with the passage of time. Bazarov quipped that "the time is not far distant when the sum of the nominal rubles will exceed the number of all atoms or electrons of which our planet is composed" (Nove 1969).

The Communists used paper money to advance their purpose. Lenin apparently held the view that the peasants could be persuaded to "loan" food to the Bolsheviks only by purchasing it with irredeemable and depreciating paper. He fully understood that what the peasants received in return for their produce represented no immediate value; there was almost nothing they could buy with it. When in 1924 the original paper rubles were at last redeemed, the rate at which they were convertible was fixed at 50 billion paper rubles for one gold ruble. This meant in practice that the peasants received no tangible value for the food they had "sold" (Hubbard 1936).

A word is needed here to explain the Communists' disregard for the peasants, who in 1920, together with others of the rural population, constituted 79 percent of the total (Clarke 1972). In communist doctrine, the class war was between the bourgeoisie (entrepreneurs) and the proletariat (wage workers). Most of the peasants were essentially self-sufficient and therefore were neither of the bourgeoisie nor the proletariat, so they did not enter directly into revolutionary confrontations. The kulaks were different. They were the larger farmers, generally with as many as two cows and two horses, and produced enough grain to sell the surplus after feeding themselves. Thus they were entrepreneurs, and so by definition enemies of the people. The "liquidation of the kulaks as a class" carried out by Stalin in 1930 was the logical consequence of Marxist doctrine. This was incomprehensible to people of the West, to whom all farmers were worthy, especially those more enterprising and efficient.

Despite the ideological irrelevance of the peasants and despite the opposition to the kulaks, Lenin used the peasants' land hunger as an integral part of the revolutionary takeover (Nove 1969).

In communist theory, price is not to be determined by the interaction of supply and demand but in accordance with the labor theory of value, a concept propounded by the early English economists and discarded by the West more than a century ago in favor of neoclassical theory (the labor theory of value has been largely discarded by modern-day Communists). In pure communist theory, the price of an article or a service—if there is a price—is determined by the amount of socially useful labor expended in its production. This value is exceedingly difficult to compute, and it is evident that prices thus derived would baffle a westerner.

Civil War, or War Communism, 1918–1920

Opposition to the Bolsheviks formed quickly. They had only about eight months to consolidate their position and nationalize large-scale industry (Hubbard 1936). In June 1918 they precipitated the Civil War, often referred to as War Communism.

Supporting the new government were the Reds, consisting mostly of the army, including draftees, the greater part of whom the Communists had won over, in addition to many peasants who had acquired land and feared losing it to their old landlords if the Whites won.

Opposed to the Bolsheviks were the Whites, consisting of the expropriated capitalists, the dispossessed landlords, the remnants of the nobility, and those who had managed somehow to sequester their wealth, plus manpower recruited from whatever source. These loyalists were supported by the few troops who remained faithful to the czarist cause. The Whites were aided by soldiers from France, Great Britain, Japan, and the United States, all of whom feared communism and hoped in vain to see the Communists overthrown.

The civil war raged for the greater part of three years, and was finally won by the Reds. Abramovitch quotes the deaths from the civil war as above 7 million from 1 January 1918 to 1 July 1920—four times the Russian losses during World War I. The civil war left both town and rural areas in chaos. Typically, grain was acquired from farmers by outright confiscation, by a "grain tax," or by purchase at fixed prices with currency of no immediate value. Supplies were inadequate. Black markets proliferated, and illegal prices soared. It was impossible to live on official rations—2 ounces of bread per person per day for workers in 1918 (Nove 1969)—so the majority of bread supplies came from the black market. Despite all efforts to requisition bread grain, in 1918–1919 60 percent of that consumed in the cities passed through illegal channels.

Urban workers experienced deprivation greater than the peasants. At times there were no wages as such; workers were paid in kind if at all. They supplemented their meager rations by barter and use of the black market. The revolution was purported to benefit the industrial workers but brought disaster instead. As industry fell into chaos (Table 2.10), the number of employed shrank by more than half, from 2.6 million in 1917 to 1.2 million in 1920. Many urban people left the city and went to their country relatives in quest of food. Reserve food supplies were raided. Sometimes the only source of food was the black market, where, in 1920, rates for articles of consumption were forty or fifty times as high as those fixed by the government (Carr 1952).

War Communism, like earlier stages of the revolution, was financed by printing paper money. Currency circulation, which stood at 22.4 billion rubles on 1 November 1917, reached 30 billion in March 1918. On 1 June that year, it reached 40.3 billion and by 1 January 1919 stood at 60.8 billion (Dobb 1948). Inflation proceeded at a rapid pace. Overall prices rose more than 200-fold from June 1918 to January 1921. According to official statistics, which one must doubt, real wages fell from an estimated 10.70 rubles per month to the incredibly low level of 0.26 rubles per month (Strumilin

Table 2.10
Production and Trade, Russia, 1913 and 1921ᵃ

	1913	1921
Gross output of all industry (index)	100.0	31.0
Large scale industry (index)	100.0	21.0
Coal (million tons)	29.0	9.0
Oil (million tons)	9.2	3.8
Electricity (billion kilowatts)	2039.0	520.0
Pig iron (million tons)	4.2	0.1
Steel (million tons)	4.3	0.2
Sugar (million tons)	1.3	0.05
Railway tonnage carried (millions)	132.4	39.4
Agriculture production (index)	100.0	60.0
Imports ("1913" rubles)	1374.0	208.0
Exports ("1913" rubles)	1520.0	20.0

Source: Vaisberg, 1934.

ᵃ Some of the figures do not refer to strictly comparable territory.

1923). Barter, payment in kind, and the black market were necessarily the means of livelihood.

On the way to oblivion, a 1,000-ruble czarist note was worth 50,000 to 60,000 Soviet rubles (Carr 1952). By March 1922, a prewar ruble exchanged for 200,000 Soviet rubles. Money lost respect. Alec Nove (1969), who grew up in the Soviet Union during the revolution, recalled giving a banknote of considerable face value to a beggar, who returned it to him saying it was worthless.

With all this confusion stemming from the paucity of hard data, questionable official prices, and unrecorded black market prices, students of the Russian Revolution resort to nonquantifiable phrases to describe the inflation: "a tide of paper" (Galbraith 1975), "ever-wilder inflation" (Nove 1969), "irredeemable and depreciating paper" (Hubbard 1936), "the realm of astronomical" (Hutchings 1971).

The New Economic Policy Beginning in 1921

By 1921 the civil war was over, the Reds triumphant, but the land was devastated and the people sullen. Drought and war had reduced the harvest. Grain production, which stood at 80 million tons in 1913, fell to 42 million tons in 1921. Famine took an estimated 5 million lives (Paarlberg 1988).

In 1921 there was a sailors' rebellion in Kronstadt. Perhaps remembering the execution of Robespierre, leader of the French Revolution who failed to sense the changing mood of the French people, Lenin ordered a strategic retreat. He said, "War Communism was thrust upon us by war and ruin. It was not, nor could it be, a policy that corresponded to the economic tasks of the proletariat. It was a temporary measure" (Dobb 1948). The new economic policy reintroduced the market. The grain delivery quota was cut in half, private trade was legalized, and entrepreneurship reemerged. The "commanding heights"—banking, foreign trade, and large-scale industry—were retained by government (Nove 1969).

Inflationary policies were retained and inflation accelerated during the new economic policy. During 1921, government expenditures were 26 trillion rubles, only 16 percent of which were met by revenue. Notes issued covered three-fourths of the deficit (Young 1925). During eleven months of the year 1921, notes were printed to the amount of 17 trillion, increased almost 500 times from the issue of 1918; 550 carloads of paper notes were distributed among the treasury offices of the government (Haensel 1930).

In an effort to suppress inflation, a Committee on Prices was appointed in August 1921 (Haensel 1930). The following are samples of the Committee's price fixing (times the prewar price).

Raw materials	20,000
Sewing machines	20,000
Nails	70,000
Window glass	150,000

With the headlong issue of paper and depreciation of the currency, however, price regulation became meaningless, and the work of the Committee on Prices was soon abandoned (Haensel 1930).

The more currency the government issued, the less the total was worth. Prices rose faster than the money supply (Young 1925). Foreign trade and the foreign exchanges were drastically out of balance. In January 1916, a U.S. dollar would buy a little more than three rubles; in December 1922, it would buy more than 3 million.

Prices shot upward. The price level increased 1 million–fold from the onset of the new economic policy in January 1921 until currency reform in early 1924.

The chief dynamic of prices in the Soviet Union during the revolutionary period was money supply. The early economists said that the demand for goods was identical to the supply of money. Think how ridiculous it would be to measure the demand for goods by the 550 carloads of paper notes churned out by the Soviet printing presses. As indicated above, the price of an article is a ratio of the value of an article to the value of money, with both free to vary independently in accordance with their respective supplies and demands.

After the credibility of money had been lost, further pursuit of the old inflationary course was impossible. In 1923 the currency was renamed *sovznaki* (Hutchings 1971). Then a new stabilized currency, the *chervonetz*, backed by gold and foreign exchange, was introduced, and for a while circulated simultaneously with the *sovznaki*. The *chervonetz* began to depreciate and from January to October lost 25 percent of its value (Dobb 1948). By March 1924, the greater part of the monetary reform was accomplished. Stabilization of the currency was made possible by financial reform, the rehabilitation of the state budget, and elimination of the practice of issuing paper money to cover the budget deficit (Young 1925).

The Soviet Union used an ancient device: when the old ruble had lost its credibility, the government renamed its currency. This paper depreciated, followed by a new ruble, which also declined in value. Transitional currency was used concurrently in Germany, where a reform government was disengaging from hyperinflation. Germany and Russia, military enemies, emulated one another in embracing inflation and then checking it. The transition to the new currency apparently was accomplished without a major new upheaval, probably partly because the old currency had approached irrelevance.

An associated price phenomenon occurred in 1922 and 1923: the famous "scissors" effect. From March 1922 to September 1923, the ratio of industrial prices to agricultural prices increased more than four times (Dobb 1948), to the grave disadvantage of the farmers. The cause of this strange price behavior was uncertain; the government policy favoring rapid industrialization and the long-standing apathy regarding agriculture were probably influential.

With the improved incentives of the new economic policy, production increased; by 1930, agricultural production exceeded prewar levels and industrial production also responded well. Iron ore production, which had been 9 million tons before the war and had fallen to 0.1 million tons by 1919, exceeded the prewar level and by 1930 reached 11 million tons (Clarke 1972). To what degree the recovery resulted from the end of the civil war and to what degree it was a consequence of the new economic policy are unanswered questions.

Collectivization of Agriculture

Russian agriculture had traditionally been technologically backward, oversupplied with labor, largely of subsistence type, and opposed to the Communist party. Stalin sought to transform agriculture into large-scale collectivized units that would be better suited to mechanization, release manpower for the Soviet effort at industrialization, be more amenable to central direction, be more easily subjected to forced grain collection, and better fit the party's concept of economic organization. Consequently, in January 1930, as part of the first Five-Year Plan, the goal was announced of complete collectivization of agriculture and the "liquidation of the kulaks as a class within three years" (Hutchings 1971). The technique employed was to ally with the poor peasants, neutralize the middle peasants, and eliminate the richer peasants, the kulaks. At least 4.5 million kulak families were deported or otherwise removed from the rural landscape (Nove 1969).

The immediate result of the collectivization, however, was that the peasants slaughtered their livestock rather than lose ownership of them to the collectives. Between 1928 and 1933, the numbers of horses and pigs declined by more than half, sheep and goats by almost two-thirds, and cattle by almost half. The lack of horses for field work, the peasants' noncooperation, and unfavorable weather led to a drop in total agricultural output. By official statistics, farm production fell 23 percent between 1928 and 1932. During 1933 and 1934, famine, comparable in severity with the famine of 1921 and 1922, took another 5 million lives (Paarlberg 1988).

The strategy for economic development was to strengthen industry and the military at the expense of agriculture and the Russian consumers by requisitioning grain from the farmers at official low prices, transferring labor from farm to industry, and emphasizing cheap basic foods such as bread and potatoes rather than expensive foods such as livestock products. Stalin succeeded in his economic development policy, as witnessed by the military buildup and the rapid growth of Russian industry. The Russian plan for economic development was later emulated by a number of Third World countries, but most of these countries lacked the cushion of potential food supply and the ruthless character of the Soviet Union. Coercing the farm people and jeopardizing the food supply were unacceptable policies in Asian and African countries that enjoyed a substantial degree of freedom and democracy.

Official prices rose as the collectivization effort went forward (Hutchings 1971):

Index

1927–1928   100.0

1928–1929	106.6
1930	132.0
1931	179.7
1932 (first half)	251.8

Free-market prices rose even more steeply to twelve to fifteen times the fixed market price for the most important items (Hutchings 1971). Rationing was implemented; 50 million people, one-third of the population, were included in a bread-rationing scheme.

During the Great Depression from 1930 to 1940, prices in the market economies throughout the world were in sharp decline and unemployment was high. Prices in the Soviet Union, however, continued to increase, and unemployment was minimal (Hutchings 1971). By controlling the exchange rate and regulating prices, the Soviet Union achieved a large measure of insulation from the price behavior of the market economies. Naum Jasny (1951), the Soviet agricultural expert, shows that during the decade of the 1930s, while prices in other countries fell, the retail price of bread in Russia rose eleven times. Despite this increase, real prices of food were low enough to shift large numbers of peasants to urban employment, as Stalin wished. Incomes of farmers and laboring people were held down while prices of consumer goods increased and a shift to production goods was encouraged, thereby speeding the industrialization process. With the collectivization of agriculture, the major sectors of the Soviet Union had been transformed in accordance with the communist plan.

What can be learned about inflation from this examination of the Russian Revolution? The following eight findings seem valid:

1. A centrally directed economy is vulnerable to inflation, as are market economies.

2. The chief losers of the Russian inflation were the commercial farmers, who were either liquidated or had their crops requisitioned at inequitable prices; the laborers, whose level of living was held down; and the well-to-do, who saw their wealth confiscated or their savings eroded away by the decline of the ruble.

3. Chief gainer was the government, which was able to finance the revolution essentially without taxes or borrowing, and was able to escape accountability by repudiating its paper currency.

4. Least affected were the subsistence farmers, who lived largely outside the exchange economy.

5. The black market was a chief means by which the people survived.

6. Manipulations of prices and wages, by using differential rates of inflation together with prescribed employment, were the policies by which the Soviet Union was able to industrialize.

7. Largely by controlling the exchange rate with other countries and manipulating its internal economy, the Soviet Union achieved something like economic autonomy.

8. In the long run and in terms of material goods, subsequent generations experienced higher living levels as a result of the sacrifices imposed on the people during the revolution.

Defenders of the Russian Revolution can point out, truthfully, that the new government was able to escape the Great Depression, that the Red Army increased in strength so that it turned back a German invasion during World War II, and that the Soviet Union, along with the United States, became a superpower. Opponents of the revolution speak of the immense cost in death and human suffering, the loss of liberty, the denial of civil rights, the threat to the free world, and the repression of religious freedom. To the standard cliché of Soviet apologists that you can not make an omelette without breaking eggs, opponents respond by deploring the egg-breaking and denouncing the omelette.

Inflation is an expression of fundamental economic forces that can accompany and assist in the achievement of liberty, as in the American Revolution, or in the denial of it, as in the Soviet Union.

By early 1992, the time of writing, the Soviet Union had been transformed. It had become the Commonwealth of Independent States, vastly more open and entrepreneurial. Glasnost and perestroika had produced a society in some ways similar to that of Lenin's New Economic Policy of seventy years earlier. Inflation had been rekindled and appeared to be headed toward multiple-digit levels.

HUNGARY, 1946: THE ULTIMATE INFLATION

The most fantastic inflation in history was that of Hungary in 1946. At their peaks, prices exceeded, astronomically, even the incredible level reached by the great German inflation of 1923. Inflation tore through the Hungarian price structure like a tornado. The price increase was too great to be shown visually. On a conventional graph, with the difference between 100 and 200 equal to an inch, the vertical scale would have to be greater than the distance from the earth to the sun. In a year's time, prices rose from a base of 100 to an index of 399,623,000,000,000,000,000,000,000,000 (Table 2.11) or, equally incomprehensible, nearly 400 octillion. The concise mathematical expression is $400 (10^{27})$.

Table 2.11
Index Numbers of Prices in Hungary, July 1945–July 1946 (August 26, 1939 = 100)

1945, July	105
1945, August	171
1945, September	379
1945, October	2,431
1945, November	12,979
1945, December	41,478
1946, January	72,330
1946, February	453,887
1946, March	1,872,913
1946, April	35,790,361
1946, May	11,267,000,000
1946, early June	862,317,000,000
1946, late June	954,000,000,000,000
1946, early July	3,066,254,000,000,000,000
1946, mid July	11,426,000,000,000,000,000,000
1946, late July	36,018,959,000,000,000,000,000,000
1946, end of July	399,623,000,000,000,000,000,000,000,000[a]

Source: Nogaro, 1948.

[a] This could also be written as 399,623 septillions or roughly as $400(10^{27})$.

The inflation escaped widespread or lasting notice. It occurred in a small country, amid the chaos that followed World War II, and was quickly ended, its virulent form having lasted only a few months. It became part of economic literature through a few articles, the most prominent of which are shown in the references.

World War II was devastating to Hungary. Forty percent of the national wealth was destroyed. The National Bank's gold reserves were appropriated by the Nazis and removed to Germany (Fekete 1982). With no backing for the currency and with revenues equal to not more than 15 percent of budget expenditures (Nogaro 1948), the government turned to the printing press. The Hungarian inflation came from both a dearth of goods and an excess of currency, mostly the latter.

The engine of inflation was a system of indexation, perhaps inadvertent. Inflation came from a desire to maintain the purchasing power of the tax revenue. This seemed a worthy goal, and the device for achieving it appeared reasonable, such as might understandably be devised by a revenue expert, but it turned on its masters as a circus lion attacking its tamer.

There had been war-associated inflation that had increased prices threefold from 1937 to 1944 (Coulborn 1950), a price increase by no means unusual for a wartime economy. Early in 1945, following the arrival of the Russian armies, with all war restrictions suspended and with the supply of commodities low, the cost of living rose to fifteen times its earlier level (Nogaro 1948). This set the stage for the most fantastic inflation ever.

The Hungarian currency was the pengö. With the pengö depreciating rapidly, considerable real tax revenue was lost between the time the tax was imposed and when it was paid. To counteract this loss, the apparently well-meaning tax authorities invented the tax pengö. Taxpayers were obligated to pay the government the amount stipulated on the tax notice multiplied by a factor based on the inflation rate since the time of tax notification. A price index was calculated and published daily. The tax pengö was launched to facilitate the payment of the tax. As a means of stabilizing the purchasing power of tax receipts, the method as it was first launched was theoretically valid, but by a fatal policy decision this tax pengö came to be used in regular business transactions. It became a fully functioning currency. Beginning in January 1946, commercial banks and savings banks opened valorization accounts in tax pengö (Nogaro 1948). The customer deposited a certain amount of pengö and was entitled to withdraw his deposit at will, multiplied by the index of the inflation rate. The government was thus obliged to print pengö in an amount required by the indexation, which reflected the inflation rate. The two fed on each other, creating the inflationary spiral. Bank customers deposited their liquid funds in the evening and drew them out, revalorized, the next morning (Nogaro 1948). If a man deposited 100 pengö on one day and the price index doubled during that day, he could draw out 200 pengö the next morning (Nogaro 1948). The process could be repeated without restraint. The government was compelled to print pengö in order the satisfy the appetite of the monster it had created. Currency issue during the inflation is shown on Table 2.12. The more money the government printed, the less the total was worth. One can hardly think of an arrangement more conducive to a price spiral. Inflation fed on itself and grew in prodigious fashion. Between the third and fourth week of July 1946, the price level rose by a factor of more than 10,000. Prices rose not just by the year, month, week, or day, but by the hour. Employees receiving their pay rushed into the street to spend it before its value eroded.

The system served to maintain the aggregate purchasing power of the public but without regard for the price consequences and without concern for how it affected individuals. The sparse literature does not record it, but the astute financial people must have gained from the opportunity for risk-less arbitrage. The poor, lacking both financial awareness and the resources with which to ride the price escalator, must have suffered miserably.

Table 2.12
Currency Issued, Hungary, December 1945–July 1946

December 31, 1945	765,400
January 31, 1946	1,646,000
February 28, 1946	5,238,000
March 31, 1946	34,002,000
April 30, 1946	434,304,000
May 31, 1946	65,589,000,000
June 30, 1946	6,277,000,000,000,000
July 31, 1946	17,300,000,000,000,000,000[a]

Source: Nogaro, 1948.

[a] This could be written as 17.3 quintillions or $173(10^{17})$.

One is inclined to conclude that the conversion of the tax pengö from a money of account into a fully functioning currency was an accident, that the multiplication of currency through the banking system resulted from inadvertence, and that the delay in correcting it resulted from bureaucratic inertia. On the other hand, the Russian conquerors, poorly educated in market behavior, may have simply failed to anticipate the working of risk-less arbitrage. Another hypothesis is that the Russians conspired to do what Lenin did in the Soviet Union nearly thirty years earlier: debauch the currency in an effort to overthrow the capitalistic system. In any case, the experience illustrates the potent forces associated with money and the profound adverse effects that can result from a bad decision, whether deliberate or inadvertent. In monetary policy, errors are catastrophic whereas good decisions go unnoticed.

The creation of currency had no equilibrating factor. It was like the sorcerer's apprentice. This legendary novice gave the magic word for the broom to bring water but could not recall the word to stop. Bad money (the tax pengö) drove out good money (the pengö) in accordance with Gresham's Law.

The pengö passed from hand to hand with enormous speed. The velocity of circulation increased at a prodigious rate. Prices rose not only because of the superabundance of currency but also in anticipation of further inflation. The attitude was, "Buy now, before prices go still higher." Expectations, a price dynamic little considered before the Age of Inflation, became the dominant form of price behavior.

The pengö depreciated against the dollar more than it depreciated in domestic trade (Table 2.13)—partly from the principle of purchasing power parity and partly from anticipation of further inflation. Apologists for

Table 2.13
Pengö per Dollar on the Black Market, Hungary, July 1945–July 1946

1945, July	1,320
1945, August	1,510
1945, September	5,400
1945, October	23,500
1945, November	108,000
1945, December	290,000
1946, January	795,000
1946, February	2,850,000
1946, March	17,750,000
1946, April	232,000,000
1946, May	59,000,000,000
1946, early June	7,600,000,000,000
1946, late June	42,000,000,000,000,000
1946, early July	22,000,000,000,000,000,000
1946, mid July	481,500,000,000,000,000,000,000
1946, late July	5,800,000,000,000,000,000,000,000
1946, end of July	4,600,000,000,000,000,000,000,000,000,000[a]

Source: Nogaro, 1948.

[a] This could be written as 4,600,000 septillions or as $46(10^{29})$.

Hungarian monetary policies attributed the inflation to foreign interests that allegedly drove down the pengö.

Sanity finally prevailed, aided by the allied occupational forces in nearby conquered Germany. Hungary's prewar gold reserve, taken by the Nazis, was found and restored to Hungary by the U.S. military authorities (Coulborn 1950). A new money, the forint, was established, equal to 75.7 milligrams of gold, at the rate of one forint to 400 octillion pengö (Nogaro 1948).

Official new prices were announced in terms of the new forint that reflected the need felt for food and for industrial revival (Nogaro 1948):

Times the 1938 Level

Price of grain	2.2
Average of farm prices	2.7
Industrial	4.4
Wages	.6
Salaries	.4
Rents	.5

The monetary reform and price fixing slowed the galloping inflation to a relative creep (Fekete 1982):

Consumer Prices
(1946 = 100)

1946	100
1949	152
1952	265
1957	259

Obviously, the virus of inflation can infect communist and market systems and peacetime as well as war economies.

The Hungarian economy recovered somewhat, even during the inflation. By the time of stabilization (August 1946), 90 percent of the railway network was again in operation, compared to 50 percent at the end of the war. Coal output had risen to 60 percent of the prewar output, and iron and metal industries to 75 percent (Fekete 1982).

The sparse literature on the Hungarian inflation yields little knowledge about how business affairs were conducted and tells us almost nothing about how the wrenching inflationary experience affected various groups in the economy. It sheds little light on how prices achieved reentry after having been in orbit. Perhaps the inflation was so rapid that deflation from the elevated level could be accommodated with less disturbance than would occur had hyperinflation become well established.

The experience indicates that economic policy should not subordinate itself to tax policy, a lesson presently useful to the United States. The Hungarian experience reveals that a wrong signal can open the floodgates that lead to chaos. Above all, it illustrates the perils of inept indexation.

CHINA AND HYPERINFLATION

The Chinese national government's efforts to finance the 1937–1945 war with Japan and to cope with the related challenge by the Communists were failures by almost any measure. Not only did the Nationalist government succumb but also the financial policies it adopted produced a runaway inflation that ranks with the most inequitable and spectacular in history. The Chinese inflation carried prices to 1,261,000,000,000,000 times the prewar base, a level almost 900 times as high as that of the better-known German inflation (Table 2.14). China's inflationary experience was like that of an

Table 2.14
Index Numbers of Prices in China (Index, January–June 1937 = 1)

Year	Index
1937, December	1.18
1938, December	1.76
1939, December	3.23
1940, December	7.24
1941, December	19.77
1942, December	66.2
1943, December	228
1944, December	755
1945, December	2,491
1946, December	N.A.
1947, December	N.A.
1948, June	176,960,000
1948, August	985,400,000
1949, March	2,430,000,000,000
1949, May	1,261,000,000,000,000

Sources: 1937-1945: Young, 1965; 1948-1949: Chou, 1963.

airplane that starts rolling down the runway, picks up speed, becomes airborne, heads for the stratosphere—and then crashes.

Background

A brief review of the war and the revolution is necessary for an understanding of the Chinese inflation. In September 1931, Japan seized Manchuria and set up a puppet regime. From this base the Japanese encroached southward along the Chinese coast. Open undeclared war began after 7 July 1937, when a clash occurred between Chinese and Japanese troops near Beijing at a site known as the Marco Polo Bridge. The Japanese advanced into south and eastern China and by the end of 1938 occupied a third of the country, regions that produced 40 percent of China's agricultural output and 92 percent of her prewar industry (Chang 1958).

The Chinese had to cope not only with the Japanese invasion but also with the civil war that had developed between the national government and the Chinese Communists. War with the Japanese ended in 1945 with the victory of the Allies over the Axis powers. The Japanese withdrew from an exhausted China. With some 50 million displaced persons awaiting return to their former homes, rebuilding had to be postponed (Chang 1958). The Civil War escalated, ending in victory for the Communists. On 1 October 1949, Chairman Mao proclaimed the establishment of the People's

Republic of China. The victors imposed harsh discipline and ended the inflation.

Hyperinflation

During 1938, the first full year of the war, the approximate price rise was a modest 50 percent. In 1939, prices nearly doubled and more than doubled during 1940. Thereafter, through 1946, prices approximately tripled each year. In 1947, hyperinflation began—prices increased to fifteen times the level of the previous year. From 1947 to mid-1948, the number of digits in the price index increased from six to nine, and by mid-1949 to sixteen. From May 1946 to March 1949, wholesale prices in Shanghai rose to 7.5 million times their earlier level (Eckstein 1977). At the end of the twelve-year inflationary span, prices had risen by a factor of more than a quadrillion, or 126 (10^{13}).

Numbers of this magnitude overwhelm one's ability to comprehend. Examining them in smaller pieces and personalizing them may help. From August 1948 to April 1949, prices in Shanghai increased at an average rate of 300 percent per month (Chou 1963). It was said that at the height of the inflation the cost of printing paper currency exceeded the purchasing power of the bills themselves. Many people lost their life savings. One story told, perhaps apocryphal, was that of a Chinese family that had been saving a substantial amount each year for the education of their son. When toward the end of the war he had his eighteenth birthday, they took all the funds and bought him a birthday cake (A. N. Young 1965).

Economic Performance

The Chinese economy performed unevenly but on the whole remarkably well during the war and inflation. Agricultural production was sustained despite the exodus of peasants into the Army (Chang 1958). Had this not been so, widespread famine would have occurred as the Chinese had little cushion with which to counter a shortfall in food production. Between 1945 and 1950, despite war and revolution, the Chinese population increased from 454 to 533 million.

Manufacturing, under forced draft during the war, generally expanded even though much destruction occurred and factories had to be relocated in the interior (Chang 1958). The well-known resilience and adaptability of the Chinese people were thus documented.

For a people accustomed to a stable currency, the maintenance and even expansion of economic activity in a country experiencing inflation is a source of wonder. Inflation seems to be associated with heightened economic activity except when price increases run totally out of control; then the economy ultimately breaks down as was the case in Germany, Russia, and China. Improved economic performance associated with moderate inflation has been observed in several of the inflations examined in this study: Spain in the sixteenth century, France in the eighteenth, and, as discussed below, Brazil in the twentieth century.

The war was financed chiefly by government deficits (Chang 1958). During the period 1937–1945, only 6 percent of government expenditures were raised by taxes (Chang 1958). In 1941, sales of bonds were only 2 percent as great as the increase in note issue. Fearing inflation, citizens were dubious about investing in fixed-value instruments. Astute people had by this time put aside the money illusion.

The government undertook "compulsory borrowing" of agricultural products, also referred to as a "land tax in kind." The government thus acquired, from 1941 to 1946, about 5 percent of the rice crop and 3 percent of the wheat crop (Chou 1963). The practice is reminiscent of grain acquisition by the Soviet Union during the Russian Revolution.

Although the government was active in "taxing" farmers, it neglected to tax others who profited greatly from the war: speculators, hoarders, profiteers, smugglers, and military officers who used their special status to further their business projects (Chang 1958). Some of these entrepreneurs served the war effort in that they helped initiate productive investments and assisted in the acquisition of needed military supplies, but their booty was not taxed. The government thus neglected a potential source of revenue. John Maynard Keynes, who understood war finance, once stated: "It is expedient to use entrepreneurs as collecting agents. But let them be agents, not principals" (Chou 1963).

Expenses for expanding the war, relocating millions of people, and building and rebuilding industry required immense government outlay. Expenditures of the government, which had stood at 5 percent of the gross national product before the war, more than doubled to 12 percent a year later. During the middle war years, government expenses for the war and war-related construction took 73 percent of total government revenue (Chang 1958). Large sums in government credit were expended for the military buildup and for financing the repair of war damages. This credit was supplied at negative real interest rates.

By far the greatest source of government finance came from printing paper notes. Historically, China had used paper money intermittently when the supply of gold, silver, and copper currencies had been deemed insufficient. The 1937 to 1949 inflation was not the first such experience.

In time of military emergency, any government must find the means to procure needed resources. A war can be financed by confiscation, increased production, savings, imports, taxes, borrowing, foreign aid, or an expanded money supply. The Chinese were disinclined to tax a people already mistrustful of government. Credit was limited. The government could not readily import because of the blockade. China was a poor country with little excess capacity. The easiest combination of alternatives was to draw down monetary reserves, confiscate needed food supplies, seek foreign aid, and, most important, print new money. China increased its issue of currency to more than 100,000 times its 1937 level. The government reduced its monetary reserves in U.S. dollar equivalent from $858 million in December 1945 to $101 million in March 1949 (Chou 1963). China received, in all, $3.5 billion in aid from the United States (Chou 1963). The government acquired substantial quantities of food by confiscation. Primarily, however, the government printed enormous amounts of money.

Although printing money was the easiest of the alternatives in the short term, the long-term consequences were difficult, and the war lasted twelve years. A few economists recommended heavier taxation and controls on consumer spending, but these suggestions were dismissed by the Ministry of Finance and the business community (Chang 1958).

When defeat by the Communists was imminent, the national government sought, in desperation, to introduce a new currency, the gold yuan. This, however, the people rejected. The exchange rate skyrocketed. In April 1949, the black market rate exceeded the official rate by a factor of four (Chang 1958). Chinese capital, estimated at the equivalent of U.S. $300 million, fled the country (A. N. Young 1965).

As prices rose, people hastened to exchange their money for goods in anticipation of further price increases. The equation of exchange is $MV = PT$; that is, quantity of money times velocity of turnover equals price times the volume of trade, a truism. In this equation, the velocity of money increased at a fantastic rate as people rushed to dispose of it. The more money the Chinese printed, the less was the value of the total amount. By December 1945, the total value of notes in circulation was only one-third as great as it had been in July 1937 before inflation began (A. N. Young 1965). Money had gone mad.

Interest rates rose as the inflation progressed: an inflation premium was added to what would ordinarily be a normal rate. The real interest rate was strongly negative. In addition, the principal of a borrowed sum was repaid with much cheaper money. The incentive to borrow from the government was therefore enormous. In response, the government poured out new money. From 1938 to 1945, the total amount of credit increased almost 1,000 times (Chang 1958).

What stands out in this story is the enormous momentum that the conventional, bureaucratic ways of doing things had, despite a war and a price upheaval that invalidated established practices. This inertia related to taxing, lending, interest rates, contractual relations, and, as discussed below, salaries and wage rates. Many of these economic phenomena were contrary to the public interest. The larger question is whether a huge government establishment, faced with the need for change but inclined toward preserving the status quo, can cope with a major inflation—even one that it had induced.

Impact of Inflation on Various Sectors

Inflation, simultaneously the world's greatest thief and benefactor, redistributed wealth. Unearned profits were reaped by speculators, borrowers, and hoarders. Manufacturers and farmers did fairly well. Holders of real estate and owners of other property were protected from inflation (A. N. Young 1965). Victimized were savers, government employees, teachers, holders of fixed-value securities, and lenders. The inequitable burden-sharing aggravated the effects of the inflation, and was the rationalization of widespread graft and corruption among public officials. Undoubtedly, the inequitable effect of the inflation was an important factor in the downfall of the Nationalist government (Chou 1963, Chang 1958, A. N. Young 1965).

The Chinese people felt that their ruler should hold power and receive their support so long as he possessed the "Mandate of Heaven," evidenced by the well being of the country. Grave problems were interpreted to mean that heaven had withdrawn its mandate, in which case government no longer merited the peoples' support.

What was the reason for the Nationalist government's failure? Was it an unworthy cause? Outright military failure? Poor leadership? Bad financial management and the inflation associated with it? Failure of China's allies to provide sufficient help? A failure of will? All of the above? Whatever the causes of the Nationalist's downfall, China's financial management failed to avert the disaster.

Wealthy people accumulated gold and foreign assets (Chou 1963). Some of the rich people fled the country. Gold proved to be the best hedge against inflation, as it moved up in price roughly parallel with the price level (Table 2.15). Teachers, civil servants, laborers, and farm workers fared very poorly, as shown in Table 2.16.

Circumstances were so bad for some workers that wages and salaries had to be supplemented with special allowances, distribution of daily necessities, and provision of housing. In some cases, petty thievery and chicanery became a necessary means of livelihood. The principle that hunger knows no law found active expression. Holders of government bonds suffered the

Table 2.15
Index Numbers of Prices of Gold and of Commodities in Shanghai,
1937–1949 (Base Period, 1937 = 1)

	Gold Price	Wholesale Price Index
1937	1	1
1941, December	11	16
1945, August	10,527	86,400
1945, October	98,600	75,726
1948, June	192,058,000	176,960,000
1948, August	925,637,000	985,400,000
1949, March	2,270,000,000,000	2,430,000,000,000
1949, May	1,252,000,000,000,000	1,261,000,000,000,000

Source: Chou, 1963.

worst loss (Chang 1958). The real value of returns on loans dwindled to almost nothing. Shareholders in banks and other financial institutions within China suffered severe reductions in real returns, whereas holders of U.S. securities received real gains.

There were gross differences in real incomes for different enterprises. In April 1944, workers in glass and tobacco industries in Chungking received wages equal to 57 percent of prewar wages in real terms, whereas workers in public utilities, engineering equipment, and printing were receiving less than 40 percent of their real prewar wages (Chang 1958). There were regional differences. In April 1944, index numbers of real wages of nonfactory workers in various cities (with prewar wages equal to 100) were as follows (Chang 1958):

Chengtu	97
Loshan	71
Chungking	66
Tzeliutsing	60
Wanhsien	48
Neikiang	42

White collar workers were badly hurt. In 1943, index numbers of real incomes (with 1936–1937 equal to 100) were as follows (A. N. Young 1965):

College teachers	10
Middle school teachers	19
Primary school teachers	27
Government officials	10

Table 2.16
Index Numbers of Real Salaries and Wages in Free China, 1937–1943
(1937 = 100)

	Civil Servants, Chungking	Teachers, Chungking	Servicemen, Chungking	Laborers	Industrial Workers, Chungking	Rural Workers, Szechwan
1937	100	100	100	100	100	100
1938	77	87	93	143	124	111
1939	49	64	64	181	95	122
1940	21	32	29	147	76	63
1941	16	27	21	91	78	82
1942	11	19	10	83	75	75
1943	10	17	57	74	69	58

Source: Chang, 1958.

Inequities were enormous. In June 1944, index numbers of real incomes for various activities (with 1937 equal to 100) were as follows (A. N. Young 1965):

Farmers	102
Farm workers	71
City workers	88
Clerks	31
Professors	11
Soldiers	9

Disaffection with the inflation led many to become disillusioned and anti-government, and contributed to the downfall of the Nationalist regime.

Prices received by farmers moved generally in step with the prices they paid but fell behind somewhat during the last stages of the Japanese war. Farmers, largely on a subsistence basis and living to some degree outside the exchange economy, were in considerable measure insulated from the inflation (Chou 1963).

Nothing in the Chinese experience with inflation conflicts with the generalizations made from the inflations examined above. Subsistence enterprises, mostly independent of the market, were little affected. Precious metals were an effective inflation hedge. Enterprises that operated with contractual arrangements (interest, rent) experienced lags in adjustment, whereas activities that operated in an active competitive market (raw materials, speculative commodities) generally had price behavior that kept up with or ahead of the inflation rate. These leads and lags reflected the degree of freedom provided in their respective markets. Price behavior in these various sectors sometimes contributed to and sometimes detracted from the general welfare. General welfare and interpersonal equity, however, were not the determining factors in the behavior of the various sectors of the economy.

Price Control

Efforts were made to control prices. Nonetheless, although the government tried everything, including benign neglect, nothing worked. Price controls proved ineffective; the government pumped out increasing amounts of paper currency and bank credit, pushing up with one hand what it was trying to hold down with the other. Inflation, immediately experienced by all, became the scapegoat for causes remote to many.

There were additional obstacles to effective price control. The people were antagonistic to controls. The guilds, logically the agencies to regulate their members and workers, were reluctant or impotent or both.

In January 1938, the Ministry of Economic Affairs was empowered to ration essential goods, but such controls were not implemented. In December 1938, the government issued a sanctimonious decree that prices of necessities should be fixed at fair levels and that hoarding and profiteering should be shunned (Chang 1958). The effort was half-hearted, and prices continued to rise.

In November 1942, a new comprehensive program was initiated, including price ceilings, rationing, governmental buying and selling of commodities, limitations on inventories, restrictions on use of scarce goods, and wage ceilings. Black markets were to be suppressed. Capital punishment or life imprisonment could be imposed for serious breaches of regulations. None of these measures worked.

Some price ceilings were too low, and others were geographically inept. As a consequence, Chungking faced a rice famine, relieved by readjusting price ceilings (Chang 1958). Rationing failed, in part because the data on population and supply of commodities were inadequate and the number of enforcement personnel was insufficient. Government rice stocks were sold to civilians at low subsidized prices in 4,083 localities in eighteen provinces (Chang 1958). The distribution of cotton, coal, charcoal, and edible oil to wholesalers was controlled in Chungking and other large cities (Chang 1958). To prevent hoarding, merchants and manufacturers were required to report inventories on some 200 items. In December 1942, wages were frozen at the levels of November 30 of that year, but the inflationary policies of currency issue and low-cost government credit continued. The control effort failed; prices in free China more than doubled each year from 1942 to 1944, and rose even more rapidly thereafter.

Efforts at price control occupied great numbers of government workers and diverted human resources from activities more supportive of the war effort. Administrative and general expenses had taken up 4 percent of governmental expenses in 1940; they took up 33 percent during 1941–1944 (Chang 1958).

After the close of the war with Japan, with the increase in the communist threat and the escalation of inflation, price and wage ceilings, which had lapsed, were reintroduced (Chang 1958). Rationing was reimposed. Fueled by mounting issues of paper, prices increased yet faster. As inflation intensified, low-income people suffered extreme hardship. The "automatic adjustment" was adopted: Wages were to be revised monthly by a complicated formula according to the cost-of-living index, a move strongly opposed by employers. Government was caught manipulating the cost-of-living index in an effort to hold down wages, and workers protested (Chang 1958). Prices rose so fast that monthly adjustments proved inadequate; half-monthly changes were made. By making inflation marginally less painful, further inflation was rationalized, thus illustrating a chief drawback of indexation.

The Emergency Regulations of February 1947 broke down, and prices that had been temporarily suppressed surged upward 70 percent in May 1947 alone (Chang 1958). During the next fourteen months, prices in Shanghai rose to 111 times the May level, while the cost of living rose 59 times (Chang 1958).

In a desperate effort to combat inflation, monetary reform was undertaken in August 1948. A new gold yuan, worth 3 million units of Chinese National currency, was proclaimed. Official prices were rolled back accordingly. Prices were as follows (Chang 1958):

	Rice (per 171 lbs.)	Flour (per 49 lbs.)	Edible Oil (per 22 gals.)
Market, 19 August 1948, Chinese National Currency, before the gold yuan	$63,000,000	$21,800,000	$190,000,000
Official 22 August 1948, gold yuan, after new gold yuan	$20	$7	$58
6 November 1948, market price, gold yuan	$240	$69	$522

The new official prices were considered ludicrously low by merchants and traders, hence the sharp increase over old official prices in just three months' time.

After these gyrations, prices skyrocketed (Chang 1958).

	Shanghai Wholesale Price Index (August 1948 = 100)	Shanghai Cost of Living Index (August 1948 = 100)
1948 November	1,365	1,170
December	1,921	1,670
1949 January	6,900	6,825
February	40,825	52,113

In this last gasp of inflation was heard the death rattle of the Chinese National government.

Stabilization

The Communists, aware that inflation had been a factor in toppling the Chinese National government, were not about to expose themselves to this same adversary. They issued jen-min-pi (people's currency), which replaced local currencies (Eckstein 1977). Stringent and quite orthodox fiscal and monetary measures were invoked. The budget was balanced, note issue was controlled, the tax system was reorganized, fiscal management was imposed, and local government functions were transferred to the central government. The purchasing power of new government securities was guaranteed (Eckstein 1977). The People's Bank pursued a harsh antiinflation policy. Black markets, speculation, and interest rates were brought under control. Bank credit was curbed.

This draconian effort to check inflation brought about a crisis. Banks failed, businesses went bankrupt, unsold inventories accumulated, and unemployment increased (Eckstein 1977). Nonetheless, the back of inflation was broken, and prices were generally stabilized. The twelve-year inflationary spiral came to an end.

Although price behavior during this period is not well documented, it appears that the worst effects of deflation were avoided.

From 1950 to 1956, official wholesale and retail prices in urban areas were as follows, in index numbers, with 1952 equal to 100:

	Wholesale	Retail
1950	85	89
1951	100	99
1952	100	100
1953	99	104

1954	99	104
1955	100	106
1956	99	106

This price stability and the associated reforms were achieved at enormous cost of life and human freedom. Landlords and bourgeoisie leaders were executed, "reconstructed," or driven into exile. There were catastrophic aftershocks: the Great Leap Forward and the Great Proletarian Cultural Revolution. Yet runaway inflation was halted.

It is said that no country will countenance a second great inflation while there is still recent memory of the first. Now, however, forty years after the revolution, that memory is apparently fading. China is again on an inflationary course. How tempting is the forbidden fruit!

The Road Not Taken

Could the Chinese inflation have been suppressed? In the views of Chang, Chou, and A. N. Young, it could have been held to moderate levels if there had been greater courage to impose taxes coupled with greater resolution to resist printing excessive amounts of money and extending credit. Based on the experience of other countries, this should have been possible. Aware of the excesses associated with World War I, most European nations, with the notable exceptions of Hungary and Greece, were able to keep inflation within reasonable bounds during and after World War II. During 1979–1982, when the U.S. inflation had reached a rate of 14 percent on an annual basis, strict monetary discipline was imposed at a great cost to the United States and other nations, thereby averting what might otherwise have become an inflationary spiral.

Inflation is like a spirited horse, manageable if kept calm but impossible to control if alarmed. Another figure of speech: inflation is like a fire in a domestic dwelling; early on it can be extinguished with a bucket of water, but once it spreads, it may have to burn itself out.

This section relies heavily on three sources: Chang Kia-Ngau (1958), who was with the Central Bank of China during the inflation; Professor Shun-Hsin Chou (1963), who was also associated with the Central Bank of China during the great inflation; and Arthur N. Young (1965), who was financial advisor to China from 1929 to 1947. It is fair to say that the counsels of these three excellent men were not evident in major decisions taken by the Nationalist government.

The statistical data supplied by these and other writers do not always distinguish among Free China, the occupied areas, and totals for the whole of the country. One must surmise that the data offered are generally comparable for the inflationary period, but in an economy as chaotic as that of war-time China, the strict comparability of statistical data can hardly be affirmed.

BOLIVIA: A COUNTRY THAT TOOK THE CURE

Many of the inflations chronicled in this study went through the roof and culminated in chaos. Bolivia, however, confronted hyperinflation and suppressed it while the spiral was at full strength. Bolivia, a landlocked country high in the Andes, the poorest nation in South America, seems an unlikely country to challenge an inflationary spiral and even less likely to check it. Nonetheless, Bolivia did both.

In August 1985, Bolivian prices stood at a level 103,000 times higher than in 1972 (Table 2.17), and the economy was sliding backward. In the midst of this price surge, Victor Paz Estenssoro, the new president, inaugurated only three months earlier, issued Supreme Decree Number 21060, which became known as the New Economic Policy (Cole 1987). Its main purposes were to check inflation and to revitalize a deteriorating economy. The rate of inflation, which had been approximately doubling each month, slowed from a gallop to a creep. From February 1986 to July 1988 the inflation rate averaged about 1 percent per month, one of the lowest rates in Latin America (Sachs and Morales 1988).

When the hyperinflation was seriously confronted, it ceased quickly. Apparently it had little momentum, as was found for the hyperinflation of Germany, Russia, Hungary, and China. According to Sachs (1989), this lack of momentum occurs because hyperinflation wipes out long-term contracts so that the country operates mostly on a day-to-day basis. With almost no long-term commitments, it can function at a stable current level. Momentum is a problem at lower rates of inflation when long-term contracts, which have anticipated inflation, are in force and call for continuity in the rate of price increase.

How did Bolivia get on the inflation track? Basic to the explanation is the extreme poverty of Bolivia's lower classes—the bottom 20 percent of the population in 1970 received 4 percent of the nation's income. The story begins with the Bolivian National Revolution of 1952, a popular uprising that overthrew the government (Malloy 1970). To reduce the enormous disparity of income between the poor and the wealthy and to generate economic growth, state enterprises were established. More than half of Bolivia's total fixed national capital investment was in the public sector.

Problems soon arose. The government lacked the administrative capability to operate the state industries efficiently. Uneconomic enterprises were set up. Patronage padded the payrolls, and corruption was rife. To placate

Table 2.17
Index Numbers of Consumer Prices in Bolivia, December 1972–April 1986
(1975 = 1)

	Consumer Price Index
1972, December	0.51
1973, December	0.69
1974, December	0.96
1975, December	1.02
1976, December	1.07
1977, December	1.19
1978, December	1.34
1979, December	1.96
1980, December	2.42
1981, December	3.03
1982, March	3.90
1982, June	4.79
1982, September	8.20
1982, December	12.03
1983, March	14.9
1983, June	18.2
1983, September	29.4
1983, December	51.6
1984, March	84.1
1984, June	209.9
1984, September	348.6
1984, December	1,174.0
1985, January	1,980.0
1985, February	5,602.0
1985, March	7,000.0
1985, April	7,826.0
1985, May	10,616.0
1985, June	18,948.0
1985, July	31,515.0
1985, August	52,460.0
1985, September	82,090.0
1985, October	80,297.0
1985, November	82,868.0
1985, December	96,866.0
1986, January	128,840.0
1986, February	137,344.0
1986, March	139,915.0
1986, April	144,969.0

Source: Cole, 1987.

Table 2.18
Money Supply in Bolivia at Year's End, 1972–1985 (in millions of pesos)

1972	2,210
1973	2,969
1974	4,257
1975	4,759
1976	6,497
1977	7,855
1978	8,831
1979	10,304
1980	14,694
1981	17,587
1982	57,827
1983	177,500
1984	3,370,100
1985	207,000,000

Source: Cole, 1987.

the people, state enterprises provided goods and services below cost, thus requiring subsidies. Government revenues fell behind income; in 1984 only 11 percent of expenditures were covered by receipts. The deficit was met largely by "seignorage," a euphemism for printing money. The presses turned out money at a prodigious rate (Table 2.18).

With this stimulation, the economy performed well for a time. The injection of new money had a buoyant effect. The prices of Bolivia's export commodities were strong. The inflation rate was creeping up, but the economy was growing. From 1952 to 1985, Bolivian economic growth averaged, in real terms, 5.4 percent per year.

Amidst this euphoria, Bolivia borrowed large sums from abroad, willingly supplied at prevailing low interest rates by foreign lenders as much deluded by the temporary economic growth as were the Bolivians.

In 1981 the breakdown of this foreign debt was as follows (Cole 1987):

Bilateral	32 percent
Multilateral	29 percent
Private	
banks	33 percent
others	6 percent
	100 percent

By 1981, the external debt equaled 89 percent of Bolivia's gross domestic product. Service on the foreign debt was equal to 26 percent of export revenue. There was also internal public debt, but the amount was relatively small. Because receipts were variable and commitments fixed, Bolivia's vulnerability to economic downturn was growing.

Jeffrey Sachs (1989), in his paper, "Social Conflict and Populist Policies in Latin America," comments, "high income inequality in Latin America contributes to intense political pressures for macroeconomic policies to raise the incomes of lower income groups, which in turn contributes to bad policy choices and weak economic performance."

Disaster came in multiple forms. The price of tin, Bolivia's chief export, fell abruptly. Interest rates rose sharply, an unfortunate occurrence for a nation heavily in debt. Anticipated profits from public investment in cotton and hydrocarbon production failed to materialize, but debt services remained. Real gross domestic production, which had earlier increased at an annual rate of 5.4 percent per year, fell 8.7 percent in 1982. Printing presses turned out more paper money. Inflation, which had been creeping, began to walk and then to gallop. The peso was repeatedly devalued against the dollar (Table 2.19), but the black market diverged increasingly and in August 1985 stood at fourteen times the official rate. Capital flight drained the country of needed financial resources. The Morgan Guaranty Trust Company estimated that by the end of 1987 Bolivian assets held abroad totaled $2 billion.

During 1980–1981 Bolivia was forced to reschedule its debt obligations. Foreign sources of capital dried up. Net resource transfer from abroad, which in 1980 had been a positive 6 percent of gross domestic production, became in 1983 a negative 6 percent.

There came a series of political upheavals. During 1979 alone there were five heads of state: Pereda, Padilla, Guevara, Busch, and Guiler. Four more passed through the revolving door between 1980 and 1982: Meza, Bernal, Torrelio, and Calderón. Siles Suazo held the presidency from 1982 to 1985. He repeatedly sought to achieve stabilization (during November 1982, November 1983, April 1984, August 1984, and November 1984), but his efforts were blocked by his political opponents in Congress and his ostensible allies in organized labor. Powerful groups had a vested interest in lax government discipline with its attendant inflation: black market dealers in foreign exchange, influential landowners who borrowed money from the government at low interest rates and wanted to repay their loans in cheap pesos, smugglers who profited by evading the controls that accompanied inflation, labor groups who feared the loss of jobs rightly expected to accompany a stabilization effort, and politicians who found it easier to go with the flow than to impose discipline.

Paz Estenssoro came to power in September 1985. He had been a leader in the revolution of 1952 and had been president three times before with a strong populist record. Paz made what seemed to many a 180-degree turn

Table 2.19
Exchange Rate in Bolivia, Selected Dates, 1981–1985 (pesos per dollar)

	Official	Black Market
1981, December	25	--
1982, March	44	48
1982, June	102	103
1982, September	229	257
1982, December	200	283
1983, March	200	457
1983, June	200	431
1983, September	200	761
1983, December	500	1,244
1984, March	500	2,800
1984, June	2,000	3,250
1984, September	5,000	14,600
1984, December	9,000	22,100
1985, January	9,000	60,100
1985, February	50,000	120,000
1985, March	50,000	121,000
1985, April	50,000	156,000
1985, May	75,000	248,500
1985, June	75,000	448,000
1985, July	75,000	801,000
1985, August	75,000	1,050,000

Source: Cole, 1987.

from his past, as had Karl Helfferich in Germany in 1923. He formed a center-right government and promptly launched a stabilization program to check inflation and jump-start the stagnant economy. The program had five elements:

1. A stable unified exchange rate based on the U.S. dollar and supported by tight fiscal and monetary policies
2. Increased public sector revenues based on tax reform
3. A reduced public sector wage bill, to be achieved by reducing both employment and wages in state enterprises
4. Elimination of debt servicing through rescheduling with official creditors and a unilateral suspension of payments to private creditors
5. A resumption of concessional financial assistance from government and multilateral institutions, based on the above reforms

Significantly, no wage or price controls were imposed. Regulations were lifted and trade was liberalized. With increased revenues and reduced expenditures, the government's deficit was cut and the printing of paper money was checked. Expectations of inflation were abated. The country bought back about half the outstanding debt owed to commercial banks at about eleven cents on the dollar and initiated negotiations to shrink its obligations on the balance. Interest payments on commercial bank debt were suspended totally. Unable to meet all its obligations, Bolivia minimized interest payment on the commercial and bilateral debt, while cultivating good relations with the multilateral agencies. This strategy, coupled with the toughness of the stabilization program, won new credits from the International Monetary Fund despite the continuing buildup of Bolivian arrears to the commercial banks. Thus, after 1985, Bolivia became one of the few debtor countries in the world to achieve a net inward transfer of resources.

Through this combination of actions, the decline in gross domestic product was turned around. In 1987, Bolivia experienced its first real output growth after seven years of decline, a modest 2.3 percent increase in gross domestic product. An increase, small but encouraging, continued in 1988.

This performance is all the more remarkable when one considers that Bolivia is contiguous to three countries—Brazil, Peru, and Argentina—all of which are currently experiencing hyperinflation and faltering growth.

When the stabilization program was first launched, organized labor protested, based on the well-founded fear that jobs would be lost. A general strike was called, and an abortive hunger strike was begun. With accelerating inflation and a growing sense of impending chaos, however, the new government clearly had the upper hand. Reluctantly, the pro-inflation groups accepted the reform. Helping mightily in this acceptance was the government's stance on loans: nonpayment of interest, renegotiation of foreign debt, and repurchase of obligations at a sharp discount. The government was able to say truthfully to its citizens that the new austerity was for the sake of Bolivians, not foreigners.

The pain of the stabilization program was intense; stopping the hyperinflation imposed harsh, inequitable consequences. The state mining operation, COMIBOL, cut employment from 30,000 workers in 1985 to 7,000 in 1987. The state hydrocarbon enterprise, YPFB, cut its payroll from 9,000 to 5,000. Twenty percent of the working force were unemployed (Hauxhurst 1989). Those living in poverty were reduced to destitution. Some of the new unemployed became involved in coca leaf production, to the dismay of both the Bolivian and the U.S. governments.

No effort was made to bring prices down; the purpose was to slow the rate of increase. Thus the problem of actual deflation, so disastrous to the United States following 1780, 1864, and 1920, was averted.

The key elements in the Bolivian stabilization program were debt adjustment, fiscal prudence, monetary discipline, privatization of inefficient state enterprises, deregulation, wage restraint, and a realistic exchange rate. None of these methods is novel; almost any good economist could have prescribed them. The key elements were the courage and resolution to put them into effect.

Bolivia became the showcase country for the World Bank and the International Monetary Fund. The country's experience is being watched with alternating hope and doubt by other debt-ridden nations undergoing severe inflation.

Were the achievements of the stabilization program worth the pain, the unemployment, and what the economist calls transaction cost? The people of Bolivia apparently answer in the affirmative. Bolivia is a country known for political volatility, having had ten presidents in as many years. But from 1985 to 1989 the country kept in office the man who launched and administered the stabilization effort, Paz Estenssoro.

Enormous problems remain: to stay the course so boldly taken, to hold the ground gained at so great a cost, to manage the remaining debt, to maintain political stability, to develop new enterprises to supplement those in decline, to reduce income disparity, to discipline the coca trade, to develop the lowlands, and somehow to integrate the Indian population into the country's social and political system. If responsible fiscal and monetary policies can be maintained, these problems will become more tractable. Planning Minister Gonzalo Sánchez de Losada defined the scope of the country's task: "Bolivia must re-invent itself" (ICEG 1989).

In a 1989 election, Jaime Paz Zamora, a leader of the leftist party, was chosen president. Zamora insisted that he would maintain the stabilization plan. In 1990, in a demonstration of anti-inflation sentiment, Bolivia planned to incinerate its redundant currency. Doubts remain, however. As the foregoing sections indicate, few inflationary episodes are final or conclusive.

BRAZIL: DEVELOPMENT AND INFLATION

Brazil was the first major country to enter the Age of Inflation and to institutionalize a rising price level. This form of price behavior began early, while Brazil was still a colony. From the early sixteenth century to 1822, the year of independence, Brazilian coins lost 80 percent of their gold content. During most of this long period, Brazil was on a metallic standard, gold and/or silver; however, this did not prevent inflation. Prices increased tenfold during those three centuries and have increased more rapidly since independence (Table 2.20). By a rough calculation, the 1987 price level in

Table 2.20
Approximate Number of Years Required for a Ten-Fold Increase in
Brazilian Prices

Period	Years Required
From early colonial times to 1822	300
1822 to 1900	80
1900 to 1950	50
1950 to 1961	11
1961 to 1965	4
1965 to 1976	11
1976 to 1981	5
1981 to 1983	2
1983 to 1985	2
1985 to 1987	2

Sources: Kahil 1973, Spiegel 1949.

Brazil, with early colonial times at an index of 1, stood at about $1(10^{10})$, or ten billion times the beginning level.

During this nearly 500-year period, Brazil used various monetary units. When one lost credibility or practicality, it was replaced by another. At one time the unit was the real, which so depreciated that it was replaced by the milreis (1,000 reals). In 1942 the milreis became the cruzeiro. In 1967 the cruzeiro gave way to the new cruzeiro, equivalent to 1,000 of the old (Kahil 1973). During the past five years, the Brazilians have had four currencies: the cruzeiro, the cruzado, the new cruzeiro, and now back to the cruzeiro.

Periods of deflation have occurred, as during the Great Depression, when the cost of living fell 15 percent. Except for early and intermittent declines, however, the trend of prices has been inexorably upward (Simonsen in Ellis 1969). Brazil may have the longest, continuous recorded inflation of any country. Table 2.21 reports Brazilian prices annually since 1937. Prices increased during all but one of those fifty-one years. In modern Brazil, general deflation is nonexistent unless it is taken to mean a diminution in the rate of price increase. The average annual rate of price increase from 1951 to 1982 was 37 percent.

Brazilians have never fully accepted conventional ideas about money, credit, banking, and prices. Endorsing this nonconformity, Dudley Seers (1962) argued that "the inflationary process in Brazil cannot be classified as one of 'cost inflation' or 'demand inflation' in the manner customary in professional discussions in Western Europe or North America [owing to the presence of] structural features and trends which are peculiar to less-developed countries." This assessment is questioned by many economists.

Table 2.21

Index Numbers of Wholesale Prices of Commodities in General in Brazil, 1937–1988 (1937 = 100)

Year	Average	% Change	Year	Average	% Change
1937	100		1963	9,690	73
1938	93	- 7	1964	18,600	42
1939	94	1	1965	28,000	51
1940	100	6	1966	38,400	37
1941	122	22	1967	48,000	25
1942	146	20	1968	59,500	24
1943	167	14	1969	72,000	21
1944	180	8	1970	87,700	32
1945	208	16	1971	105,000	20
1946	248	19	1972	124,000	18
1947	299	21	1973	145,000	17
1948	347	16	1974	187,000	29
1949	384	11	1975	212,000	13
1950	441	15	1976	336,000	59
1951	534	21	1977	472,000	40
1952	597	12	1978	656,000	39
1953	658	10	1979	1,020,000	55
1954	858	30	1980	2,040,000	100
1955	967	13	1981	4,530,000	122
1956	1,160	20	1982	8,450,000	87
1957	1,300	12	1983	24,100,000	185
1958	1,460	12	1984	81,200,000	237
1959	2,010	38	1985	272,000,000	235
1960	2,640	31	1986	706,000,000	160
1961	3,650	38	1987	2,170,000,000	207
1962	5,590	53	1988[a]	8,000,000,000	269

Sources: 1937-1952: Wegner, 1953; 1953-1988: calculated by David Camp from various
issues of the United Nations Monthly Bulletin of Statistics.

[a] First nine months of 1988.

Economic Growth

In Brazil, economic development is imperative. The relationship between inflation and economic development is in professional dispute. Hans Singer, the well-known United Nations economist, said in one of his Brazilian lectures: "There never was to my knowledge a successful case of economic development coupled with inflation" (Eugenio Gudin in Ellis 1969). Sir Arthur Lewis, however, winner of the Nobel Prize for economics, maintains that "inflation which is due to the creation of money for the purpose of accelerating capital formation results in accelerated capital formation"

(Kahil 1973). The evidence in Brazil seems to favor the positive relationship stated by Lewis. Year-to-year changes in the rates of inflation and economic growth are not closely related, but over time inflationary Brazil has experienced pronounced economic growth. Table 2.22 shows the annual rate of growth in the real gross domestic product. From 1951 to 1981, the average annual rate was 6.8 percent, approximately twice that of the United States.

Money Supply

Table 2.23 reports the annual rate of growth in the money supply from 1951 to 1987. The increase averages 65 percent, fairly close to the average of the annual rates of price increase for the same years, 60 percent. Arguments about alleged structural causes of inflation will have to be judged against evidence that the money supply and the price level rose at very similar rates. Both the annual rates of change in money supply and real growth are erratic. The dominant fact is the high average levels of both variables. The basic cause of the Brazilian inflation, as in the cases previously studied, is the extraordinary outpouring of new money. This openhanded monetary policy appears to have accommodated development as well as inflation, but after decades of such indulgence, has also brought Brazil to the brink of financial chaos.

In most of the inflationary case histories examined in this book, national budgetary deficits have been basic to increases in the money supply and to inflation. Hardly so in Brazil. Reported annual federal deficits during the period 1951 to 1974 averaged only 1.5 percent of the gross national product; during four of the twenty-four years there was a surplus (Krause and Salant 1977). Brazilian budgets are, however, misleading. Only about one-third of the central government's finances are included in the formal budget (Ellis 1969). The extension of credit and the issue of paper money are not clearly accountable. According to Ellis (1969), "monetary control scarcely existed."

Interest Rates

The real interest rate charged to industrial developers was negative during much of Brazil's history. Kahil wrote in 1973: "The elimination of a positive real rate of interest and its replacement by an increasingly generous subsidy meant that new ventures became profitable, even if wholly uneconomic, provided that the expected annual loss did not exceed 4 percent in the early 1950s, 10 percent in the middle of the decade, and 25 percent from the late 1950s onward." That rapid industrialization would occur

Table 2.22
Annual Percentage Change in Real Gross Domestic Product in Brazil, 1951–1985[a]

Year	Rate of Growth
1951	6.0
1952	8.7
1953	2.5
1954	10.1
1955	6.9
1956	3.2
1957	8.1
1958	7.7
1959	5.6
1960	9.7
1961	10.3
1962	5.3
1963	1.5
1964	2.9
1965	2.7
1966	5.1
1967	4.8
1968	9.3
1969	9.0
1970	9.5
1971	11.1
1972	10.4
1973	11.4
1974	9.5
1975	5.6
1976	9.7
1977	5.4
1978	4.8
1979	6.8
1980	7.9
1981	-1.9
1982	0.9
1983	-3.2
1984	4.5
1985	8.3

Sources: 1951–1974: Krause and Salant 1977, 1975–1981: Pereira 1984, 1982–1985: Baer 1989.

[a] In Brazil, as in other countries with rampant inflation, statistics that reflect price behavior must be adjusted for inflation. Comparison of price-related data over any expanse of time is meaningful only in real terms.

Table 2.23
Annual Percentage Changes in the Money Supply, Brazil, 1951–1987

Year	Currency in the Hands of the Public Plus Demand Deposits, Percentage Change
1951	16.4
1952	15.4
1953	19.3
1954	23.7
1955	16.4
1956	21.9
1957	32.1
1958	23.0
1959	42.9
1960	38.8
1961	52.5
1962	64.1
1963	64.6
1964	81.6
1965	79.5
1966	13.8
1967	45.7
1968	39.0
1969	32.5
1970	25.8
1971	32.3
1972	38.3
1973	47.0
1974	34.0
1975	42.8
1976	37.2
1977	37.5
1978	42.2
1979	73.6
1980	70.2
1981	73.0
1982	70.2
1983	95.0
1984	203.5
1985	328.2
1986	306.7
1987	133.3

Sources: 1951–1974: Krause and Salant 1977, 1975–1987: Baer 1989.

with such incentives is not surprising. That misallocation of resources would follow from such subsidized interest rates is equally obvious.

Institutional Changes

We come now to the heart of this section: How has Brazil been able to cope with an inflation that has continued—irregular but escalating—for nearly 500 years? Most economic institutions have evolved during times of generally stable prices. Traditional and respected economic deportment comes under stress when its foundation—relative stability in the value of money—is eroded. Necessarily, institutional changes had to be invented. These we now examine.

Indexation

From 1964 on, many of Brazil's economic sectors were tied to changes in the price level in order to reduce the price distortions resulting from inflation (Lemgruber in Krause and Salant 1977). Savings, loans, debts, rents, assets, insurance, interest, wages, housing, and the exchange rate were all made responsive to price level changes in what was called "monetary correction." This correction was either "prefixed," based on a prediction of the subsequent inflation rate, or "postfixed," reflecting what had actually happened. Escalated upward in step with changes in the price level were the normally lagging economic sectors such as rents and insurance. Monetary correction thus reduced the asymmetry ordinarily associated with inflation, making it less painful, thereby weakening resistance to it. By the 1980s, the inflation rate had climbed from a two-digit to a three-digit level, indicating that indexation accommodated rather than checked the inflationary trend.

There was chicanery. The government jockeyed the statistics in an effort to reduce the inflationary impact of price increases. The cost-of-living index, the basis for monetary correction, was purged of "accidental events" so that in 1984 the adjusted cost-of-living index in Rio de Janeiro rose by 190 percent compared with the unadjusted increase of 197 percent.

Development of a System with Two Units of Account

During the mid-1960s, when monetary correction was adopted, the Brazilian economy began functioning with two units of account: the common monetary unit (the cruzeiro) and the constant purchasing power unit (the UPC) (Baer 1983). Nominal assets, including ordinary money and financial instruments prefixed for inflation, are denominated in cruzeiros; long-term index-linked assets are computed in UPCs. This innovation makes possible reliance on the cruzeiro for ordinary purchases, whereas long-term financial ventures are served by UPCs, without which the building industry and capital investment could hardly function.

Use of two units of account, operating in an inflation-prone economy with indexation, sometimes produced strange price behavior. The price of farm land (an inflation hedge) was financed by borrowing with constant purchasing power UPCs. In 1986, monetary correction was eliminated, and the real price of farm land suddenly doubled. In 1987 monetary correction in the form of UPCs was reintroduced, and real land prices fell (Brandao 1988).

Variable Exchange Rates

With inflation rampant in Brazil and prices tilted irregularly upward in the rest of the world, Brazilian exchange rates were necessarily both volatile and deteriorating. The Brazilians tied their exchange rate to the dollar by what was known as a "trotting peg." In 1974, the cruzeiro was devalued eleven times. The purpose was to keep the cruzeiro related to the dollar on the purchasing power parity principle, thus equilibrating the rates of price change in the two countries (Lemgruber in Krause and Salant 1977).

The equating of domestic and external prices could have been accomplished in a free market by allowing the exchange rate to fluctuate in accordance with the supply and demand for Brazilian and other currencies. The Brazilians prefer to control the exchange rate, however, which they do with their "trotting peg."

The purchasing power parity principle, which once served to equate the price levels among trading countries, no longer performs this function reliably. Exchange controls, quotas, differentiated exchange rates, black markets, and surging international financial transactions obfuscate what formerly were clear-cut relationships. Price levels in various countries, which once found equilibrium through the channels of trade in much the same fashion as water, now respond more sluggishly, like molasses.

In the United States and Great Britain during the nineteenth and early twentieth centuries, the stable exchange value of the national currency was defended with passion. For Brazil, pride in maintaining the exchange value of the currency has eroded; currency devaluation has been depoliticized.

Purchasing Power Bonds

When the rate of inflation moved to the double-digit level and the inflation risk of bond purchases was borne entirely by the buyer, voluntary purchases of cruzeiro-denominated government bonds dwindled to an insignificant amount. After index-linking, with its purchasing power bonds, the inflation risk was borne entirely by the federal treasury (Baer 1983), and bond purchases shot upward by a factor of thirteen, from 59 billion old cruzeiros in 1964 to 743 billion two years later (Ellis 1969). That the government should bear the risk of deteriorating bond values had moral justification; the government had caused the deterioration by its inflationary policies.

The advent of purchasing power bonds deprived the government of the opportunity to reduce its real internal debt burden by inflation. This deprivation became painfully obvious with the rampant inflation of the 1980s. Renegotiation and/or debt repudiation are the remaining alternatives.

Selective Escape from Regulation

During the stress of the Great Depression in 1933, Brazil passed a "gold-clause law," forbidding contractual payments except in domestic currency at its legal value and thus prohibiting monetary correction. Inflation made this law archaic, and it was simply ignored. Also in 1933, a law was passed prohibiting interest charges in excess of 12 percent per year, a law made inoperable by inflation (Simonsen in Ellis 1969). Nonetheless, the populist appeal of these two laws is such that politicians have been unable or unwilling to change them.

The law prohibiting interest greater than 12 percent has been circumvented by ingenious subterfuge (Simonsen in Ellis 1969), conveniently and necessarily overlooked by the authorities, via the following techniques:

1. *Reinterpretation of the law.* The 12 percent has been interpreted to mean real, not nominal interest.
2. *Interest on the outside.* In addition to the legal rate, an extra rate is charged, not entered on the books.
3. *Surcharge on banking commissions.* Greatly inflated fees and commissions are charged, which elevate the cost of money to the desired level.
4. *Tied accounts.* The borrower is obliged to take out a loan greater than desired, to pay interest on the entire sum, and to leave part of the funds in the bank in a tied account that pays no interest.

Laws, outdated by inflation, can thus stay on the books, while ingenuity and lax enforcement circumvent the original intent.

Black Markets

Brazil's black market foreign exchange rate is substantially different from the official rate. In December 1984, the black market rate was 19 percent above the official rate.

Price control was imposed to hold down prices of food products, drugs, medicines, electric rates, transportation rates, and industrial products (Ellis

1969). Wages were both pushed up and held down. Price controls were imposed with the mistaken notion that prices could be held down by law even while excessive amounts of paper money were being issued. The misallocations resulting from inflation made price ceilings unenforceable. Black markets arose, thereby giving expression to the inflationary forces engendered by the government. Thus the economy was able to function, though with difficulty. Had the price ceilings been strictly enforced, the economy would have been crippled; price relationships would have been distorted and incentives dulled.

Barter

When official price relationships became unreasonable and the relevance of the currency eroded, people engaged in barter, thus establishing individualized value relationships not subject to control but suited to the respective utilities of the goods exchanged. This was practiced extensively internationally as well as in rural areas. The effects of inflation were thus bypassed, as values were not denominated in the diminishing value of the cruzeiro.

Barter is a cumbersome means of exchanging goods and services, relying as it does on the simultaneity of supply of the particular commodity on the part of one party with demand for that same commodity on the part of the other, coupled with reciprocal supply and demand regarding another commodity. Resorting to barter means turning the calendar back 3,000 years to a time before money was invented. Nonetheless, barter may be necessary if money loses its credibility.

Other Adjustments

Other institutional changes were brought about by inflation. Citizens with political and economic power coped with inflation by investing in real assets such as land or by sending their money out of the country. Institutions that have developed during a time of price stability must be modified during major persistent inflation. Countries embarked on an Age of Inflation can take note.

All of these methods of coping with inflation—monetary correction, variable exchange rates, the two-money system, purchasing power bonds, indexed interest rates, selective escape from regulation, black markets, barter, exporting capital, and investing in real assets—can be useful in living with inflation. Their adoption means acceptance of inflation as a way of life, however. They do nothing to check inflation and in all likelihood contribute to it.

Development and Inflation

Most of the advanced countries of Europe and North America achieved gradual economic development based largely on individual decision making, accumulated savings, a fairly open competitive system, and a reasonably stable price level. Not so Brazil. Brazil's economic development occurred with a large measure of central planning, a preponderance of state enterprises, semiauthoritarian governments, heavy borrowing from abroad, open-handed subsidies, import substitution, and rampant inflation (Bergsman and Candal in Ellis 1969). That Brazil has achieved major development with so different a system continues to puzzle many people of the North Atlantic community.

Brazilian economic development relied on three organizational forms (Baer 1983):

1. Domestic dominance of industries such as housing construction, communications, clothing, agriculture, wood products, and retail food sales

2. Foreign dominance of other industries, especially automobile assembly, pharmaceuticals, petroleum distribution, hygienic goods, transportation products, and plastics. In the late 1970s, 50 percent of the total assets in manufacturing were owned by multinationals (Hewlett 1980).

3. State dominance of public utilities, chemicals, mining and steel production

Brazil's economic development model is capital intensive and employs relatively little labor. In the development process, the focus has been on areas that were well endowed, aggressive, and politically powerful, such as those in the south, whereas the less favored northeast has lagged significantly.

A favorite liberal myth is that private enterprise exploits the poor and that if an activity can be moved from the private to the public sector the poor people will be better served. The Brazilian case gives little support for this belief; the poor have been bypassed.

Trickle-Down Development Policy

The accurate though pejorative term for Brazil's development model has been "trickle down." It has indeed been a trickle rather than a flow. The income gap between the rich and the poor is enormous. Brazil's is a two-sector economy with a small, developmentally favored, wealthy class and large numbers of poor, readily visible in the slums on the outskirts of Rio. The skewness of income in Brazil is among the greatest in the world, and it appears to be growing (Table 2.24).

Table 2.24
Distribution of Income among the Economically Active Population, Brazil

	Percentage of National Income Received	
	1960	1970
Poorest 20 percent	3.9	2.8
Poorest 50 percent	17.4	12.6
Richest 10 percent	39.6	50.9
Richest 5 percent	28.3	37.9
Richest 1 percent	11.9	16.9

Source: Pereira, 1984.

Brazil has not invested heavily in human development. In 1973 the country spent twice as much on roads and public works as it did on education and health combined (Hewlett 1980). In 1960, less than 10 percent of persons active in agriculture had completed the primary educational course of four years (Ellis 1969).

If the overall rate of economic growth is the criterion, Brazil's development policy, assisted or at least accompanied by inflation, has been successful. But this has been achieved at high risk, with great inequity and with wrenching results. The often quoted quip about Brazil is that it hosts an enclave like Belgium in a country like India.

Hinge Points

The three major economic events in Brazil's post–World War II history all relate to inflation. They can be characterized as the revolution of the 1960s, the miracle of the 1970s, and the crisis of the 1980s.

The Revolution of the 1960s

In response to growing unrest, Brazil in 1960 elected a populist president, Jânio Quadros, and an equally populist vice-president, João Goulart (Roett 1972). In March 1961, the government launched an anti-inflation program. The exchange rate system was reformed, subsidies on essential imports were lowered, government spending was cut, and the cruzeiro was sharply devalued. It was more change than the dominant interests could accept. Five months later Quadros resigned under pressure, and Vice-President Goulart was sworn in.

Goulart, likewise a reformer, launched his own anti-inflationary program. He moved to nationalize all private oil refineries, to expropriate all "underutilized" properties (Roett 1984), and to institute agrarian reform, which was not implemented. This also was too much. A political revolution was launched in March 1964. The armed forces assumed control and ousted President Goulart. The military establishment held power with a succession of military presidents.

Amid the political turmoil, the economy slid into recession. The emerging judgment was that the import-substitution plan of economic development had failed (Roett 1976). By 1963, the annual rate of economic growth, which had been around 10 percent, fell to 1.5 percent. Despite the anti-inflation campaign, by 1964 the annual rate of price increase, which had been creeping up from the 30 percent range, rose to 92 percent. From 1960 to 1963, real minimum wages declined 32 percent (Pereira 1984). The prevailing economic belief was that forced savings and tight wage policies were required for economic growth (Roett 1984).

General Castello Branco, who replaced Goulart, brought in both military men and technocrats, a government of the middle class. Unfortunately, the industrial workers, the students, the left-leaning groups, and the entrepreneurs lacked representation (Pereira 1984). Branco placed monetary stabilization as his primary objective and was ready to sacrifice development in order to fight inflation. The money supply, which had increased at an 80 percent rate in 1965, rose only 14 percent in 1966. The inflation rate came down from 92 percent in 1964 to 21 percent in 1969. Real economic growth, which had slipped to 2 percent in 1963, crept up to around 5 percent by 1966 and 1967, still short of the performance during the 1950s. For some ten years following the changes associated with the revolution, the inflation rate held to 20 to 30 percent, modest for a country such as Brazil.

The retrenchment and self-discipline of the 1960s helped set the stage for the prosperity of the 1970s.

The Brazilian Miracle

The rate of economic growth, which had fallen to about 2 percent, rose during the early 1970s to about 11 percent. Exports and imports both soared. Delfim Netto, minister of finance and architect of the "miracle," attributed the change to flexible exchange rates, the introduction of incentives, and the casting off of crippling restrictions (Netto 1974).

The oil shock of 1973 and the worldwide economic decline of 1974 were not enough to erase the Brazilian miracle; the country borrowed to overcome the hurt. Huge amounts of petrodollars resulting from revenues flowing to the oil-producing nations were banked in the industrialized countries and were available for lending at low rates of interest. Banks in Europe and the United States, flooded with oil money and impressed by the "Brazilian Miracle," pushed loans to Brazil, which were avidly taken up. Brazil's foreign debt, denominated in U.S. dollars, rose from $3 billion in 1960–1964 to $22 billion in 1975 (Roett 1976).

Euphoria arising from the "Brazilian Miracle" led to extravagant projects. Among them were Daniel Ludwig's effort to grow pulpwood in the Jari River area of the Amazon basin; a 180,000-acre project near Belo Horizonte to grow manioc for alcohol as motor fuel; a land settlement venture at Altamira on the Xingu River, served by the new Trans-Amazon Highway; a $62 billion undertaking on the Carajas River to develop iron deposits, electricity, transport, agriculture, and industry (Coffey and Correa do Lago 1988; Hall 1987). At least the first three of these four projects have fallen into trouble (Paarlberg 1984).

Crisis of the 1980s

By the late 1970s ominous events began to occur. As the discipline of the 1960s set the stage for the "miracle" of the 1970s, so the excesses of the 1970s ushered in the debacle of the 1980s. Hyperinflation, long a threat, became a fact. The rate of economic growth, which had averaged 6.7 percent during the late 1970s, fell to −1.9 percent by 1981, the first decline within living memory. The second oil shock, coming in 1979, jolted import-dependent Brazil. In that same year, the United States boosted the interest rate to check U.S. inflation; interest rates rose worldwide, a disaster for debt-ridden Brazil. In 1982, following the anti-inflation policy in the United States, there came a general economic slow down throughout the world. An international decline in dollar-denominated wholesale prices of raw materials reduced Brazil's agricultural export earnings. Brazil's per capita economic growth was negative during the early 1980s (Brandao 1988).

A painful lesson is being learned. Autonomy in macroeconomic policy, which nations once had or thought they had, is no more. To paraphrase John Donne, no nation is an island, sufficient unto itself. Each is a part of the main.

The magnitude and severity of Brazil's debt burden increased. Brazil's total external debt, which had stood at U.S. $3 billion in 1960–1964 (Roett 1976), rose to U.S. $107 billion in 1985 (Coffey and Correa do Lago 1988), having grown at an average annual rate of more than 20 percent for fifteen years. In 1985, Brazil's total debt equaled more than half the gross national product. Servicing the public debt absorbed more than a quarter of the country's earnings from exports of goods and services.

Between 1970 and 1976, Brazil borrowed money to increase investment and for consumption. Between 1978 and 1980, Brazil borrowed to maintain consumption. Since 1981 the country borrows not so much for investing and consuming but primarily to pay interest (Pereira 1984).

Under pressure from the International Monetary Fund, Brazil agreed to an austerity program, that is, to cut the balance-of-payment deficit, bring down the rate of inflation, restrain wage increases, phase out farm subsidies, devalue the cruzeiro, and reduce government spending on large investment projects (Roett 1984). The agreement was not consummated. Despite attempts at retrenchment, intended in part to make Brazil credit worthy in world financial markets, net direct foreign investment to Brazil declined from U.S. $1.556 billion in 1983 to U.S. $655 million in 1986 (Coffey and Correa do Lago 1988). Foreign investors were disinclined to "throw good money after bad."

With soaring prices, erratic exchange rates, and an uncertain future, capital fled the country. This loss was estimated to total U.S. $8 billion from 1983 to 1986 (Coffey and Correa do Lago 1988).

On 28 February 1986, President Sarney announced Decree Law 2283, the "Cruzado Plan," intended to kill Brazilian inflation in a dramatic blow (Baer 1989). This plan, seemingly successful in the early stages, soon failed. By the middle of 1987, the yearly rate of inflation was well over 1,000 percent (Baer 1989). By February 1989, Brazilian bonds were selling in the secondary market at 34 percent of face value (Sachs 1989).

Traditionally, heavily indebted countries have been able to reduce their real debt by inflating their prices. This route was denied to Brazil. The domestic debt was indexed, as mentioned above. The foreign debt is denominated in dollars. In neither case would Brazilian inflation reduce the real debt burden. Renegotiation is one alternative; repudiation is the other.

In 1987, Brazil declared a moratorium on debt payments. In February 1988, following months of negotiations, Brazil ended the moratorium and concluded a twenty-year rescheduling agreement with creditors, including $5.2 billion in new bank money to cover interest payments (Hayes 1989).

In March 1990, Fernando Collor de Mello became president. He moved immediately to curtail inflation. He froze approximately 70 percent of the money circulating in the economy. Deprived of cash, consumers stopped buying, companies stopped producing, and exporters stopped exporting. Alarmed, the government started reinjecting money into the system to the point that some feared a revival of inflation, and then closed the tap again.

Previous anti-inflation plans have failed in Brazil. It remains to be seen whether the most recent one will do better. By mid-1990 the monthly inflation rate, which had stood at 84 percent, had fallen to 13 percent (*Wall Street Journal*, September 24, 1990). Since then it rose again.

Fifty years ago Professor Frank A. Pearson said that a country would not experience hyperinflation so long as its production plant was intact and it escaped both war and revolution. If that is the generalization, Brazil is the exception.

The lesson is clear. Capital-intensive development, undertaken by a pre-industrial country with the help of heavy debt and inflation, is a gamble. It can succeed, but at a high risk, with great inequity and at great cost. Brazil's "success" (before the debt crisis) has led many pre-industrial countries to attempt forced-draft economic development. The inflation so general in Third World countries is thus in part explained.

In 1796 France had a double-digit rate of annual price increase—an increase greater than 9 percent but less than 100 percent. France corrected the upsurge by burning its paper currency. Germany had seven-digit inflation in 1923 and curbed it by replacing its policymaking officials. The Soviet Union experienced a three-digit rate of price increase in 1924 and checked it by imposing authoritarian monetary reform. Hungary reached a fantastic twenty-five-digit level of annual price increase in 1946 and overcame it by wiping out an ill-advised policy of indexation. China's inflation rose to the three-digit level in 1949; the increase was halted when the Communists took over. Bolivia reached a four-digit level in 1986 and suppressed it with orthodox austerity. The United States moved to a two-digit annual rate of price advance in 1979 and checked it by curtailing the creation of new money and by a sharp increase in the interest rate. In the late 1980s, Brazil's inflation reached a three-digit level which it has been unable to check. Every country now has some degree of inflation. Those with a one-digit rate of annual price increase—a price increase of less than 10 percent—have generally decided to live with it.

U.S. INFLATION: 1933 AND AFTER

The 1930s saw a revolution in price behavior, ushering in the Age of Inflation. The upheaval was worldwide and lasting. Each country had its own version, in some ways similar to that of others and in some ways unique. The U.S. experience provides a good example.

Yearly data on U.S. price levels are available for the two centuries from 1790 to 1990 (Table 2.25, Figure 2.1). During the first 140 years of that period, prices fluctuated around a fairly stable level, approximately doubling with each major war and declining thereafter to prewar levels or lower. Price increases were generally accompanied by economic expansion, whereas declines were associated with contraction. Prices waxed and waned with the level of gold production.

The most recent sixty-one years have departed markedly from this pattern. During the Great Depression, from 1929 to 1932, wholesale prices of all commodities fell 32 percent for reasons not yet agreed upon. The rate of price decline was a staggering 12 percent per year, compounded for three years. During the next fifty-eight years, prices rose to more than nine times

Table 2.25
Index Numbers of the Wholesale Prices of All Commodities in the United States, 1786–1990 (1910–1914 = 100)

Year	Average	Year	Average	Year	Average	Year	Average
1786	90[a]	1837	115	1888	86	1939	110
1787	90	1838	110	1889	81	1940	112
1788	--	1839	112	1890	82	1941	129
1789	86	1840	95	1891	82	1942	157
1790	90	1841	92	1892	76	1943	174
1791	85	1842	82	1893	78	1944	176
1792	--	1843	75	1894	70	1945	182
1793	102	1844	77	1895	71	1946	210
1794	108	1845	83	1896	68	1947	257
1795	131	1846	83	1897	68	1948	277
1796	146	1847	90	1898	71	1949	255
1797	131	1848	82	1899	77	1950	268
1798	122	1849	82	1900	82	1951	299
1799	126	1850	84	1901	81	1952	281
1800	129	1851	83	1902	86	1953	260[c]
1801	142	1852	88	1903	87	1954	250
1802	117	1853	97	1904	87	1955	240
1803	118	1854	108	1905	88	1956	245
1804	126	1855	110	1906	90	1957	248
1805	141	1856	105	1907	95	1958	253
1806	134	1857	111	1908	92	1959	240
1807	130	1858	93	1909	99	1960	240
1808	115	1859	95	1910	103	1961	243
1809	130	1860	93	1911	95	1962	238
1810	131	1861	89	1912	101	1963	235
1811	126	1862	104	1913	102	1964	233
1812	131	1863	133	1914	99	1965	245
1813	162	1864	193	1915	101	1966	260
1814	182	1865	185	1916	125	1967	246
1815	170	1866	174	1917	172	1968	250
1816	151	1867	162	1918	191	1969	267
1817	151	1868	158	1919	202	1970	277
1818	147	1869	151	1920	226	1971	284
1819	125	1870	135	1921	143	1972	315
1820	106	1871	130	1922	141	1973	429
1821	102	1872	136	1923	147	1974	484
1822	106	1873	133	1924	143	1975	486
1823	103	1874	126	1925	151	1976	506
1824	98	1875	118	1926	146	1977	529
1825	103	1876	110	1927	139	1978	592
1826	99	1877	106	1928	141	1979	677
1827	98	1878	91	1929	139	1980	751
1828	97	1879	90	1930	126	1981	812
1829	96	1880	100	1931	107	1982	788
1830	91	1881	103	1932	95	1983	797
1831	94	1882	108	1933	96	1984	814
1832	95	1883	101	1934	101[b]	1985	759
1833	95	1884	93	1935	111	1986	691
1834	90	1885	85	1936	118	1987	736
1835	100	1886	82	1937	132	1988	759
1836	89	1887	85	1938	112	1989	811
						1990	852

[a] The index numbers for 1786-1933 are for wholesale prices of all commodities and were obtained from Warren and Pearson, 1935, Tables 1 and 2.

[b] The index numbers for 1934-1952 are for wholesale prices of raw materials and were obtained from Wegner, 1953, Table 1.

[c] The index numbers for 1953-1990 are also for wholesale prices of raw materials and were obtained from David Camp's working paper.

Source: Compiled by David Camp, Department of Agricultural Economics, Purdue University.

Figure 2.1
Wholesale Prices in the United States, 1790–1990 (1910–1914 = 100)

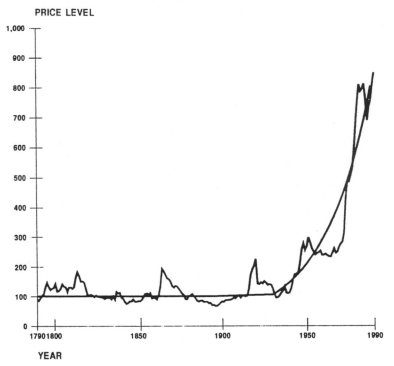

Source: David Camp, Dept. of Agricultural Economics, Purdue University, West Lafayette, IN.

the 1932 level from an index of 95 to an index of 852. Prices rose during forty-three of those fifty-eight years.

Beginning in 1929 the method of determining prices underwent a major transformation. The theses of this section are that the Great Depression brought institutional changes to the U.S. economy that committed the country to an uptilt of the price level, and that this change is not confined to the United States but is worldwide.

The Great Depression

The beginnings of U.S. inflation, and indeed the inflations for most of the thirty countries whose price levels are reported in Chapter 3, are to be found largely in the worldwide deflation of 1929–1932. For this reason the dimensions of that disaster are taken as the beginning point of this section. The U.S. experience is lifted up because the institutional changes associated with the Great Depression and the subsequent inflation are more readily identified in the United States than elsewhere; and as the world's largest producer and trader, the United States may logically be expected to exert a proportionate economic influence on world events.

The onset of the Great Depression is usually dated from the 1929 crash of common stock prices on the New York market, which had earlier experienced an enormous boom, unwarranted by underlying economic conditions. Thursday, 24 October 1929, Black Thursday, was by general consent the day on which the stock market is considered to have crashed. Nearly 13 million shares of stock changed hands compared with a precrash volume the preceding September of around 4–5 million. From the September peak to the following November, two months' time, security prices fell by one-third and continued irregularly to decline for more than three years. Investors sold stocks out of fear of further decline. This dumping of shares further reduced prices, and this led to margin calls. Rather than pay the calls, investors sold, thereby further forcing prices down and uncovering other margin calls and more stop-loss orders. The expectation of price decline, like the earlier expectation of price increase, became a self-fulfilling prophecy. Ultimately, common stock prices fell to 16 percent of the peak.

The economy had been weakening before the stock market fell, but the two went down together after Black Thursday. Under this pressure the credit system collapsed, the money supply shrank, prices fell, farms failed, factories shut down, jobs disappeared, banks went into receivership, mortgages were foreclosed, bankruptcies multiplied, equities vanished, tax revenues shriveled, and the incumbent administration was voted out of office. The author was in his twenties during this terrible decade and the events are indelibly etched in his memory.

The Federal Reserve Board used its long-established tool, the interest rate, for coping with recession. It reduced the bank rate from 6.0 to 1.5 percent, but prices were falling so fast that few people wanted to borrow. A borrower would have to repay a greater real value than he had received. Nor did people want to invest or make loans; business prospects were so poor that a loan might not be repaid. With falling prices, money hidden in the mattress gained greater value than could reasonably be expected from investment, and hoarding of money was widespread. As a consequence, the velocity of its circulation diminished. Deprived of both deposits and loans, banks failed. People pulled their money out of suspected banks, and more banks failed. Bank failures took on epidemic proportions. In 1929,

659 banks failed; in 1930, 1,352; and in 1931, 2,294. By the end of 1933, nearly half the nation's banks had closed.

From the cyclical peak in August 1929 to the cyclical trough in March 1933, the stock of money fell more than one-third. The crying need, however, was for more money. Now a remark that is only half facetious: needed at that time was a syndicate of several thousand counterfeiters scattered about the country, each turning out millions of paper dollars to make up for those extinguished by the financial system. There were indeed some counterfeiters, who were thrown into jail; a triumph of law over economics. Actually, there was an official form of counterfeit: school teachers were paid with scrip called tax anticipation warrants, which passed as legal tender.

The disastrous German inflation, only a decade earlier, was still a vivid memory in the minds of monetary authorities. The conventional wisdom was that an upward price spiral was to be avoided at all costs. A balanced budget was the goal set by the politicians, when in fact a large deficit with the attendant injection of new money was the urgent need.

Had prices fallen equally there would have been little problem. But they did not. From 1926 to 1932 the changes were as follows (Warren and Pearson 1935):

Prices of thirty basic commodities	−49%
Retail prices of food	−37%
Cost of living	−22%
Hourly wages	−19%
Long-term mortgages	0%
Salaries of government employees	+ 6%

The wrenching effect of the Depression, experienced in some fashion by every industrialized country, contributed to the overthrow of representative governments in Italy and Germany and aroused concern about the political stability of the United States. Spread by international trade, fueled by fear, and translated through exchange rates, price deflation radiated throughout the world. From 1929 to 1932 basic commodity prices changed by the following amounts (Warren and Pearson 1937):

Netherlands	−53%
United States	−52%
Canada	−45%
Belgium	−45%
France	−38%

Germany	−36%
Italy	−35%
England	−34%
Sweden	−31%
Australia	−26%
Finland	−21%
New Zealand	−21%
Spain	−6%
Mexico	−6%
World, in terms of gold	−50%

The worldwide Depression produced an enormous and controversial literature. The author has tabulated forty-three different published explanations of the disaster, each of which was sufficiently credible to be brought into print by a reputable publisher.

Which, if any, of these alleged causes were valid? What was to be done? A frenzied effort was made to cope with this disaster. Economists divided into two camps. The orthodox neoclassical economists, dominant at the time, numbered among their adherents most of the members of the Federal Reserve Board. Traditional economic theory had postulated an economic order that was equilibrating; it was thought to have natural shock absorbers. Economic oscillations, it was believed, served a useful purpose. Whereas inflation and its attendant prosperity were thought to provide incentives for the launching of needed new ventures, deflation and recession purportedly shook out inefficient enterprises and improved the economic health of the economy. In this analysis, nothing special was to be done during an economic downturn; it was the system's way of pruning off the inefficient. The 1929 to 1932 downturn, however, broke through the constraints that were supposed to confine it. The economy plunged into something like a free-fall, defying conventional economic theory. Traditional theory was without explanation or remedy for the disaster.

The second group of economic thinkers was made up of radicals who espoused either unorthodox explanations for the disaster or unconventional remedies or both. Among these were Irving Fisher of Yale, G. F. Warren and F. A. Pearson of Cornell, and Benjamin Graham, the securities analyst. John Maynard Keynes, the most prestigious of the group, came to prominence only later. Though these people differed greatly from each other, they were united in their opposition to economic orthodoxy. Their proposals were all inflationary, appropriate at that time.

The Beginnings of the Age of Inflation

The radicals carried the day. The mood of the country changed. Concern about inflation gave way to apprehension about deflation. President Franklin Roosevelt was one of the converts. He initiated changes that helped check the free-fall of the economy. His methods were experimental and pragmatic, lacking, at that time, theoretical respectability. The changes that resulted set the stage for the Age of Inflation, the major worldwide economic phenomenon of the past half-century.

The balance of this section treats the institutional changes that flowed from the Great Depression. Their combined effect on the price level was to ratchet it upward, diminishing the downward adjustments that had characterized all previous U.S. economic history.

Abandonment of the Gold Standard

The United States had adhered to the gold standard throughout its history, that is, its currency was redeemable in gold at a fixed amount per dollar. Brief departures, associated with the War of 1812, the panics of 1837 and 1857, and the Civil War had occurred, but after each departure, redeemability was restored.

Before the Great Depression, the U.S. dollar was the equivalent of 23.22 grains of fine gold, and the official price of gold was $20.67 per ounce. The paper dollar was redeemable in gold, and gold was convertible into paper notes at these fixed rates. The Great Depression drove the country off gold. Early in 1933 the dollar could no longer be defended at the old rate; confidence had been diminished, and people were drawing gold out of the banks. More paper dollars were required to purchase an ounce of fine gold in the free market, and the price of gold rose. The government called in all the privately held monetary gold and issued paper money in exchange for it. On 1 February 1934, the official price of gold was fixed at $35 an ounce, an increase of 69 percent. Domestically the government refused any longer to pay out gold in exchange for paper dollars. A quip of the times was that paper money was still redeemable; you could take your paper dollar to the bank and exchange it for another paper dollar with a different serial number. Internationally, gold was still paid out for paper. Other countries followed similar systems. There was a worldwide flight from gold. Internationally, we were on a gold exchange standard.

This state of affairs continued until July 1944, when, at Bretton Woods, New Hampshire, representatives from forty-four countries agreed to stabilize their national currencies by an "adjustable peg fixed rate system," which made the dollar, not gold, the world's international monetary standard (Brittan in Hirsch and Goldthorpe 1978, Fleming in Hirsch and

Goldthorpe 1978). This revised system came under pressure and began to weaken during the late 1960s. The dollar could no longer be defended at the $35 per ounce of gold rate. The system was transformed by stages during 1971 and 1973 to a "managed floating rate" system, thus formally ending both gold convertibility and reliance on the dollar (Brittan in Hirsch and Goldthorpe 1978, Lindberg and Maier 1985). The consensus view of the world monetary community was that we now had central banking with the knowledge and the ability necessary to manage both money and prices; we needed neither gold nor a fixed value of the dollar any longer.

When, after 1971–1973, the United States no longer had to defend the dollar at a fixed rate, domestic macroeconomic policies became less disciplined. After the monetary systems of the world were officially detached from both the gold and the dollar standards, prices skyrocketed. From 1971 to 1981, the price of gold increased eleven-fold, the supply of money nearly doubled, and the price level nearly tripled.

Conventional wisdom attributed the near tripling of the wholesale price index to such easily understandable events as the OPEC cartel, the disappointing crop yields of the early 1970s, and profiteering by middlemen. The abandonment of gold, the end of the dollar standard, and the expansion of the money supply were little noticed. The price-related events of the 1970s were largely beyond the understanding of the public and the media.

With the collapse of the Bretton Woods system, the last link with gold was broken. Price and monetary discipline were relaxed. Exchange rates, once held stable by hard-money principles, readily changed, permitting any or all countries to follow open-handed economic policies.

By steps, various countries moved gradually, over a forty-year period, away from convertibility of paper notes into gold and to inconvertible paper currency.

Keynesian Economics

Into the void left by the Depression-born collapse of traditional economics rushed what was called "The New Economics," the product of the mind of the English economist John Maynard Keynes. For our purposes, the chief attribute of the new economics was its endorsement of deficit financing as a way of providing the increments to income needed to lift a country out of depression. The proper course, said Keynes, was to stabilize the economy by balancing the national budget over the business cycle, incurring a deficit during slack times and running a surplus when times were good.

Unhappily, the executive and legislative branches of government soon overlooked the admonition to run a surplus when times were good. Keynesian ideas were corrupted to the point that the master, had he lived, would have had difficulty recognizing them as his own. Warped ideas about government finance were adopted throughout the world.

In time, Keynesian ideas were used to stimulate a U.S. economy that was already running a fever. More was asked of the economy than it could provide. Weary, like a horse flogged beyond the capability to respond, the economy stumbled into stagflation, a combination of inflation and stagnation not foreseen by Keynesian economics. Designed to cope with deflation, which it did well, Keynesian economics was carried over into times of inflation, thus undoing its earlier success.

The Supply Siders

Keynesian economics had focused on stimulating demand and by the late 1970s had led to stagflation. So, in the 1980s, a new economic doctrine called supply-side economics, by intent and by name opposed to Keynesianism, was introduced. The idea was to cut government expenses, stimulate production, increase the supply of goods, build tax revenues, and thereby reduce the government deficit. By increasing supply and reducing the deficit, the rate of inflation logically should subside. This happy outcome was to be achieved by disciplining the budget and simultaneously reducing the tax *rate*. More money would then be available for private investment, according to the theory. The economy would throw off its sluggish behavior and move into increased production. Advocates claimed that following a cut in the tax *rate*, production and general economic activity would pick up so tax *revenues* would increase, thus achieving a variety of desirable economic consequences. Econometric models were built, based on these assumed relationships (Stockman 1986).

Some conservatives argued that if tax *rates* were cut, tax *revenues* would also diminish. Reduced revenues would in turn discipline spending so the size of government would also diminish. Conservatives saw this as a desirable outcome. The politicians, little concerned with theory, opted for a reduced tax rate as being good in itself.

Thus the proposal won the support of businesspeople who wanted greater economic growth, of conservatives who wanted less government, of the public who wanted less taxes and less inflation, and of the politicians who wanted more votes. Most economists were dubious.

So the tax rate was cut. What ensued? Tax revenues, government expenditures, and the deficit all increased. The price level first surged upward, then fell back, and then renewed its upward creep. The gross national product weakened, then recovered, then weakened again. The performance was as controversial as the prescription had been.

One important legacy left by supply-side economics was that the desire for low tax rates was seemingly made respectable.

The Debt

During the fifty-nine years from 1933 to 1992, there were only eight years of budget surplus. The federal debt, which had stood at $17 billion in 1929, increased to over $4 trillion in 1992. Even after correcting for changes in the price level and the increase in the population, this is still a 18-fold increase.

In addition, the government lends almost as much money as it borrows, so that its vulnerability is greater than the official debt figures. From 1980 to 1988, when cumulative federal budget deficits totaled $1.41 trillion, the government had also issued $394 billion of direct loans and an additional $756 billion of primary loan guarantees. These figures omit secondary guarantees, the activities of government-sponsored enterprises, and vulnerability to the cost of the savings and loan bailout. On top of all this came the costly Middle East war.

In 1990 the interest charge on the official debt, was $182 billion, 14 percent of total federal outlays. This sum must be raised from the public and paid to bond holders to maintain the credit of the U.S. government. With continuing federal deficits the share of tax revenues going to bondholders will continue to grow. To citizens, the purchase and holding of bonds is a reward for postponing consumption, for doing without. To bankers who take the bonds that the public will not buy, it is in fact a means of stoking the fires of inflation by increasing the amount of money they can lend. These bonds in the hands of banks become the basis for expanding loans, thus creating more of the medium of exchange. The federal deficit can sidestep these inflationary consequences if most of the bonds by which it is financed are bought by the public rather than the banks. Bonds bought by the public wipe out, at least for some years, money that would otherwise be used to support expenditures for consumption. This has been possible only in part because U.S. citizens have proved unwilling to purchase all the bonds issued.

A 6 percent interest rate is approximately twice the average rate of economic growth, growth being the product not only of capital but also of labor, land, technology, and management. The only methods by which an economy can pay a 6 percent return on capital, over time, and on the average, are the following:

- Transfering some of the social dividend to capital and away from the other factors of production
- Reducing the real rate of interest by inflation and so diminishing the burden of repayment
- Defaulting on the debt

The first and second devices are commonly resorted to as they are preferable to the third, which lacks subtlety.

The larger the debt, the greater becomes the drag on the economy, transferring income away from those who produce goods and services and to those whose incomes are derived by clipping their bond coupons. This lesson the Third World countries are learning, and the United States may yet learn.

A large and growing part of the debt is held by foreigners; the U.S. savings rate has become so low that only part of the bonded indebtedness can be sold to the public. Foreign capital came in to help fill the gap. By 1988 the United States was the world's largest debtor; its net international investment position was a negative $532 billion. This financial overhang could be pulled out of the country on short notice, making the country vulnerable to a shift in overseas perceptions of the stability or instability of the U.S. economy.

As individual banks had been vulnerable due to fear of their inability to pay their obligations during the Depression, so the nation became vulnerable to a similar fear sixty years later. As the individual banks were protected from fear by the Federal Deposit Insurance Corporation, so the nation is in the process of developing an international system of protection.

Attitudinal Changes

John Goldthorpe, a sociologist and a Fellow of Nuffield College at Oxford, England, maintains that there have been subtle changes in modern society that make it inflation prone (Hirsch and Goldthorpe 1978). Goldthorpe believes that the common people are increasingly egalitarian in their concepts and that they increasingly insist upon receiving what they see as their entitlements. No longer are they willing to accept deflationary policies as a means of checking economic excesses. They are increasingly able to demand what they consider to be their just due. The dedication to the common good that previously had characterized the ordinary citizen has been eroding, says Goldthorpe. Waiting, saving, and accepting—attitudes characterized by an earlier day—have been replaced. Instead of waiting, consume; instead of accepting, demand; instead of paying cash, buy on credit; instead of saving, spend. The present low rate of saving has some logic to it. If inflation will erode away the value of your savings, why save? Savings lag. Investment is inhibited. We are eating up the seed corn.

The average citizen now wants to live like the affluent, whose life-styles are constantly paraded by the media. Increasingly he expresses this urge. The political means of doing so have been, in part, opened to him. There has been a revolution of rising expectations.

Ronald Inglehart, a political scientist writing in 1977, reports a generational shift in values away from hard work, self-discipline, production, public order, and patriotism, toward self-expression, self-realization, political participation, and concern for the "quality of life." The traditional or "materialist" values, says Inglehart, were related to a high priority on control of inflation. These values are still held by older people, but less so by the younger "postmaterialist" generation. This attitudinal change, says Inglehart, helps tilt the price level upward. With the downside of price fluctuation sharply reduced and the upside made tolerable, the price level is pushed upward.

Concentration of Advocacy and Dispersal of Opposition

"Buy low, sell high" is the popular advice for success in trading. One might reason that for every buyer there is a seller, and that in aggregate terms the desire for a low price would offset the desire for a high price. So, one might conclude that the inclination in the long term would be for the price level to be stable. This reasoning overlooks the fact, however, that the average person sells only one or two things, be it his labor or the corn he grows, in which he has concentrated interest and for which he tries to obtain a high price. The average buyer purchases a thousand things, in which his interest is dispersed. The buyer of cornflakes and of articles that reflect increased wage rates has limited interest in these items and is unlikely to resist a modest price increase. The seller of cornflakes or labor, however, has concentrated interest in that particular item and will do his best to push up the price. The structure of modern society accommodates this urge. This unequal battle contributes to inflation. One should beware, therefore, of public clamor for a stable price level, and not be deceived by its own self-deception.

Full Employment

Shortly after World War II, Congress, convinced that Keynesian ideas had enabled the country to have a continuously thriving economy with a fully employed labor force, passed the Employment Act of 1946. The Act made clear the objective of full employment but said nothing about price behavior.

Since that date Congress and the executive branch have sought to prod the economy into employing the entire labor force, acknowledging the existence of frictional unemployment resulting from people being between jobs, first considered to be 3 percent of the total. But the 3 percent target has not been attainable over any long period. With unemployment insurance, food stamps, and other benefits, unemployment is not the disaster it once was. David Piachaud has reported (Hirsch and Goldthorpe 1978) that in

Figure 2.2
The Relation between Unemployment and the Rate of Change of Money Wage Rates in the United Kingdom, 1861–1957

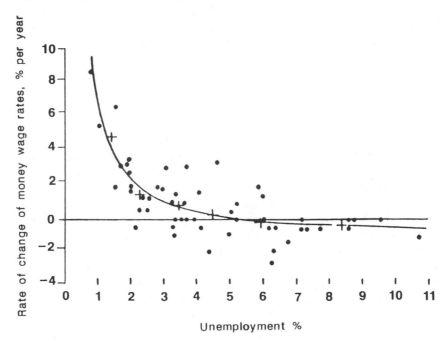

Source: Phillips, 1958.

Britain the after-tax income of a household while the male is out of work is 72 percent as great as when the male is employed. Hence, achieving full employment is more difficult than formerly. With the new safety net and with the new attitude toward entitlements, the economy must be flogged harder by open-handed monetary policy in an effort to achieve the full employment objective. Inflation results.

In 1958, Professor A. W. Phillips published a curve, here reproduced, that showed the unemployment rate to fall as wage rates increased (Figure 2.2).

Phillips's paper stirred great interest. Were the wage rates dependent on employment? Or was employment dependent on the wage rate? Do they interact with one another? Is the relationship spurious? My opinion is that rising employment and rising wage rates are both influenced by a force that does not appear in the figure: a rising price level. An increase in the price level boosts both employment and wage rates.

Defenders of the Full Employment Act point out, correctly, that since this law was placed on the books, the country has not experienced depression or unemployment such as had occurred earlier. Keynesian ideas, deficit financing, and full-employment policies helped to avert a recurrence of the free fall from 1929 to 1932, a contribution of incalculable value. Postwar deflation, which had occurred after every previous war, was avoided after World War II, a gain of enormous importance. There have been seven recessions since the passage of the Employment Act of 1946: 1953–1954, 1957–1958, 1960–1961, 1969–1970, 1974, 1982, and 1990–1992. None of these approached the disastrous proportions of 1929–1932. The 1987 drop in the stock market led to a fear that 1929 would be repeated, but it was not. In 1989 came a lesser drop in the stock market, and again a downward spiral was avoided. Each time the economy slowed, older people, who remembered the debacle of 1929–1932, said "here we go again!"—but it did not happen. Downward vulnerability had been lessened, but at a cost of increased vulnerability on the upside. The Employment Act of 1946, although it gave stability to the work force and to business, clearly contributed to the inflationary trend that has marked the last half of the twentieth century.

The inflationary effect is considered here as a fact, neither as an indictment nor as an endorsement of the Act.

Money Supply

In 1932, the total of deposits and currency was $45 billion. In 1990 the figures were as follows:

M1	(chiefly currency and demand deposits)	$826 billion
M2	(M1 plus mostly small time deposits)	$3,323 billion
M3	(M2 plus mostly large time deposits)	$4,094 billion

Thus from 1932 to 1990, the money supply has increased enormously, no matter how it is calculated. Clearly the Age of Inflation is associated with huge increases in the money supply.

Inflation is generally a monetary phenomenon (Lindberg 1985). Nonmonetary factors are said to affect inflation in the long run only as they affect monetary policy (Hirsch and Goldthorpe 1978).

The money supply must increase over time to meet the needs of a growing economy. Milton Friedman has calculated that it should increase by not less than 3 nor more than 5 percent per year to give a stable price level. But the annual rate of increase in the money supply from 1930 to 1987 was 6 percent, more than appropriate for price stability and clearly inflationary.

With the advent of paper money, we were able to create this precious item by the stroke of a pen, a much less costly method than digging it from the earth. To create so valuable a thing at near zero cost is enormously appealing; small wonder we make so much use of it.

Special Interests

The Roosevelt Administration dealt with the Great Depression not only with macroeconomic policies but also with legislation in behalf of specific interests:

- *Labor:* The Wagner Act, giving the right of collective bargaining to hired labor, and unemployment insurance to help those who could not find jobs
- *Farmers:* Price supports to boost farm income
- *The financial community:* the Federal Deposit Insurance Corporation, the Federal Savings and Loan Insurance Corporation, the Reconstruction Finance Corporation (RFC), and the Glass-Steagall Act, permitting government bonds to be used as collateral for the Federal Reserve System
- *Business:* The National Industrial Recovery Act (NIRA) to stabilize prices and production for the business world
- *The elderly:* Social Security

These laws were enacted to cope with deflation and low income. They did so, by increasing prices or wages or both, directional changes appropriate at the time. All but the NIRA and the RFC were continued after the deflation had been reversed. They extended their price and wage boosting effect into what was already an inflationary period.

Further special interest legislation was added, arising not from the Depression but from social concerns: Aid to Families with Dependent Children, food stamps, health benefits, housing, transportation, education, and much else.

The special interests organized lobbies to protect and exploit the gains made. Logrolling, an ancient legislative practice, increased. Political action committees were organized that bestowed their funds primarily on incumbent senators and congressmembers, not on those who challenged them, in effect an endorsement of the inflationary policies being pursued. Congress reorganized itself to accommodate these demands. It reduced the power of party leadership, clipped the wings of the committee chairmen, created many more subcommittees, and gave each member a fiefdom of sorts. It tripled the staff of the House. The increased staffs invited and accommodated increased lobbying efforts. The overall committee chairmen, shorn of much of their power, were unable to discipline the subcommittees. They responded to the demands of their respective subcommittees with little regard for their compatibility. The national interest was fragmented. That such a structure would produce overspending and inflation was inevitable.

The well-known Iron Triangle was reinforced: lobbies of the special interests, their friends in the administration, and the congressional committees that had jurisdiction. No effort has been sufficient to convince special interest groups that altered circumstances have reduced legitimate reasons for their existence. Once the process started, more special interest groups joined in, if for no other reason than to protect themselves from the others. When one of the special interests felt that its budget was being threatened, the others perceived that they also were in jeopardy and rushed forward to support the one in danger. It was one for all and all for one. This system seems to have public approval; more than 90 percent of congressmembers seeking reelection are returned to office. A wise man once said that democracy would succeed until the people learned that they could vote themselves largesse from the public purse. The people may be on the threshold of that discovery.

The case is one of the cost-raising special interests versus the cost-bearing general interests, a concentration of advocacy and a dispersion of opposition—an unequal struggle that puts greater demands on the economy than it is able to meet at face value, thus resulting in inflation, which reduces the real value of each claim.

Big Government

In 1929, federal outlays were $3 billion. In 1990, they were $1.251 trillion. Even after allowing for population increase and the change in price level, this is still a thirty-four-fold real increase. In 1929, federal outlays constituted 3 percent of the gross national product. In 1990, they amounted to 23 percent.

This enormous expansion of the federal government transferred huge chunks of the economy from the private to the public sector. Economic activities in the private sector are highly cost-conscious and subject to the discipline of competition. Transferred to the public sector, competition is diminished and cost discipline is relaxed. The government bailed out banks that would have failed, provided more health services than private medicine would have done, spent billions for weapons that the public could not purchase, propped up farms that would have gone under, moved in to save corporations that would have experienced bankruptcy, and kept in existence transportation services that could not pay their way. These operations added to the cost of goods and services. Money was created to support these interventions, thus contributing to inflation. We have privatized profits and socialized losses. We are knocking at the door of Alice's Wonderland world, where all have won and each must have a prize.

My intent is to assess the directional price behavior that results from big government. Advocates of big government contend that these governmental interventions are worth all they cost. I do not examine that doubtful case. All that I contend here is that the trend toward big government has been and continues to be inflationary.

The Government's Stake in Inflation

Government officials publicly deplore inflation but by their actions promote it. We know how to check inflation: reduce the rate of growth in the supply of money over which the government has a monopoly. Why are public officials reluctant to apply the brakes? The answer is that the alternatives to inflation are so bleak that, though having the knowledge and the implements with which to check it, officials choose not to travel that road.

Contrary to the popular view, government has its reasons for favoring inflation.

Inflation reduces the real burden of public debt. Government, the biggest debtor, gains from inflation, as do private borrowers. A thirty-year government bond, priced at $100,000 and sold to a loyal citizen in 1957 could be repaid, in 1987, in real terms, for $33,700, about one-third of its face value.

Inflation is a penalty placed on savers. It is the debtor's surrogate for the Year of Jubilee reported in Chapter 25 of Leviticus; Scripture prescribed that every fiftieth year debts should be wiped out and a new start begun.

Full repayment in real terms of long-term debt plus the going rate of interest is expectation beyond realization. The economy does not have such capability, though lenders continue to assert it. Public and private borrowers need some form of escape from such a system. Inflation helps provide it.

With inflation, progressive income taxes lead to "bracket creep," an alternative to a tax increase. Other things equal, with progressive income taxes, inflation nudges the taxpayer into a higher income bracket, yielding more income for the government without an overt tax increase, a strategy that politicians relish and are reluctant to forego.

Inflation escalates the economy out of specific commitments. Wage negotiations and farm price supports frequently have clauses that carry specific dollar-denominated increases beyond the year of their enactment. Inflation makes possible the achievement of these targets even though they may be unwarranted by increased productivity. Enough remains of the money illusion to make this a relatively painless process.

Inflation can contribute to economic growth. An increase in the money supply and the accompanying inflation, if moderate, are often accompanied, at least in the short run, by increased economic growth. Other methods of achieving growth, such as structural change and improved efficiency, are more difficult and less attractive. Thus there is the inclination to increase the money supply, stimulate the economy, and deny the resulting inflation or accept it as a reasonable cost.

Inflation can reduce invidious comparisons. A vocational group will often look with envy at a different group, comparing its own wage or income unfavorably with the other. With inflation, nominal incomes of both groups will probably increase, so that awareness shifts from envy to gratification. This kind of psychological betterment can come even if there is no increment to real economic growth and no real improvement for the respective parties. The money illusion accommodates the perception. Such a manner of dealing with perceived inequity is much more attractive to politicians than is taking from one group to give to another. When economic growth cannot keep up with expectations, inflation can disguise the lag.

Inflation is an attractive surrogate for taxes. Taxes are overt, visible, and painful. Inflation is subtle, for the most part invisible, and results, at least temporarily, in an enjoyable increase in nominal income. So public officials often prefer it to taxes.

For the greater part, this is an illusion. In an economy approaching full employment, people do not escape tax increases if the government, facing huge deficits, fails to increase taxes and borrows from the banks. People pay taxes in the form of reduced purchasing power resulting from inflation. People are deprived of goods and services much as though taxes had been increased. They may bid for goods and services in the market, but the government, with bank-created money, will outbid them. The rival bids, the government's versus the people's, will drive up the price. Inflation is a subtle form of taxation. Not one person in a thousand realizes that escaping a tax increase is likely to mean accepting some increment of inflation as well as accepting some increase in debt and the burden of bearing it.

There is a circumstance in which debt creation is preferable to taxes: when there are falling prices, substantial unused resources, and severe unemployment. This was the situation addressed by John Maynard Keynes fifty years ago, a special circumstance. Debt creation produced inflation even then, which was much needed at that time.

Inflation can improve prospects for reelection. Contrary to popular opinion, elected governments often are returned to office after having followed inflationary policies. It is unlikely that politicians who opt for inflationary policies misread their constituents.

The popular perception is that even modest inflation, say of the single-digit type, will hurt an incumbent government. This view emanates from bondholders, salaried folk, and especially from people of the media. The anchorman sees that inflation hurts him personally and generalizes therefrom for the body politic. These people speak and write out of proportion to their numbers and create a misleading perception.

Of the forty-two U.S. presidential elections since 1828, there were twenty-four preceding which prices had been high or rising. In nineteen of the twenty-four cases, the party in power was returned to power. There were eighteen elections preceding which prices had been low or falling. In thirteen of these, the party in power was turned out of office (Table 2.26).

Of the presidential elections beginning in 1932, the generalization holds, though less firmly than before. Of the fifteen, nine conformed to the historic pattern: if prices had been strong, incumbent parties were returned to office; if prices had been weak, incumbents were displaced. Overall, during the 160-year period, three-fourths of the cases supported the above proposition. Hence voting patterns appear not to confirm the peoples' aversion to inflation depicted so prominently in cartoons, editorials, and political statements.

This experience occurred while inflation was generally of moderate proportions, mostly of the one-digit type. What electoral results would be with inflation in the two-digit or three-digit range is another matter. Nonetheless, with inflation having so many attractions to government, it is small wonder that the price level is tilted upward.

Inflation has been called "the democratic disease." Although a democratic country such as the United States is clearly vulnerable to inflation, as this section shows, the problem is not unique to democracies. Inflation occurred in Rome, an empire, in the third century A.D. It occurred in feudal Europe during the 1300s. France, a kingdom, experienced inflation in 1720. Our American colonies saw inflation before the Revolution. The Soviet Union, a communist country, had hyperinflation from 1917 to 1924. Brazil, while a military dictatorship, underwent severe inflation. Virtually all countries for which statistics are available, of whatever kind of government, are now experiencing price increases. Apparently no form of government is proof against it.

This discussion of the stake that government has in inflation does not consider the ethical question as to the moral connotations of altering, by subtle means, for better or for worse, the real wealth of helpless citizens. The author's aversion to this form of deceit will be obvious to the reader, however.

Indexation

Rising prices erode wage contracts and retirement benefits; inflation reduces the real returns of any loan that has a considerable time dimension. Hence indexation is utilized to tie wage contracts to the cost of living, escalate social security payments, and increase food stamp benefits as inflation

Table 2.26a
Presidential Elections during Periods of Rising or High Prices in Which the Incumbent Party Was Reelected, 1832–1984[a,b]

Election Year	Incumbent[c]	Candidates Victorious	Defeated
1832	Jackson (D)	Jackson (D)	Clay (W)
1836	Jackson (D)	Van Buren (D)	Harrison (W)
1856	Pierce (D)	Buchanan (D)	Fremont (R)
1864	Lincoln (R)	Lincoln (R)	McClellan (D)
1868	Johnson (D)[d]	Grant (R)	Seymour (D)
1872	Grant (R)	Grant (R)	Greely (D)
1880	Hayes (R)	Garfield (R)	Hancock (D)
1900	McKinley (R)	McKinley (R)	Bryan (D)
1904	Roosevelt (R)	Roosevelt (R)	Parker (D)
1908	Roosevelt (R)	Taft (R)	Bryan (D)
1916	Wilson (D)	Wilson (D)	Hughes (R)
1924	Coolidge (R)	Coolidge (R)	Davis (D)
1928	Coolidge (R)	Hoover (R)	Smith (D)
1936	Roosevelt (D)	Roosevelt (D)	Landon (R)
1940	Roosevelt (D)	Roosevelt (D)	Willkie (R)
1944	Roosevelt (D)	Roosevelt (D)	Dewey (R)
1948	Truman (D)[d]	Truman (D)	Dewey (R)
1972	Nixon (R)	Nixon (R)	McGovern (D)
1984	Reagan (R)	Reagan (R)	Mondale (D)
		Exceptions	
1852	Fillmore (W)	Pierce (D)	Scott (W)
1912	Taft (R)	Wilson (D)	Roosevelt (PR)
1952	Truman (D)	Eisenhower (R)	Stevenson (D)
1976	Ford (R)[d]	Carter (D)	Ford (R)
1980	Carter (D)	Reagan (R)	Carter (D)

[a]   The direction of the movement in commodity prices 48, 36, 24, and 12 months before the election and the level of prices at elections were taken into consideration.

[b]   The table from 1824-1944 was obtained from Pearson and Myers, 1948; 1948-1988 compiled by David Camp, Department of Agricultural Economics, Purdue University.

[c]   RD, Republican-Democrat; D, Democrat; W, National Republican or Whig; R, Republican; PR, Progressive Republican.

[d]   These men were not elected president but came into office upon the death of the president or the vacancy of the office in the middle of the term.

Table 2.26b
Presidential Elections during Periods of Declining or Low Prices in Which the Incumbent Party Lost Power, 1824–1988[a,b]

Election Year	Incumbent[c]	Candidates Defeated	Victorious
1828	Adams (RD)	Adams (W)	Jackson (D)
1840	Van Buren (D)	Van Buren (D)	Harrison (W)
1844	Tyler (D)[d]	Clay (W)	Polk (D)
1848	Polk (D)	Cass (D)	Taylor (W)
1860	Buchanan (D)	Douglas (D)	Lincoln (R)
1884	Arthur (R)	Blaine (R)	Cleveland (D)
1888	Cleveland (D)	Cleveland (D)	Harrison (R)
1892	Harrison (R)	Harrison (R)	Cleveland (D)
1896	Cleveland (D)	Bryan (D)	McKinley (R)
1920	Wilson (D)	Cox (D)	Harding (R)
1932	Hoover (R)	Hoover (R)	Roosevelt (D)
1960	Eisenhower (R)	Nixon (R)	Kennedy (D)
1968	Johnson (D)	Humphrey (D)	Nixon (R)
		Exceptions	
1824	Monroe (RD)	Jackson (D)	Adams (RD)
1876	Grant (R)	Tilden (D)	Hayes (R)
1956	Eisenhower (R)	Stevenson (D)	Eisenhower (R)
1964	Johnson (D)[d]	Goldwater (R)	Johnson (D)
1988	Reagan (R)	Dukakis (D)	Bush (R)

[a] The direction of the movement in commodity prices 48, 36, 24, and 12 months before the election and the level of prices at elections were taken into consideration.

[b] The table from 1824-1944 was obtained from Pearson and Myers, 1948; 1948-1988 compiled by David Camp, Department of Agricultural Economics, Purdue University.

[c] RD, Republican-Democrat; D, Democrat; W, National Republican or Whig; R, Republican; PR, Progressive Republican.

[d] These men were not elected president but came into office upon the death of the president or the vacancy of the office in the middle of the term.

carries the consumer price index up. This eases the burden of inflation for those with sufficient political clout to win indexation. On the other hand, by reducing the pain of politically powerful groups, indexation diminishes the government's resistence to inflation, which in turn aggravates the problems of small businesspeople, unorganized workers, and others whose incomes are not indexed.

The overall effect of indexation is controversial. It certainly creates inequities between protected and unprotected groups. It is a tinkering response to the problems of inflation, certainly not a correction.

Inflation's Impact on Particular Groups

Inflation often is positively correlated with economic growth and employment, so its individual effect is difficult to differentiate. Generally helped by inflation are the government, borrowers, holders of real property, entrepreneurs, and farmers. Usually hurt by inflation are lenders, bondholders, beneficiaries of life insurance policies, receivers of annuities, salaried workers, and the rentier class.

Speculation focuses on the relative impact of inflation on low-income, high-income, or middle-income groups. Is inflation like Robin Hood, robbing the rich to give to the poor? Or is it like a medieval tyrant, piling up wealth for the rich by exploiting the poor? It is hard to generalize. The particular case is more important than the generalization. Among low-income people, manual laborers can get more jobs but the unprotected poor face a higher living cost with little or no increase in income. Among high-income people, the enterprising industrialist is helped whereas the wealthy retired bondholder is hurt. Among middle-income people, the farmer is helped but the professional salaried person is injured.

Ever since the Keynesian revolution, the emphasis has been on macroeconomics, that is, the overall performance of the economy. This has had the unfortunate consequence of obscuring microeconomic phenomena, the fallout for particular individuals.

There is much speculation as to whether the Age of Inflation with its accompanying institutional change has widened or reduced the relative income gap between the high and the low quintile. The evidence seems to be that the gap was widened, perhaps not for reasons of inflation, but because of demographic, political, and social changes (Phillips 1990). The situation is so complex that it is possible, by using selected evidence, either to condemn or to condone inflation on the basis of whether, in an overall sense, it reduces or widens the income gap between rich and poor.

Bankruptcy

Bankruptcy, which occurs for private firms, is not experienced by government. A private firm in financial stress undergoes bankruptcy, writes down its liabilities to equal its assets and pays off, say, 50 cents on the dollar. Government, when in financial stress, does not undergo bankruptcy; by inflation it writes up its assets so as to carry its liabilities and pays off an illusory 100 cents on the dollar.

Worldwide Inflation

The United States does not bear sole responsibility for launching inflation on the world. Keynes, perhaps the person most responsible for the Age of Inflation, was British, and his ideas have been applied (and misapplied) throughout much of the world. Bretton Woods, the World Bank, the International Monetary Fund, Special Drawing Rights, and the Smithsonian agreements all in some way added to international liquidity. These international financial agencies provide a worldwide central banking system in fact if not in name, and it possesses the inflationary potential of any banking system. Inflation has developed its own dynamic, the result of institutional changes described above. It has become self-generating.

When worldwide inflationary trends are under way, traditional price behavior analysis is inappropriate. No longer is money without force of its own, or countries autonomous as regards price behavior, or institutions unchanged over time. No longer are year-to-year changes the heart of the matter, or passing physical phenomena such as crop failure and oil shocks the prime forces bringing inflation. One of the effects of the Age of Inflation was to jar economic analysis off its historic circumscribed assumptions. Salant stated, "to study world inflation by beginning with analyses of national inflations and then studying international transmission is like studying inflation in the United States by first studying inflation in each of the twelve Federal Reserve districts, and then analysing the process of transmission among them. It can be done, but with the degree of integration that exists in the United States, it is not the best approach" (Krause and Salent 1977).

Restraining Inflation

There are basically three strategies for disciplining inflation: exhortation, price control, and restraint of the money supply.

Exhortation

Exhortation as a strategy is easily dismissed. It serves primarily to alert the public that inflation is imminent and causes people to rush to the market and buy up things "before the hoarders get them."

Price Control

In 1971 the dollar, which had been made the basis of the international financial system, could no longer be defended. An adverse trade balance had placed it in jeopardy. Prices were increasing throughout the world, including in the United States (Table 3.1). On 15 August 1971, President Nixon "closed the gold window," cut loose from gold, and imposed price controls, which were finally terminated in April 1974.

The effort at price control was offset by an expansion in the money supply and the debt. Despite controls, prices rose, moderated, and then moved up to double-digit levels.

	Wholesale Price Index, % Change from Preceding Year
1971	3
1972	11
1973	36
1974	13
1975	0
1976	4
1977	5
1978	12
1979	14
1980	11
1981	8

The surge in 1973 was primarily a result of the jump in the price of crude oil, felt throughout the world (Table 3.1).

This experience of the early 1970s illustrates one of the chief difficulties regarding price controls. The imposition of controls and their temporary effectiveness creates the illusion that inflation has been overcome and that fiscal-monetary stimulus can be provided with safety, pumping up the economy and assuring full employment without inflation. Price control, often accompanied by rationing to make it work, can suppress inflation for a time. But misallocation of resources grows and pressure builds, so controls are removed. When that happens, accumulated savings are poured into the market, and delayed inflation occurs.

Restraint of the Money Supply

Economic stimulation, with an accompanying inflationary effect, is sometimes used by an incumbent government prior to an election in order to improve the likelihood that it will succeed itself. The inducement to take this course is heightened by the fact that the stimulus to the economy resulting from an increased money supply occurs rather quickly, whereas the effect on prices generally lags somewhat. During 1971 and 1972, prior to the 1972 election, the Federal Reserve Bank kept the interest rate so low relative to inflation that member banks paid nothing for borrowing and in effect were paid to borrow from the Federal Reserve (Lindberg and Maier

1985). The money supply grew at an 8.5 percent rate in 1972, thus stimulating the economy.

Edward Tufte noted that economic stimulus seems to be associated with elections. In twenty-seven democracies there were nineteen in which "short-run accelerations in real disposable income per capita were more likely to occur in election years than in years without elections" (Barry in Lindberg and Maier 1985).

The most effective strategy for restraining inflation is to restrict the growth of the money supply. The Federal Reserve System is the one agency that offers real hope for inflation control, although, as has been shown, it sometimes shifts over to stimulate inflation rather than suppress it.

Restraining the money supply may be both the most necessary and the most difficult task in government, as the experience of the early and mid-1980s illustrates. During 1979 and 1980, the wholesale price index, responding in part to monetary excesses of earlier years, climbed into the double-digit range.

	% Change in Wholesale Price Level
1979	14
1980	11

Interest rates had been low during the 1970s, as low as 4 percent for three-month Treasury Bills, a negative real rate. Money growth had been excessive. Debt had been growing at a double-digit rate. The value of the dollar had been falling against other currencies in the international exchanges, in part an expression of concern about U.S. inflation.

The country had been exceeding the speed limit, and the Federal Reserve Board felt that it had to apply the brakes. Interest rates on three-month Treasury Bills, which had been 5 percent in 1977, were pushed up to 10 percent in 1979 and 14 percent in 1981. Monetary growth was restrained. The dollar rose in foreign exchange markets, thus encouraging imports and making exports difficult.

The results were harsh. Wholesale prices fell 7 percent from 1981 to 1985. Net farm income, which had stood at $32 billion in 1979, fell to $15 billion in 1983. Unemployment, which had been 5.8 percent of the labor force in 1979, climbed to 9.5 percent in 1982 and 1983. Corporate profits, which had been $88.5 billion in 1981, fell to $58 billion in 1982. Banks failed or were rescued by deposit insurance. The recession was worldwide, in part the consequence of tightening monetary policy in the United States. Third World countries were unable to pay their debts.

When the Federal Reserve Board applied the brakes, it indeed brought the country down within the speed limit, but it threw the passengers against the windshield. Such is the pain of applying restraint, needful as it may be. Understandably, the regulatory authorities are reluctant to cool off the economy. What inflation the Federal Reserve System does not cause, it condones. The Federal Reserve Board is like a bartender called on to close the bar just when the party gets rolling.

We are on a long-time inflationary trend, but there may be short-run dips great enough to bankrupt a firm that bets on inflation, as illustrated by the experiences of the early 1980s. When the Federal Reserve System applies the brakes there is no way to know whether it will reduce the rate of speed—the desired outcome—or whether it will throw the vehicle into a skid, as during 1982–1983. Yet such is the force of the price-raising tendencies that even after drastic restraint during the early 1980s, during 1987–1992, prices were moving up again.

The price-increasing forces of the new institutions are built into the economy and must be held in check. Unlike the pre-1929 circumstances, there are no automatic inhibitors of the new inflationary institutions. Unless self-control is applied, inflation is likely to escalate. If discipline is applied early, inflation can be checked, though with pain. If inflation is indulged too long, checking it may result in severe recession, domestic and foreign, as in 1982–1983.

There is this subtlety to inflation: its stimulating effect on the economy, described variously in this section, comes only if inflation is greater than anticipated. (After more than half a century of an inflationary trend, the money illusion is somewhat eroded. There is now some anticipation of inflation.) If a 5 percent inflation rate is expected, the realization of 5 percent inflation is economically neutral; inflation must be greater than 5 percent to provide its increment to growth. If 5 percent inflation is expected and none occurs, this is relative deflation. This is why, once embarked on an inflationary course, the temptation is to advance the rate of price increase in the hope of satisfactory economic performance. If and when the annual rate of inflation moves up to the two-digit or three-digit level, the Latin American type, capital is exported, middle- and upper-class consumers and savers become alarmed, and unproductive subsidies are adopted.

There is an absolute bottom to prices and the price level—zero—but there is no absolute top. In July 1946, Hungary had a price level, with the July 1945 level equal to one, of $400(10^{25})$, or 400 followed by twenty-five zeroes (Nogaro 1948). Prices might have gone still higher had not reason prevailed. "What goes up must come down" was a familiar comment about prices during earlier days, when the price level fluctuated around a fairly stable level. This is no longer true. What goes up may stay up, or go higher.

The U.S. experience since 1933 demonstrates that the runaway tendencies inherent in inflation can be restrained, though diligence is needed and costs are great.

With modern finance a country can have whatever price level it wants—if it is willing to accept the consequences: economic distress if it is overzealous in curbing inflation or utter chaos if it allows inflation to run rampant. There need be no mystery about this. The principles that determine price levels are known, though not always acknowledged.

Economic Performance

The inflation from 1932 to 1987 was slow, irregular, and gradual, averaging about 4 percent per year, compounded—in sharp contrast to the well-known hyperinflation of Germany, when prices doubled in a month's time. It was gradual enough so that adjustments could be made with relative ease. This situation was much more in keeping with the public interest than the thirty-year deflation from 1864 to 1896, when prices fell at an average compounded rate of 3 percent per year. The complaints came from different people: from the entrepreneurs and debtors during deflation and the lenders and salaried people during inflation.

The standard of living rose during the inflationary time, as any open-minded observer can see. Inflation was held to a creep; it did not lead to political upheaval as the 1929–1932 deflation threatened to do. Monetary collapse was avoided. Income was redistributed from savers to spenders in a moderate fashion, not enough to incite critical sectoral disorder. Economic inefficiency occurred, but the dynamism of new technology was enough to overcome it. Economic growth continued at rates comparable with those of earlier years and with fewer oscillations. Harold Shapiro concluded (Krause and Salant 1977): "The bad reputation inflation has among the U.S. public rests in part on not quite relevant historical experiences together with a deep desire for stability, rather than on a convincing demonstration that inflation causes economic slowdowns. The German experience of the early 1920s—the picture of inflation destroying the middle class and causing a general economic breakdown—has had an extraordinary influence on U.S. thinking. The hyperinflation of that time however, does not teach us much about the U.S. inflation of the last two decades."

The gains described have come at a cost, however, the bill for which may be presented at some unknown future date. The wish to satisfy current desires has given the United States a low saving rate. We are consuming more than we produce, importing the difference. In this process we have incurred a huge net foreign debt, which stood at more than $500 billion in 1988. The Japanese alone bought 40 percent of our government bonds. This debt makes us vulnerable to people from abroad who might wish to exercise their claims against us and suddenly pull their financial assets out of the country, creating a monetary crisis. We have acquired an enormous federal debt, equal to more than half our gross national product, plus a huge federal deficit, and a major adverse balance of trade. In a number of enterprises, we have lost our competitive edge to foreign firms.

Deportment of this kind results from relaxation of discipline, public and personal. Some part of this attitudinal change is associated with the new institutions described above. As this is written, the bill for these excesses has not yet been presented. Defenders of the new institutions maintain that the bill will never be put forward or, if it is, we shall find some way to cope. Those troubled by the Age of Inflation note our vulnerability, as witnessed by the severe recession of 1982–1983. The stock market crash of 1987 was thought by some to be the first shoe to drop. But this alarm, now several years behind us, was either premature or unfounded. The Federal Reserve System wisely intervened, made more money available, and forestalled disaster. Nonetheless, an ominous note is sounded: in all but one of the fifteen inflations reported in this book (the Black Death is the exception), governments had acquired huge deficits or similar financial obligations.

The institutional changes that have led to the Age of Inflation are so firmly in place that a stable price level is impossible unless the institutions are changed, a most difficult and unlikely event. Advocates of stabilizing the price level while leaving in place the institutions that are responsible for its upward tilt have a hopeless cause. Equally bleak are the prospects for reinstituting the old institutions for the new. Given our new institutional arrangements, the alternatives to inflation are so unattractive that we had best learn to live with it, holding it to a single digit, which we have the demonstrated capability to do.

Counsel

How can individuals cope with inflation? Those who are wealthy, young, ambitious, venturesome, and anxious to pass on a goodly estate to their heirs and able to withstand a temporary setback in income should invest, preferably as owners, in enterprises they understand. They should acquire common stocks, which, though variable in price and earnings, are likely in the long run to ride the inflationary trend. They should be wary of bonds, life insurance, and certificates of deposit, which pay back dollar for dollar and fail to reflect inflation.

Those who are elderly, poor, conservative, and living on pensions can do little about inflation. They should scale their life-styles to their incomes and forget about leaving money to their heirs.

Many combinations of age, wealth, health, ambition, venturesomeness, and family responsibility are possible. How to cope with inflation is an intensely personal matter. A generalized recommendation is likely to be wrong in an individual case.

Nonetheless, one generalization is of central importance: despite the fact and prospect of general inflation, there can be short-run periods of deflation, as economists well know. One of these can wipe out the fortunes of those who bet on inflation and went deeply into debt.

3

Prices in Thirty Countries,
1937–1988

Table 3.1 shows the price series for thirty countries, all those for which prices are continuous or nearly so, from 1937 to 1988, as reported by the *United Nations Monthly Bulletin of Statistics.* Each of the thirty countries experienced inflation. Eighteen had unbroken series, from 1937 to 1988. Of the eighteen, the least amount of inflation is shown by Switzerland, whose prices nevertheless increased by a factor of about four. The United States was the next lowest: prices increased by a factor of about six. The unweighted geometric average increase for the eighteen countries was seventy-nine-fold.

Prices increased in developed economies, in Third World economies, and in newly industrialized market economies. Although communist countries do not generally report prices, it is common knowledge that prices have increased in China, in the former Soviet Union, and in the formerly communist countries of Eastern Europe. That the world has entered the Age of Inflation is amply clear from Table 3.1. Inflation is not merely a localized infection; clearly, it is in the global bloodstream.

Table 3.1
Index Numbers of Wholesale Prices of Commodities in General in Thirty
Countries, in Terms of Their Respective Currencies, 1937–1988 (1937 = 100)[a]

	Australia, A. Pound	Belgium, Franc	Brazil, Cruzeiro	Canada, Dollar	Chile, Peso	Costa Rica, Colon	Denmark, Krone
1937	100	--	100	100	100	100	100
1938	100	--	93	95	95	97	94
1939	100	--	94	92	93	99	99
1940	110	--	100	100	102	95	145
1941	117	--	122	108	119	101	171
1942	132	--	146	114	162	132	179
1943	138	--	167	119	179	165	180
1944	139	--	180	121	184	173	182
1945	140	--	208	123	196	189	179
1946	141	330	248	129	227	190	176
1947	150	355	299	151	292	220	195
1948	170	389	347	179	335	224	213
1949	189	370	384	184	383	222	218
1950	224	388	441	196	449	250	246
1951	277	471	534	222	586	258	313
1952	313	443	597	209	720	233	305
1953	321	416	658	204	793	222	285
1954	314	408	858	200	1400	231	285
1955	314	420	967	202	2200	238	294
1956	331	433	1160	208	3600	240	302
1957	343	441	1300	210	5120	240	302
1958	336	420	1460	210	6400	240	299
1959	339	420	2010	212	8320	238	299
1960	360	424	2640	212	8770	242	299
1961	346	420	3650	214	8830	252	305
1962	336	425	5590	220	9540	250	314
1963	343	437	9690	225	14,700	259	323
1964	353	458	18,600	227	22,100	263	332
1965	363	462	28,000	230	27,000	261	342
1966	378	473	38,400	239	33,800	262	352
1967	386	468	48,000	243	40,300	270	355
1968	388	469	59,000	248	52,600	291	368
1969	391	492	72,000	260	71,900	282	378
1970	424	516	87,700	264	97,800	305	410
1971	451	516	105,000	264	114,000	330	426
1972	472	513	124,000	286	193,000	348	448
1973	510	572	145,000	347	1,200,000	405	515
1974	609	658	187,000	424	13,500,000	565	629
1975	627	705	212,000	453	78,000,000	676	665
1976	705	760	336,000	472	253,000,000	739	717
1977	805	778	472,000	515	471,000,000	795	775
1978	904	763	656,000	562	673,000,000	856	809
1979	1350	812	1,020,000	575	1,010,000,000	1010	882
1980	1440	858	2,040,000	653	1,290,000,000	1250	1030
1981	1550	940	4,530,000	718	1,530,000,000	2060	1090
1982	1700	1000	8,450,000	764	1,800,000,000	4300	1440
1983	1840	1060	24,100,000	796	2,140,000,000	5430	1460
1984	1940	1130	81,200,000	823	2,640,000,000	5850	1770
1985	2070	1130	272,000,000	855	--	6450	1520
1986	2190	--	706,000,000	862	--	--	1420
1987	2350	1030	2,170,000,000	888	--	--	1420
1988	2520	1090	11,300,000,000	901	--	--	1430

Table 3.1
(continued)

	Egypt, E. Pound	El Salvador, Colon	Finland, Markka	France, Franc	India, Rupee	Ireland, Pound	Israel, I. Pound	Italy, Lira	Japan, Yen
1937	100	100	100	--	100	--	100	100	100
1938	99	87	93	100	90	100	94	107	105
1939	100	73	98	105	100	105	93	112	117
1940	124	63	132	139	112	132	115	130	130
1941	156	83	161	171	123	148	158	145	140
1942	200	100	199	201	151	170	231	163	152
1943	254	--	226	234	206	189	282	245	162
1944	300	131	250	265	228	198	298	918	184
1945	318	150	359	375	231	198	298	2203	278
1946	308	176	562	648	252	198	310	3084	1292
1947	292	215	676	989	282	219	320	5518	3824
1948	316	241	893	1712	349	232	422	5821	10,160
1949	298	243	900	1917	362	231	407	5528	16,580
1950	330	328	1037	2070	381	244	349	5248	19,490
1951	367	347	1482	2645	419	283	384	5996	27,127
1952	357	337	1465	2780	366	299	658	5646	27,737
1953	347	--	1410	2640	373	299	966	5590	27,800
1954	332	--	1410	2600	351	292	1140	5530	27,600
1955	338	--	1400	2600	325	302	1200	5590	27,200
1956	375	--	1450	2700	362	302	1260	5700	28,400
1957	406	106[b]	1590	2860	384	323	1450	5760	29,200
1958	402	100	1730	3180	392	336	--	5650	27,300
1959	402	94	1750	3340	405	336	--	5480	27,600
1960	402	94	1800	3400	435	336	--	5530	27,800
1961	410	92	1820	3560	384	339	--	5530	28,100
1962	406	91	1850	3590	392	353	--	5700	27,600
1963	402	93	1900	3720	388	356	100[c]	5990	28,100
1964	422	99	2060	3780	410	380	101	6210	28,100
1965	450	98	2130	3830	460	393	105	6290	28,400
1966	488	98	2180	3920	520	401	110	6380	29,100
1967	523	97	2250	3890	598	412	111	6370	29,600
1968	537	98	2490	3940	594	402	114	6400	29,800
1969	546	97	2580	4280	605	470	116	6640	30,500
1970	559	106	2690	4650	644	496	124	7140	31,600
1971	581	100	2830	4750	704	522	135	7430	31,300
1972	584	106	3060	4970	759	578	151	7740	31,600
1973	607	128	3600	5760	906	682	180	8990	36,600
1974	718	161	4480	7360	1090	762	273	12,700	48,100
1975	772	163	5080	6360	1130	957	384	13,700	49,500
1976	793	220	5660	7190	1110	1150	502	16,900	52,000
1977	870	325	6260	7760	1190	--	696	19,800	53,000
1978	1030	249	6570	7880	1190	--	1070	21,500	51,700
1979	1090	295	7010	8910	1400	--	1920	24,800	55,400
1980	1440	303	8160	9380	1600	--	4800	30,000	65,300
1981	1460	321	9270	10,400	1840	--	10,000	35,000	66,500
1982	1770	345	9870	11,700	1980	--	15,600	39,900	67,300
1983	1890	--	10,400	12,800	2160	--	37,200	43,800	66,000
1984	2090	409	11,000	13,200	2160	--	--	48,300	66,000
1985	2360	467	11,500	13,400	2270	--	--	51,900	65,300
1986	2760	--	10,900	13,400	2400	--	--	51,300	60,100
1987	--	--	10,900	13,100	2540	--	--	52,800	57,500
1988	--	--	12,400	13,200	2610	--	--	55,200	57,500

149

Table 3.1
(continued)

	Mexico, Peso	Netherlands, Guilder	New Zealand, Pound	Norway, Krone	Portugal, Escudo	South Africa S.A. Pound	Spain, Peseta
1937	--	100	100	100	100	100	100
1938	--	94	101	98	97	103	112
1939	100	97	105	100	98	101	128
1940	102	120	117	131	124	112	153
1941	109	138	128	160	145	123	181
1942	121	145	139	170	168	138	199
1943	146	148	148	172	209	150	222
1944	178	151	152	174	235	155	239
1945	199	267	155	174	228	158	265
1946	229	232	155	166	223	161	319
1947	242	250	161	172	235	169	373
1948	260	260	180	178	233	181	400
1949	285	271	179	181	239	191	428
1950	311	304	194	206	236	204	515
1951	385	372	227	255	259	233	648
1952	400	364	252	271	275	268	656
1953	393	348	250	271	271	270	700
1954	429	354	247	274	257	272	704
1955	487	356	250	282	257	281	728
1956	511	362	260	295	266	284	798
1957	534	372	262	306	271	290	931
1958	556	365	270	300	271	290	1050
1959	562	369	275	300	268	290	1050
1960	589	361	275	303	276	293	1070
1961	595	358	275	306	276	290	1100
1962	606	361	275	312	279	293	1160
1963	612	369	283	312	279	296	1210
1964	634	394	297	327	282	299	1240
1965	650	406	299	334	293	313	1370
1966	658	424	302	340	305	324	1410
1967	677	424	303	346	316	277	1410
1968	690	428	325	349	330	281	1450
1969	707	432	342	362	338	286	1480
1970	749	456	360	384	352	296	1510
1971	778	460	390	402	359	310	1600
1972	800	477	433	414	380	335	1710
1973	926	537	498	447	422	379	1880
1974	1130	717	515	529	542	557	2220
1975	1250	730	575	576	615	525	1500
1976	1530	791	721	622	732	604	1880
1977	2160	820	830	666	1030	682	3370
1978	2500	776	888	691	1240	748	3850
1979	2960	860	1030	753	1610	863	4410
1980	3710	940	1240	864	1710	--	5230
1981	4590	1030	1440	964	2090	--	6070
1982	7200	1050	1640	1020	2480	--	6800
1983	15,000	1080	1670	1080	--	--	7740
1984	25,000	1120	1770	1150	3950	--	8730
1985	39,100	1090	2170	1200	4770	--	9410
1986	--	1010	2290	1240	5220	--	9520
1987	--	1000	2480	1310	--	--	9520
1988	--	1000	--	1380	--	--	9830

Table 3.1
(continued)

	Sweden, Krona	Switzerland, Franc	Thailand Baht	Turkey, T. Pound	United Kingdom, Pound	Venezuela, Bolivar	United States, Dollar
1937	100	100	--	100	100	--	100
1938	97	96	100	100	93	100	85
1939	101	100	116	102	95	101	83
1940	128	129	171	127	126	98	85
1941	151	165	225	176	140	104	98
1942	166	188	249	341	147	116	119
1943	172	196	314	592	150	129	132
1944	172	200	411	461	153	134	133
1945	170	198	--	446	155	135	138
1946	163	193	--	429	161	137	159
1947	175	201	1731	435	176	156	195
1948	188	209	1649	468	202	174	210
1949	189	199	1541	505	212	165	193
1950	199	196	1571	454	242	165	203
1951	263	219	1698	482	295	174	227
1952	278	213	1781	487	301	177	215
1953	261	205	1680	501	303	172	192
1954	259	207	1630	548	297	176	189
1955	269	208	1900	596	312	177	182
1956	280	211	1970	696	321	174	186
1957	287	215	1970	822	315	172	188
1958	281	209	1070	945	294	174	192
1959	281	205	1950	1130	297	179	182
1960	289	207	1900	1190	297	179	182
1961	295	207	2070	1230	294	183	184
1962	301	213	2190	1290	294	191	180
1963	309	222	2050	1350	300	198	178
1964	323	226	1920	1340	312	205	177
1965	337	226	1990	1470	316	212	186
1966	346	228	2260	1550	324	216	197
1967	346	231	2440	1660	322	219	186
1968	349	231	2340	1740	352	222	189
1969	365	238	2380	1840	364	226	202
1970	389	248	2380	1970	378	229	210
1971	401	253	2380	2280	395	237	215
1972	424	263	2570	2690	413	245	239
1973	471	291	3160	3250	546	260	325
1974	587	338	4080	4220	813	304	367
1975	622	330	4230	4640	879	347	268
1976	677	328	4400	5370	1120	372	383
1977	731	329	4630	6650	1280	413	401
1978	778	317	5100	10,000	1270	444	448
1979	864	330	5670	16,600	1560	485	513
1980	976	346	6810	34,300	1870	560	569
1981	1080	367	7460	47,000	2120	638	615
1982	1230	377	7560	58,800	2240	689	597
1983	1360	377	7700	76,800	2360	739	604
1984	1460	391	7420	117,000	2360	868	617
1985	1540	398	7420	122,000	2320	997	575
1986	1500	384	7420	158,000	2370	1160	524
1987	1540	374	7830	209,000	2410	1700	558
1988	1670	384	8500	--	2410	--	569

Table 3.1
(continued)

[a] Index numbers for 1937-1952 were obtained from Wegner, 1953. Numbers for 1953-1988 were calculated by David Camp, Department of Agricultural Economics, Purdue University, from the following volumes of the United Nations Monthly Bulletin of Statistics:

1953-1954, 9(12):115-118 (1955);
1955-1957, 13(2):125-132 (1959);
1958-1964, 20(1):130-140 (1966);
1965-1970, 25(4):148-159 (1971);
1971-1974, 29(7):150-160 (1975);
1975-1978, 33(7):148-158 (1979);
1979-1981, 36(2):150-160 (1982);
1981-1984, 39(9):190-200 (1985);
1985-1987, 42(12):264-274 (1988);
1988, 44(15):270-279 (1990).

[b] The index for El Salvador begins with a base year 1958 = 100.

[c] The index for Israel in 1963 shifts to a base of 1963 = 100.

4

Summary

In this journey through price history we find little validation for the various macroeconomic theories as explanations for behavior of the price level. For example:

- The theory that explained the price level by the supply of gold was outmoded by the advent of central banking and the collapse of the gold standard.
- Neoclassical economics failed to explain the Great Depression or to find a remedy for it.
- The purchasing power parity principle, which related price levels in various trading countries to one another through the exchange rate mechanism, is now crippled by exchange control, quotas, black markets, and surges in international capital flows.
- The Austrian school, exponents of classical orthodoxy in its purest form, never achieved general acceptance.
- Keynesian economics failed to explain stagflation and offered no corrective.
- Supply-side economics produced economic stimulus chiefly through increased deficits, thereby undermining its own postulates and corroborating the central idea of its Keynesian adversary.

Like the economic principles that form the foundation of economics, these various theoretical systems are valid if their assumptions are granted. The difficulty is that their many assumptions, building one upon the other, take them so far from reality as to reduce their relevance. The theoretical systems are internally consistent, which enhances their appeal in academic circles, but when the assumptions are violated, as they are in the practical world, fatal flaws can appear. The error is in presuming that internal consistency conveys outward relevance.

The best candidate for explaining price level behavior is that nonsystem, *institutional economics*, which enjoyed brief popularity early in the twentieth century and then fell into professional disrespect. Its lack of attractiveness derives from its inability to accommodate rigorous analysis and because it is ill suited to building econometric models. Its usefulness arises from its ability to deal with whatever forces exist rather than focusing on a selected few while purporting to hold the others constant, as the rigorous systems do. Institutional economics becomes increasingly useful with more-rapid institutional change. Better than the formal systems, institutional economics can deal with attitudinal changes on the part of the public; forces resulting from the drive for full employment; regulatory activity; international quotas and exchange controls; the shift from hard to soft money; the fragmentation of the general interest; the rise of special interests; the growth of government; and endemic inflation.

Institutional economics has become more appropriate as government-created or condoned institutions partially replaced the free market. The kind of economics now practiced by government officials is necessarily of an institutional sort, a kind of eclecticism, pragmatic rather than doctrinaire, using what seems relevant from various systems. Although this approach unsettles the dogmatists, it is the best possible policy given the failure of the formal systems.

This review of fifteen inflations reveals the present inappropriateness of ideas that once had gained significant acceptance: the money illusion; the notion that money is neutral, having no force of its own; and the belief that a single country can act autonomously in macroeconomic policy.

Popular explanations of the price level have some usefulness in explaining individual prices but are less useful in explaining changes in the price level over time. Among these widely held notions are the following: that history simply repeats itself; that wages create the price level; that government price fixing determines the overall level of prices; that monopoly, speculation, or conspiracy determine price levels; and that the price level can be explained by episodic events such as poor crops or an oil embargo.

The one clear conclusion that emerges from this study is that the supply of money overwhelmingly determines the general level of prices. With modern finance the supply of money is a government monopoly, subject to control by the monetary authorities. The remedy for inflation is known: limit the creation of money. If we fail to apply the remedy, the fault lies not in some vague, unknown, or malevolent force but in our inability to cope with the institutions we have allowed to develop.

5

Alternatives for Coping

In 1984, Milton Friedman summarized the then sixty-nine-year-old record of the Federal Reserve Board, the heart of our money system: "Two major war-time inflations; a banking panic far more severe than was ever experienced before the Federal Reserve System was established; a succession of booms and recessions; a post–World War II roller coaster marked by accelerating inflation and terminating in four years of unusual instability—the whole relieved by relative stability and prosperity during the two decades after the Korean War."

Other observers have commented less harshly while still others view the Bank's record as quite positive. Nonetheless, there is sufficient dissatisfaction with the record that alternative money systems have been proposed. For the greater part, however, these systems give insufficient attention to the institutional changes that have brought on or accompanied the Age of Inflation: government's vested interest in inflation, unwillingness to tax, institutionalizing of the federal debt, internationalizing of finance, atrophy of commitment to stable international exchange rates, loss of national autonomy in macroeconomic policy, growing discounting of the future, politicization of special interests, and the demonstrated wish of the public for some degree of inflation—denied in conversation but confirmed by deeds.

Theoreticians can disregard these troublesome matters, but responsible governmental officials cannot. No monetary system can overcome inflation unless the institutions that perpetuate it are dealt with. These institutions are so deeply imbedded in public and social life that they are unlikely to be dislodged in a country depending upon a representative form of government. Furthermore, the evidence is that major changes in monetary systems come only during a crisis. At the time of writing there is no crisis. A crisis may indeed come, and it may lead to demand for change in our money system, but any such change would probably modify the present system rather than adopt another form. Despite the unlikely prospect for basic change, four proposed alternatives to the present system bear examination.

RETURN TO THE GOLD STANDARD

Those who note that the Age of Inflation dates from the abandonment of the gold standard have suggested a return to the gold standard. Advocates decry the growth of government accommodated by paper money. They propose injecting a time-honored discipline into the money supply and therefore into price behavior. They argue that gold stocks are large relative to annual gold production, which allegedly should give a certain stability to a currency based on gold. Proponents point out that gold could be officially priced at such a level as to achieve a smooth price transition from the present monetary system to a gold standard.

Advocates of a return to a gold standard are of one of two persuasions: those who propose a pure 100 percent gold standard with full gold backing for the circulating currency, and those who favor a fractional reserve system such as obtained in the United States prior to the 1930s. I believe that a 100 percent gold standard is anachronistic, obsolete now for centuries, and impossible to implement. A move to the fractional reserve form, with a fixed official price for gold, is also beset with problems.

Historically, a gold standard has not provided price stability. Despite having monetary systems based on precious metals, Rome, medieval Europe, Spain, and colonial Brazil all experienced inflation. From 1896 to 1920, while the United States was on the gold standard, prices tripled. While on the gold standard, from 1879 to 1896, prices declined 24 percent. They fell 58 percent from 1920 to 1933 while we were on the gold standard.

Although the supply of gold is likely to be fairly stable, the demand is not. A move by a significant number of nations to reestablish the gold standard would increase the demand for gold, thereby increasing its value and lowering prices denominated in gold-based currency. On the other hand, a diminution in the demand for gold, for whatever reason, would reduce its value and raise prices based on gold.

Legislative action could change the official gold equivalent of a gold-based currency. To prevent such action, some people advocate writing a fixed gold standard into the U.S. Constitution. Such action, if it could be accomplished and respected, might trap the United States into a secular decline in prices, as occurred with an unchanged official price of gold during the late nineteenth century and again after World War I, or it might propel the country into an increase in prices, as occurred during the first two decades of the twentieth century, when the United States was on a fixed gold standard.

Given the present international money system, a gold standard would have to be adopted by a number of countries to be effective. There is little prospect that a significant number of countries could be persuaded to return to gold. Some countries now have insufficient reserves of gold on which to base their currencies.

A modified version of the gold standard is the compensated dollar, an idea advocated by professors Warren and Pearson during the Great Depression and partly implemented by President Roosevelt during 1933–1934. This theory allows the official price of gold to be changed periodically to stabilize a country's price level, that is, to be increased when the price level is falling and decreased when inflation threatens. The exchange rate against other currencies would change accordingly.

Stabilizing a country's price level by destabilizing the price levels of other countries was considered a form of international anarchy half a century ago. "Beggar thy neighbor" was the phrase used to describe the practice. In the current, more interdependent system of international finance, with the United States so dominant in the volume of international trade, it would be considered even more offensive.

Simultaneous change in the gold equivalents of the currencies of many countries to counteract worldwide inflation or deflation is theoretically possible but would be diplomatically difficult and of doubtful effectiveness.

The gold standard poses problems, whether on a fixed or a variable base for the dollar. Monetary systems have enormous inertia. A change so great as a return to the gold standard, in whatever form, would encounter immense opposition even if the case for it were clear, which it is not. The arguments against a return to the gold standard outweigh those in favor.

A BUNDLE OF COMMODITIES AS A MONETARY BASE

The vulnerability of a single commodity, even one as stable in quantity as gold, to fluctuations in supply and demand and therefore value, with resultant fluctuations in the price level, has led to proposals that money be based on a fixed bundle of basic commodities such as steel, copper, lumber, and wheat. The argument is that the average value of such a bundle would probably be more stable than would the value of gold, a single item. This also is an old idea, promoted without success by Benjamin Graham, the securities analyst, during the 1930s. The scheme entails numerous, difficult problems: the idea is novel, it would be difficult to manage, administering such a stock would be awkward, the cost of accumulating and carrying the stock would be great, the mix to be chosen would be contentious, and pricing the various items would be controversial. Would the government stand ready to buy and sell the various items at fixed prices? How would currencies be redeemed in such a system, or would they? How would international balances be settled? The system would seem to have, in exaggerated form, all the problems of bimetallism, which over a span of time has proved to be unsatisfactory.

NONDISCRETIONARY PAPER MONEY

The major proponent of nondiscretionary paper money is Milton Friedman, who contends that government officials lack the wisdom to regulate the money supply and so to result in stable prices. The proposal is to take the power to regulate money out of the hands of central bank officials; prescribed monetary deportment should be provided either by legislation or by being written into the Constitution. A suggested provision is that the money supply should be allowed to increase automatically at from 3 to 5 percent per year to accommodate economic growth, changes in velocity, and changed efficiency in the use of money arising from alterations in financial institutions. The hoped-for result of such a nondiscretionary system would be a stable price level. It would not be necessary to hold a stock of gold or a bundle of commodities; the currency need not be redeemable.

Here a related comment is appropriate. The merit of a stock of gold or a stock of something else lies not in redeemability itself but in the restraint imposed by redeemability on the amount of money that can be issued. The most critical attribute of money is acceptability, which has been shown to be possible in the absence of redeemability. Clearly, however, if limitation on the issue of money is constrained by redeemability, the desired effect—price stability—would more likely be achieved. The critical question with nondiscretionary paper money is the mandated rate of annual increase in the stock of money. Too high a rate and inflation is locked in; too low, and deflation becomes inescapable.

Public officials are highly unlikely to surrender their responsibility for managing the major component of our macroeconomic affairs. Even if they did, the results might be disappointing. The discretionary latitude between 3 and 5 percent might be inadequate. After the stock market crash of 1987, the Federal Reserve System wisely and quickly expanded the supply of money and helped to avert what might otherwise have been a major economic downturn. Had the United States been on monetary "automatic pilot," such new money creation might have been impossible. More likely, the law would have been quickly changed. "What the Congress has done the Congress can undo," noted Tip O'Neill, former speaker of the House of Representatives. To avert such legislative tampering, some commentators advocate writing nondiscretionary monetary policy into the Constitution. This advice seems impossible to put into place.

Nondiscretionary paper money would deprive the government of the opportunity to provide liquidity as a lender of last resort in the event of a financial panic or to check monetary growth at the onset of an ill-founded inflationary spiral.

Certainly nondiscretionary paper money, with a limit on the amount to be created, addresses the central issue regarding inflation. The logic of it is compelling, but its acceptance seems highly improbable.

DENATIONALIZING MONEY

A small group of economists, chiefly libertarians, propose taking the monetary system out of the hands of government and leaving it to private enterprise. Theoretically, the market would discipline the supply of money to keep its value at a stable level. This proposal has won acclaim from only a few. "Money cannot manage itself," said Bagehot, a nineteenth-century economist. Early in the past century, the United States had something like free banking: chaos prevailed because unscrupulous promoters set up all manner of small banks that issued notes in great numbers and variety. Needless to say, many of these banks failed, thereby making their notes worthless and so defrauding their holders. Denationalizing money may appeal to the ideological positions of a few, but it is impractical and highly dangerous to the many.

CONCLUSION

The present monetary system, with some modifications that would not do violence to its essential features, seems preferrable to any of the proposed alternatives. After all, the United States has clearly experienced less inflation than all but one of the thirty nations whose price experience has been reported in this study. With what is essentially the present U.S. system, deflation was averted after World War II, a great accomplishment. None of the postwar recessions degenerated into depressions. The economy grew and living levels rose during the Age of Inflation. The inequities of inflation posed no political problems that were beyond the nation's ability to cope.

RECOMMENDATIONS

The present system could be strengthened by changes that would make it less inflation-prone and less vulnerable to panic:

- Each of us, individually and collectively, limits the demands made of the federal government.
- Give the president the line-item veto.
- Rewrite the guidelines for administering the Employment Act of 1946 so as to include stable prices as an objective.
- Prohibit senators and congressmembers from receiving contributions from political action committees. Members of the executive and judicial branches of the government are prohibited from taking such money; members of the legislative branch should likewise be restrained.
- Limit the terms of office for senators and congressmembers as we do for the president.
- Develop a standby system to interrupt international capital flows that result from unwarranted volatility in the international exchanges. This system could be patterned after the "circuit breakers" that operate in the stock market.

Possibly someday, when economic literacy is greater, enlightened self-interest is more widespread, and citizens are more aware of the inequity of inflation, or if a major economic downturn should arise, development of a new monetary system that would provide greater price stability might be possible. Until then, it is better to cope with present evils than to fly to evils we know not of.

References

ANCIENT ROME: DEBASEMENT OF COINS AND INFLATION

Durant, Will. 1944. *Caesar and Christ.* New York: Simon and Schuster.

Frank, Tenney. 1923. *A History of Rome.* New York: Holt, Rinehart and Winston.

Galbraith, John Kenneth. 1975. *Money: Whence It Came, Where It Went.* Boston: Houghton Mifflin.

Gibbon, Edward. 1776. *The Decline and Fall of the Roman Empire.* Great Books of the Western World. Nos. 40, 41. Chicago: Encyclopaedia Britannica.

Haskell, H. J. 1939. *The New Deal in Old Rome.* New York: Knopf.

Jones, A.H.M. 1970. *A History of Rome Through the Fifth Century.* Vol. 2, *The Empire.* London: Macmillan.

————. 1974. *The Roman Economy: Studies in Ancient Economic and Administrative History.* Ed. P. A. Brunt. Totowa, N.J.: Rowman and Littlefield.

Lacy, Mary. 1923. "Food Control During Forty-Six Centuries." *Scientific Monthly* 16, no. 6.

Levi, Paul. 1927. *Ancient Rome At Work.* London: Routledge and Kegan Paul.

Rostovtzeff, M. 1926. *The Social and Economic History of the Roman Empire.* Vols. 1 and 2. Oxford: Clarendon.

Toynbee, Arnold J. 1946. *A Study of History.* Abridgement of Vols. 1–6 by D. C. Somervell. London: Oxford University Press.

THE BLACK DEATH AND PRICE BEHAVIOR

Bowsky, William M. 1971. *The Black Death: A Turning Point in History.* New York: Holt, Rinehart and Winston.

Coulton, G. G. 1974. *The Black Death.* Folcroft, Pa.: Folcroft Library Editions.

Cowie, Leonard W. 1972. *The Black Death and the Peasants' Revolt*. London: Wayland.

Duplais, Nicole. 1988. Fleas, the lethal leapers. *National Geographic* 173, no. 5.

Gregg, Pauline. 1976. *Black Death to Industrial Revolution*. New York: Barnes and Noble.

Hamilton, Earl J. 1936. *Money, Prices, and Wages in Valencia, Aragon, and Navarre, 1351–1500*. Cambridge: Harvard University Press.

Levett, Ada Elizabeth. 1974. *The Black Death*. New York: Octagon Books.

Rogers, J.E.T. 1908. *Six Centuries of Work and Wages: A History of English Labour*. London: Swan Sonnenschein and Co.

United States Department of Agriculture. 1923. *United States Department of Agriculture Yearbook of Agriculture 1922*. Washington, D.C.: Government Printing Office.

Warren, G. F., and F. A. Pearson. 1935. *Gold and Prices*. New York: Wiley.

SPAIN, SILVER, AND THE PRICE REVOLUTION

Durant, Will, and Ariel Durant. 1961. *The Age of Reason Begins*. New York: Simon and Schuster.

Galbraith, John Kenneth. 1975. *Money: Whence It Came, Where It Went*. Boston: Houghton Mifflin.

Hamilton, Earl J. 1934. *American Treasure and the Price Revolution in Spain, 1501–1650*. Cambridge, MA: Harvard University Press.

―――――. 1936. *Money, Prices, and Wages in Valencia, Aragon, and Navarre, 1351–1500*. Cambridge: Harvard University Press.

Harrison, Joseph. 1978. *An Economic History of Modern Spain*. New York: Holmes and Meier.

Kennedy, Paul. 1987. *The Rise and Fall of the Great Powers: Economic Change and Military Conflict*. New York: Random House.

Klein, Julius. 1964. *The Mesta: A Study of Spanish Economic History, 1273–1836*. Port Washington, N.Y.: Kennikat Press.

Warren, G. F., and F. A. Pearson. 1935. *Gold and Prices*. New York: Wiley.

JOHN LAW AND PAPER CURRENCY

Angell, Norman. 1930. *The Story of Money*. London: Cassell.

Galbraith, John Kenneth. 1975. *Money: Whence It Came, Where It Went*. Boston: Houghton Mifflin.

Groseclose, E. E. 1961. *Money and Man*. New York: Frederick Ungar.

Hamilton, Earl J. 1936. "Prices and Wages at Paris under John Law's System." *Quarterly Journal of Economics* 51:42–70.

Hyde, H. Montgomery. 1969. *John Law: The History of An Honest Adventurer*. London: W. H. Allen.

Law, John. 1705. *Money and Trade Considered, With a Proposal For Supplying the Nation With Money.* Reprints of Economic Classics. New York: Augustus M. Kelly, 1966.

———. 1726. Histoire des Finances pendant la Régence. In *John Law, Oeuvres Complètes.* Ed. Paul Harsin. 3 Vols. Publisher unknown, 1934.

Minton, Robert. 1975. *John Law: The Father of Paper Money.* New York: Association Press.

Train, John. 1985. *Famous Financial Fiascos.* New York: Crown Publishers.

THE AMERICAN REVOLUTION AND CONTINENTAL CURRENCY

Bezanson, A., R. D. Gray, and M. Hussey. 1935. *Prices in Colonial Pennsylvania.* Research Studies Vol. 26. Philadelphia: University of Pennsylvania Press.

Bogart, E. L. 1927. *An Economic History of the United States.* New York: Longmans, Green and Company. Fourth ed.

Bullock, C. J. 1900. *Essays on Monetary History of the United States.* New York: Macmillan.

Cole, A. H. 1938. *Wholesale Commodity Prices in the United States, 1700–1861.* Appendix A. Boston: Harvard University Press.

Davis, A. M. 1905. *The Limitation of Prices in Massachusetts, 1776–1779.* Vol. 10. Colonial Society of Massachusetts.

Dewey, D. R. 1931. *Financial History of the United States.* New York: Longmans, Green and Company.

Felt, J. B. 1839. *An Historical Account of Massachusetts Currency.* Perkins and Marvin.

Fisher, W. C. 1913. "The Tabular Standard in Massachusetts History." *Quarterly Journal of Economics* 27: 417–454.

Franklin, Benjamin. (undated). *A Modest Inquiry into the Nature and Necessity of a Paper Currency.* (Printed anonymously but later acknowledged).

———. 1764. *Remarks and Facts Relative to American Paper Money.*

Gould, C. P. 1915. *Money and Transportation in Maryland.* Johns Hopkins University Studies in Historical and Political Science. Series 33, no. 1. Baltimore: Johns Hopkins University Press.

Hepburn, A. B. 1924. *A History of Currency in the United States.* New York: Macmillan.

Lester, R. A. 1939. *Monetary Experiments.* Princeton, N.J.: Princeton University Press.

Macfarline, C. W. 1896. *Pennsylvania Paper Currency.* Annals of the American Academy of Political and Social Science, Vol. 8.

Pearson, F. A. 1948. History of prices in the United States. Unpublished.

Phillips, H. 1972. *Historical Sketches of American Paper Money.* Clifton, N.J.: A. M. Kelly.

Ramsay, D. 1789. *The History of the American Revolution.* Vol. 2, Ch. 17. Philadelphia: Raitkin and Sons.

Smith, Adam. 1776. *Wealth of Nations.* Book 2, Ch. 2. London: W. Strahan and T. Cadill.

Sparks, J. 1836. *The Works of Benjamin Franklin.* Vol. 2. New York: A. M. Kelley.

Spaulding, E. W. 1932. *New York in the Critical Period, 1783–1789.* New York State Historical Series. New York: Columbia University Press.

Sumner, W. G. 1874. *A History of American Currency.* New York: Henry Holt and Company.

Van Doren, C. 1945. *Benjamin Franklin.* New York: Viking Press.

Warren, G. F., and F. A. Pearson. 1931. "Prices of commodities in Philadelphia, 1720–1775." *Farm Economics* No. 3.

Webster, Peletiah. 1791. *Political Essays.* Philadelphia: Crukshank.

THE FRENCH REVOLUTION AND THE ASSIGNATS

Bax, E. Belfort. 1907. *The Story of the French Revolution.* London: Swan Sonnenschein and Co.

Caron, François. 1909. *Tableau de Depreciation du Papier Monnaie dans le Department de la Seine.* Paris: 386.

Durant, Will, and Ariel Durant. 1967. *Rousseau and Revolution.* New York. Simon and Schuster.

Galbraith, John Kenneth. 1975. *Money: Whence It Came, Where It Went.* Boston: Houghton Mifflin.

Greenlaw, Ralph W., ed. 1958. *The Economic Origins of the French Revolution: Poverty or Prosperity.* Boston: D. C. Heath.

Harris, Seymour E. *The Assignats.* Harvard Economic Studies. Vol. 33. Cambridge: Harvard University Press.

Keynes, John Maynard. 1935. *The General Theory of Employment, Interest, and Money.* New York: Harcourt Brace.

Labrousse, C. E. 1876. *The crisis in the French economy at the end of the old regime.* In Greenlaw, 1958.

Shepard, William Finley. 1953. *Price Control and the Reign of Terror, France, 1793–1795.* Berkeley: University of California Press.

Thiers, Adolphe. 1868. *History of the French Revolution.* New York: Appleton.

White, Andrew Dickson. 1876. *Fiat Money Inflation in France: How It Came, What It Bought, and How It Ended.* Reprint. San Francisco: Cato Institute, Paper No. 11, 1980.

THE AMERICAN CIVIL WAR, NORTH: INFLATION AND DEFLATION

Bresciani-Turroni, Constantine. 1937. *The Economics of Inflation: A Study of Currency Depreciation in Post-War Germany.* London: Allen and Unwin.

Dewey, Davis R. 1968. *Financial History of the United States.* New York: Augustus Kelley.

Friedman, Milton, 1992. *Money Mischief.* New York: Harcourt, Brace, Jovanovich.

Galbraith, John Kenneth. 1975. *Money: Whence It Came, Where It Went*. Boston: Houghton Mifflin.

Hamilton, Earl J. 1934. *American Treasure and the Price Revolution in Spain, 1501–1650*. Cambridge: Harvard University Press.

Hepburn, A. Barton. 1915. *A History of Currency in the United States*. New York: Macmillan.

Mitchell, Wesley C. 1960. *A History of the Greenbacks*. Chicago Reprint Series. Chicago: University of Chicago Press.

Paarlberg, Don. 1942. *Commodity Prices in Mexico*. Master's thesis, Ithaca, New York: Cornell University.

Pearson, F. A. 1948. History of Prices in the United States. Unpublished.

Pearson, F. A., and W. I. Myers. 1948. "Prices and Presidents." *Farm Economics* 163: 4210–4218.

Studenski, Paul, and Herman Krooss. 1952. *Financial History of the United States*. New York: McGraw-Hill.

Unger, Irwin. 1964. *The Greenback Era: A Social and Political History of American Finance, 1865–1879*. Princeton, N.J.: Princeton University Press.

Warren, G. F., and F. A. Pearson. 1935. *Gold and Prices*. New York: John Wiley.

————. 1937. *World Prices and the Building Industry*. New York: John Wiley.

Wegner, Walter. 1953. *Relationships Among Price Levels in Various Countries*. Ph.D. diss. W. Lafayette, Ind.: Purdue University.

THE AMERICAN CIVIL WAR, SOUTH: INFLATION AND DISASTER

Eggleston, George C. 1875. *A Rebel's Recollections*. Reprint. Bloomington, Ind.: Indiana University Press. 1959.

Galbraith, John Kenneth. 1975. *Money: Whence It Came, Where It Went*. Boston: Houghton Mifflin.

Lerner, Eugene M. 1955. "Money, Wages and Prices in the Confederacy, 1861–1865." *Journal of Political Economy* 63, no. 1: 20–24.

Pearson, F. A. 1948. A history of prices in the United States. Unpublished.

GERMANY AND THE CLASSIC INFLATION

Bresciani-Turroni, Constantine. 1937. *The Economics of Inflation: A Study of Currency Depreciation in Post-War Germany*. London: Allen and Unwin.

Galbraith, John Kenneth. 1975. *Money: Whence It Came, Where It Went*. Boston: Houghton Mifflin.

Graham, Frank D. 1931. *Exchange, Prices and Production in Hyperinflation: Germany, 1920–1923*. Princeton, N.J.: Princeton University Press.

Haberler, Gottfried. 1966. *Inflation, Its Causes and Cures, With a New Look at Inflation in 1966*. Revised and enlarged ed. Washington, D.C.: American Enterprise Institute for Public Policy Research.

Hirsch, Fred, and John H. Goldthorpe. 1978. *The Political Economy of Inflation.* Cambridge: Harvard University Press.

Laursen, Karsten, and Jorgen Pedersen. 1964. *The German Inflation 1918–1923.* Amsterdam: North Holland Publishing Company.

Mill, John Stuart. 1848. *Principles of Political Economy With Some of Their Applications to Social Philosophy.* London: J.W. Parker.

Ricardo, David. 1817. *Principles of Political Economy.* London: J. Murray.

Ringer, Fritz K., ed. 1969. *The German Inflation of 1923.* New York: Oxford University Press.

Sennholz, Hans 1979. *Age of Inflation.* Belmont, Mass.: Western Islands.

Warren, G. F., and F. A. Pearson. 1935. *Gold and Prices.* New York: John Wiley.

_____. 1937. *World Prices and the Building Industry.* New York: John Wiley.

Young, John Parke. 1925. *European Currency and Finance.* Commission on Gold and Silver Inquiry, United States Senate. Serial 9, vols. 1 and 2. Washington, D.C.: Government Printing Office.

THE RUSSIAN REVOLUTION AND PLANNED INFLATION

Abramovitch, Raphael R. 1962. *The Soviet Revolution, 1917–1939.* New York: International Universities Press.

Carr, Edward Hallett. 1952. *The Bolshevik Revolution 1917–1923.* Vol. 2. New York: Macmillan.

Clarke, Roger A. 1972. *Soviet Economic Facts, 1917–1970.* New York: John Wiley.

Cowden, Morton H. 1984. *Russian Bolshevism and British Labor, 1917–1921.* New York: Columbia University Press.

Dobb, Maurice. 1948. *Soviet Economic Development Since 1917.* New York: International Publishers.

Galbraith, John Kenneth. 1975. *Money: Whence It Came, Where It Went.* Boston: Houghton Mifflin.

Haensel, Paul. 1930. *The Economic Policy of Soviet Russia.* London: P. S. King and Son.

Hazlitt, Henry. 1965. *What You Should Know About Inflation.* 2d. ed. New York: Van Nostrand.

Heenan, Louise Erwin. 1987. *Russian Democracy's Fatal Blunder: The Summer Offensive of 1917.* New York: Praeger.

Hubbard, L. E. 1936. *Soviet Money and Finance.* London: Macmillan.

Hutchings, Raymond. 1971. *Soviet Economic Development.* New York: Barnes and Noble.

Jasny, Naum. 1949. *The Socialized Agriculture of the U.S.S.R.: Plans and Performance.* Stanford, Calif.: Stanford University Press.

_____. 1951. *The Soviet Price System.* Stanford, Calif.: Food Research Institute, Stanford University Press.

Kaiser, Daniel K., ed. 1987. *The Workers' Revolution in Russia, 1917: The View From Below.* New York: Cambridge University Press.

Laird, Betty A., and Roy D. Laird. 1976. *To Live Long Enough: The Memoirs of Naum Jasny, Scientific Analyst.* Lawrence: University Press of Kansas.

Lindberg, Leon N., and Charles S. Maier, eds. 1985. *The Politics of Inflation and Economic Stagnation: Theoretical Approaches and International Case Studies.* Washington, D.C.: Brookings Institution.

Macey, David A. J. 1987. *Government and Peasant in Russia, 1861–1906: The Prehistory of the Stolypin Reforms.* DeKalb: Northern Illinois University Press.

Nove, Alec. 1969. *An Economic History of the USSR.* London: Penguin.

Paarlberg, Don. 1988. *Toward a Well-Fed World.* Ames: Iowa State University Press.

Reed, John. 1919. *Ten Days That Shook The World.* Rpt. Dallas, Pa.: Penguin Books, Offset Paperback Manufacturers 1982.

Strumilin, S. G. 1923. "Wages and labor productivity of Russia, 1913–1922." *Voprosy Trlida*, No. 17–19. (Problems of Labor). Moscow: Library of Labor.

Timoshenko, Vladimir P. 1932. *Agricultural Russia and the Wheat Problem.* Stanford, Calif.: Food Research Institute, Stanford Research Institute.

Vaisberg, P. 1934. *Etapy Ekonomicheskoi Politik USSR.*

von Laue, Theodore H. 1971. *Why Lenin? Why Stalin? A Reappraisal of the Russian Revolution, 1900–1930.* New York: Lippincott.

Warren, G. F., and F. A. Pearson. 1935. *Gold and Prices.* New York: John Wiley.

————. 1937. *World Prices and the Building Industry.* New York: Wiley.

Young, John Parke. 1925. *European Currency and Finance.* Commission on Gold and Silver Inquiry. United States Senate. Serial 9, Vols. 1 and 2. Washington, D.C.: Government Printing Office.

HUNGARY, 1946: THE ULTIMATE INFLATION

Coulborn, W.A.L. 1950. *A Discussion of Money.* London: Longmans, Green.

Fekete, János. 1982. *Back to the Realities: Reflections of a Hungarian Banker.* Budapest: Akademiai Kiado.

Kaldor, N. 1946. Inflation in Hungary. *Manchester Guardian,* Weekly. 7 and 13 December.

Nogaro, Bertrand. 1948. "Hungary's Recent Monetary Crisis and Its Theoretical Meaning." *American Economic Review* 38, no. 4: 526–542.

CHINA AND HYPERINFLATION

Chang, Kia-Ngau. 1958. *The Inflationary Spiral: The Experience of China, 1939–1950.* Cambridge: Technology Press of Massachusetts Institute of Technology; New York: John Wiley.

Choh-Ming Li. 1959. *Economic Development in Communist China.* Berkeley: University of California Press.

Chou, Shun-Hsin. 1963. *The Chinese Inflation, 1937–1949.* New York: Columbia University Press.

Eckstein, Alexander. 1977. *China's Economic Revolution.* London/New York: Cambridge University Press.

Republic of China. 1948. *Statistical Yearbook.* Nanking.
U.S. Government. 1981. *China, A Country Study.* Foreign Area Studies. Washington, D.C.: American University.
Wu, Kang. 1958. *The Historical Materials Relating to the Inflation in Old China.*
Wu, T. Y. *The Economics of Price Rises* (in Chinese).
Young, Arthur N. 1965. *China's Wartime Finance and Inflation, 1937–1945.* Cambridge: Harvard University Press.
Young, John Parke. 1925. *European Currency and Finance.* Commission on Gold and Silver Inquiry, United States Senate. Serial 9, Vols. 1 and 2. Washington, D.C.: Government Printing Office.

BOLIVIA: A COUNTRY THAT TOOK THE CURE

Cole, Julio Harold. 1987. *Latin American Inflation: Theoretical Interpretations and Empirical Results.* New York: Praeger.
Hauxhurst, Joan. 1989. "Argentina's Course for Economic Reform." *Christian Science Monitor* (September 22): 2C
International Center for Economic Growth. 1989. "The Bolivian Miracle." *Newsletter* (July) 3: 1.
International Currency Analysis. 1986. *1985 World Currency Yearbook.* Brooklyn.
Malloy, James M. 1970. *Bolivia: The Uncompleted Revolution.* Pittsburg: University of Pittsburg Press.
Sachs, Jeffrey. 1989. "Social Conflict and Populist Policies in Latin America." *National Bureau of Economic Research, Working Paper* (March), 2897.
Sachs, Jeffrey, and Juan Antonio Morales. 1988. *Bolivia, 1952–1986.* Country Studies No. 6. San Francisco: International Center for Economic Growth.

BRAZIL: DEVELOPMENT AND INFLATION

Bacha, Edmar Lisboa, and Carlos F. Diaz Alejandro. 1982. "International Financial Intermediation: A Long and Tropical View." *Essays in International Finance* (May), 147.
Baer, Werner. 1983. *The Brazilian Economy: Growth and Development.* 2d ed. Praeger Special Studies. New York: Praeger.
————. 1989. *The Brazilian Economy: Growth and Development.* 3d ed. New York: Praeger.
Brandao, Antonio Salazar P. 1988. "The Behavior of Land Prices and Land Rents in Brazil." Vol. 3: 24–31. *20th Congresso International de Economistas Agrarios.* Oxford, England: IAAE.
Business Latin America, April 30, 1990. *Weekly Report to Managers of Latin American Operations.* São Paulo, Brazil.
Clements, Benedict J. 1988. *Foreign Trade Strategies, Employment, and Income Distribution in Brazil.* New York: Praeger.
Cline, William R., and associates. 1981. *World Inflation and the Developing Countries.* Washington, D.C.: Brookings Institution.

Coffey, Peter, and Luis Correa do Lago. 1988. *The EEC and Brazil: Trade, Capital Investment and the Debt Problem*. London: Pinter.

Ellis, Howard S. 1969. *The Economy of Brazil*. Berkeley: University of California Press.

Fritsch, Winston. 1988. *External Constraints on Economic Policy in Brazil, 1889–1930*. Pittsburgh: University of Pittsburgh Press.

Hall, A. 1987. "Agrarian Crisis in Brazilian Amazonia: The Grande Carajas Programme." *Journal of Development Studies* 23, no. 4 (July): 533.

Hayes, Margaret Daly. 1989. "The U.S. and Latin America: A Lost Decade?" *America and the World, 1988–1989, Foreign Affairs*, 68, no. 1: 180–198.

Hewlett, Sylvia Ann. 1980. *The Cruel Dilemmas of Development: Twentieth Century Brazil*. New York: Basic Books.

Kafka, Alexandre. 1967. "The Brazilian Stabilization Program, 1964–1966." *Journal of Political Economy* 75, no. 4 (part 2, supplement): 596–631.

Kahil, Raouf. 1973. *Inflation and Economic Development in Brazil, 1946–1963*. Oxford: Clarendon Press.

Krause, Lawrence B., and Walter S. Salant, eds. 1977. *World-Wide Inflation: Theory and Recent Experience*. Washington, D.C.: Brookings Institution.

Lewis, W. A. 1957. *The Theory of Economic Growth*. London: Allen and Unwin.

Netto, Delfim. 1974. Lessons of Brazilian Agricultural Development. *The Future of Agriculture: Fifteenth International Conference of Agricultural Economists, Papers and Reports*. Oxford: Oxford Agricultural Economics Institute/Alden Press. 436–441.

Paarlberg, Don. 1984. *Farmers of Five Continents*. Lincoln: University of Nebraska Press.

Pereira, Luiz Bresser. 1984. *Development and Crisis in Brazil 1930–1983*. Boulder, Colo.: Westview Press.

Roett, Riordan. 1984. *Brazil: Politics in a Patrimonial Society*. 3d ed. New York: Praeger.

––––––––, ed. 1976. *Brazil in the Seventies*. Washington, D.C.: American Enterprise Institute for Public Policy Research

––––––––, ed. 1972. *Brazil in the Sixties*. Nashville, Tenn.: Vanderbilt University Press.

Sachs, Jeffrey. 1989. "Making the Brady Plan Work." *Foreign Affairs* 68, no. 3 (Summer): 87–104.

Sachs, Jeffrey, and Juan Antonio Morales. 1988. *Bolivia 1952–1986*. San Francisco: International Center for Economic Growth. Country Studies no. 6.

Salazar-Carrillo, Jorge, ed. 1985. *The Brazilian Economy in the Eighties*. New York: Pergamon Press.

Schuh, G. Edward. 1970. *The Agricultural Development of Brazil*. New York: Praeger.

Seers, D. 1962. Inflation and growth: "A Summary of Experience in Latin America." *EBLA* 2, no. 1 (February).

Silveira, Antonio M. 1973. "Interest Rates and Rapid Inflation: The Evidence from the Brazilian Economy." *Journal of Money, Credit, and Banking* 5, no. 3: 794–805.

Spiegel, Henry William. 1949. *The Brazilian Economy: Chronic Inflation and Sporadic Industrialization.* Philadelphia: Blakiston.

Wall Street Journal. 1990. "Brazil's chief to reach out to world in U.N. address." A16.

Wegner, Walter O. 1953. "Relationships Among Price Levels in Various Countries." Ph.D. diss. W. Lafayette, Ind.: Purdue University.

Wiarda, Howard J. 1987. *Latin America At The Crossroads: Debt, Development, and the Future.* Boulder, Colo.: American Enterprise Institute for Public Policy Research/Westview Press.

World Bank. 1983. *Brazil: Industrial Policies and Manufactured Exports.* World Bank Country Study. Washington, D.C.: World Bank.

U.S. INFLATION: 1933 AND AFTER

Cagan, Phillip. 1974. *The Hydra-Headed Monster: The Problem of Inflation in the United States.* Washington, D.C.: American Enterprise Institute for Public Policy Research.

Daly, John Charles, moderator. 1977. *Does the Government Profit From Inflation?* Washington, D.C.: American Enterprise Institute for Public Policy Research.

Dreyer, Jacob S., Gottfried Haberler, and Thomas D. Willett, eds. 1982. *The International Monetary System: A Time of Turbulence.* Washington, D.C.: American Enterprise Institute for Public Policy Research.

Dusenberry, James S. 1974. *Can We Control Inflation?* Eighth Annual William K. McInally Lecture. Ann Arbor, Mich.: Graduate School of Business Administration, University of Michigan.

Ellis, Howard S. 1978. *Notes on Stagflation.* Washington, D.C.: American Enterprise Institute for Public Policy Research.

Fink, Richard H., ed. 1982. *Supply-Side Economics, A Critical Appraisal.* Frederick, Md.: Aletheia Books, University Publications of America.

Fink, Richard H., and Jack C. High, eds. 1987. *A Nation in Debt.* Frederick, Md.: University Publications of America.

Fisher, Irving. 1933. *After Reflation, What?* New York: Adelphi.

Friedman, Milton. 1959. "The Demand For Money: Some Theoretical and Empirical Results." *National Bureau of Economic Research* Occasional Paper 68. New York.

_____. 1965. *The Great Contraction, 1929–1933.* Princeton, N.J.: Princeton University Press.

Friedman, Milton, and Anna Jacobson Schwartz. 1963. *A Monetary History of the United States, 1867–1960.* National Bureau of Economic Research. Princeton, N.J.: Princeton University Press.

Galbraith, John Kenneth. 1954. *The Great Crash 1929.* Boston: Houghton Mifflin.

_____. 1975. *Money: Whence It Came, Where It Went.* Boston: Houghton Mifflin.

Gale, William G. 1989. "The Big Debt Overhang." *Wall Street Journal* 25 October: A22.

Goodwin, Craufurd D., ed. 1975. *Exhortation and Controls: The Search for a Wage-Price Policy, 1945–1971.* Washington, D.C.: Brookings Institution.

Harris, S. E. 1933. *Twenty Years of Federal Reserve Policy.* Vol. 2, *The Monetary Crisis.* Cambridge: Harvard University Press.

Hirsch, Fred, and John H. Goldthorpe, eds. 1978. *The Political Economy of Inflation.* Cambridge: Harvard University Press.

Hoover, Herbert. 1952. *The Memoirs of Herbert Hoover: The Great Depression, 1929–1941.* New York: Macmillan.

Horwich, George. 1989. Personal correspondence.

Humphrey, Thomas M., ed. 1980. *Essays on Inflation.* 2d ed. Richmond, Va.: Federal Reserve Bank of Richmond.

Inglehart, Ronald. 1977. *The Silent Revolution: Changing Values and Political Styles Among Western Publics.* Princeton, N.J.: Princeton University Press.

Keynes, John Maynard. 1936. *The General Theory of Employment, Interest, and Money,* New York: Harcourt Brace.

Kosters, Marvin H. 1975. *Controls and Inflation, An Economic Stabilization Program in Retrospect.* Washington, D.C.: American Enterprise Institute for Public Policy Research.

Krause, Lawrence B., and Walter S. Salant, eds. 1977. *World-Wide Inflation: Theory and Recent Experience.* Washington, D.C.: Brookings Institution.

Laughlin, J. Laurence. 1931. *Money, Credit, and Prices.* Vols. 1 and 2. Chicago: University of Chicago Press.

Lindberg, Leon N., and Charles S. Maier, eds. 1985. *The Politics of Inflation and Economic Stagnation: Theoretical Approaches and International Case Studies.* Washington, D.C.: Brookings Institution.

Meiselman, David I., and Arthur B. Laffer, eds. 1975. *The Phenomenon of World Wide Inflation.* Washington, D.C.: American Enterprise Institute for Public Policy Research.

Nogaro, Bertrand. 1948. "Hungary's Recent Monetary Crisis and its Theoretical Meaning. *American Economic Review* 33, no. 4: 526–542.

Paarlberg, Don. 1968. *Great Myths of Economics.* New York: New American Library.

Pearson, F. A. 1948. History of Prices in the United States. Unpublished.

Pearson, F. A. and W. I. Myers. 1948. "Prices and Presidents." *Farm Economics,* no. 163: 4210–4218.

Phillips, A. W. 1958. "The Relation Between Unemployment and the Rate of Change in Money Wage Rates in the United Kingdom, 1861–1957." *Economica,* vol. 25.

Phillips, Kevin. 1990. *The Politics of Rich and Poor.* New York: Random House.

President's Economic Report, Annually, 1948–1986. Council of Economic Advisors, Office of the President, Washington, D.C.

Robbins, Lionel. 1934. *The Great Depression.* New York: Macmillan.

Salant, Walter S. 1987. *A Critical Look at Supply-Side Theory and a Brief Look at Some of its International Aspects.* Brookings Reprint 425. Washington, D.C.: Brookings Institution.

Samuelson, Paul A. 1964. *Economics: An Introductory Analysis.* 6th ed. New York: McGraw-Hill.

Sennholz, Hans. 1979. *Age of Inflation.* Belmont, Mass.: Western Islands.

Shanahan, Eileen, moderator. 1974. *Indexing and Inflation*. Washington, D.C.: American Enterprise Institute for Public Policy Research.

Sparling, Earl. 1930. *Mystery Men of Wall Street*. New York: Blue Ribbon Books.

Stockman, David A. 1986. *The Triumph of Politics: How the Reagan Revolution Failed*. New York: Harper and Row.

United States Senate. 1934. *Stock Exchange Practices*. Report of The Committee on Banking and Currency, Pursuant to Senate Resolution 84. Washington, D.C.: Government Printing Office.

Warren, G. F., and Frank A. Pearson. 1935. *Gold and Prices*. New York: Wiley.

————. 1937. *World Prices and the Building Industry*. New York: Wiley.

Wegner, Walter O. 1953. *Relationships Among Price Levels in Various Countries*. Ph.D. thesis. Purdue University, W. Lafayette, Ind.

Index

Abramovitch, Raphael R., 69, 74
Academics, injured by inflation, 59
Adjustments, in Brazil, 112
Advocacy of rising prices concentrated, 129, 133
Age of Inflation, xiii, 124, 147, 155. *See also* Inflation
Agreements, Smithsonian, 140
Agriculture, German, 60
Alternatives: for coping, 155–59; when overburdened by debt, 127
American Revolution. *See* Revolution, American
Anarchy, in Rome, 8
Angell, Norman, 25
Annuitants, 139
Arbitrage, riskless, 83
Argentina, hyperinflation in, 102
Aristocracy, French, 41
Asia, Russian model in, 71
Assignats, 37–43; depreciation of, 40; repudiated, 42. *See also* Revolution, French
Assumptions, importance of, 153
Austerity: alternative to inflation, 4; in Bolivia, 102; in Brazil, 117
Australia, prices in, 148

Austria, French war with, 37, 43
Austria-Hungary, and Triple Alliance, 69
Autonomy, loss of, 48, 155

Baer, William, 107, 108, 109, 113, 117
Bagehot, Walter, 159
Balance of payments, German, 61
Bank notes: counterfeited, 44; exceeding reserves, 24
Bank shares, value reduced, 26
Bank stock, 25
Banking, central, inflationary, 140
Bankruptcies, 121; private and public, 139
Banks: failures, 121, 142; private, undisciplined, 43–44; reserves, carried off, 81
Banque Générale, 22, 23
Banque Royal, 23
Barter: in Brazil, 112; as means of survival, 75; pre-monetary, 112
Bastille, overthrow of, 37, 39
Bavarian "Beer Hall Putsch," 64
Bax, E. Belfort, 38
Bazarov, 72
"Beggar Thy Neighbor," 157

About the Author

DON PAARLBERG is Professor Emeritus in the Department of Agricultural Economics at Purdue University. In addition to teaching, he has served in the administrations of Presidents Eisenhower, Nixon, and Ford. Dr. Paarlberg is the author of seven books including *Great Myths of Economics* (1968) and *Toward a Well-Fed World* (1988).